NEW DIRECTIONS
IN AMERICAN INTELLECTUAL HISTORY

JOHN HIGHAM AND PAUL K. CONKIN
Editors

NEW DIRECTIONS IN AMERICAN INTELLECTUAL HISTORY

THE JOHNS HOPKINS UNIVERSITY PRESS
BALTIMORE AND LONDON

Publication of this book has been aided by a
grant from the National Endowment for the Humanities

Manufactured in the United States of America

The Johns Hopkins University Press, Baltimore, Maryland 21218
The Johns Hopkins Press Ltd., London

Library of Congress Catalog Number 78–21563
ISBN 0–8018–2183–5 (hardcover)
ISBN 0–8018–2460–5 (paperback)

Originally published, 1979
Second printing, 1980

Johns Hopkins paperback edition, 1980

Library of Congress Cataloging in Publication data will be found on the last
printed page of this book.

This book,
like the conference from which it emerged,
is dedicated with esteem and affection
to
MERLE CURTI

CONTENTS

vii

CONTENTS

•III•
HISTORY OF CULTURE

ACKNOWLEDGMENTS

This book results from the Wingspread Conference on New Directions in American Intellectual History held at Racine, Wisconsin, in December 1977. It is thus a product, albeit an incomplete one, of the thought, energy, and good will of all those who made the conference possible.

First among them is the scholar in whose honor we met, the dean of American intellectual historians, Merle Curti, in the year of his eightieth birthday. Curti played a central role in numerous earlier conferences that dealt in one way or another with the direction of research in American history. The first and still the most comprehensive of these took place in 1931. Many of its recommendations retain an amazingly contemporary ring.* Thus Curti's presence at Wingspread not only graced our deliberations but also linked them with a wider, enduring quest. Those who were present will always remember the modesty and simplicity of his recollections, after dinner one evening, of the spirit in which the pioneers in the field went about their work.

Our indebtedness to Merle Curti was enlarged by the crucial support we received from the Johnson Foundation. It willingly hosted a meeting recognizing one of Wisconsin's first citizens, provided us with a beautiful meeting place, took from our shoulders all the burdens of local arrangements, and taped for its archives a permanent transcript of our discussions. In particular we thank Vice-President Henry M. Halsted. Hardly less indispensable was a grant from the National Endowment for the Humanities, which paid the cost of travel and lodging for all of the participants and secretarial assistance for the organizers.

Our fundamental intellectual debt is to our participating colleagues: to those whose papers will be published elsewhere as well as those whose contributions could fit within the compass of this book. For advice, counsel, and encouragement we are further indebted to Michael Kammen and Thomas Bender, and for assistance in early stages of the planning to David A. Shannon, Richard S. Kirkendall, Laurence Lerner, Ray Billington, Arthur Link, Richard Leopold, and David Levy.

J.H.

P.K.C.

---

* Committee of the American Historical Association on the Planning of Research, *Historical Scholarship in America: Needs and Opportunities* (New York: R. Long & R. R. Smith, 1932).

INTRODUCTION

⎯⎯ ◑ ◐ ⎯⎯

JOHN HIGHAM

In the 1930s and 1940s the study of American intellectual history enjoyed its heroic age. The excitement started with Vernon L. Parrington's *Main Currents in American Thought*. Two volumes came out in 1927, the third in 1930, and the thrill this great swashbuckling work sent tingling through the classrooms and seminars of American universities lasted for about twenty years. Nothing else a young scholar could undertake in those decades matched the challenge of discovering for oneself some of the dreams and purposes Parrington assured us of finding in the turbulent adventures of the American people. Among professional historians Merle Curti and Ralph Gabriel emerged as the outstanding pioneers. Their ranging syntheses—the most impressive of many—established the legitimacy of the field in a notably conservative profession. At Harvard, Perry Miller wrought a stunning transformation in the intellectual history of New England. And by the late 1940s a younger generation, led by Richard Hofstadter and Arthur Schlesinger, Jr., was rewriting the story of American politics with methods and insights of intellectual history.[1]

Throughout the next decade, the 1950s, the study of the American past was dominated by intellectual historians and their varied allies, the general historians who relied, as Hofstadter, Edmund Morgan, David Potter, and Daniel Boorstin did, primarily on cultural interpretations. The fruits of their common success accumulated on every hand: literary prizes, flocks of eager students, lavish contracts for textbooks, invitations to pronounce on the state of the nation. The buoyant mood prompted one leading intellectual historian, H. Stuart Hughes, to announce: "The chair of speculative social thought is nearly everywhere without an occupant. Historians have peculiar qualifications to fill it, and they are already beginning to do so."[2]

Some of them were indeed. The most exciting, as well as the most controversial, single achievement of intellectual historians in the 1950s was a fresh vision of the meaning of America—a vision that comprehended the whole of American history and thus illuminated the present also. According to this approach, a unifying framework of ideas and values had created a distinctive American people. It explained the

INTRODUCTION

durability of their society and institutions. The crucial task of historians was to define the matrix of beliefs and attitudes that shaped American history. Intellectual history gave the bite of scholarship to a broad quest for the American character.

The vogue of this quest for national definition proved devastatingly brief. In a few years of the early and midsixties what was called "consensus" history suddenly lost credibility. The entire conceptual foundation on which it rested crumbled away. As an analytic construct, national character was largely repudiated in all of the social sciences in which it had flourished. Simultaneously, in sociology, anthropology, and history, two working assumptions that were closely related to the idea of national character came under withering attack: first, the assumption that societies tend to be integrated, and second, that a shared culture maintains that integration.[3] Intellectual historians had by no means ranged themselves solidly behind either of these assumptions. Some had been among the leading critics of the consensus approach; most were sensitive to its limitations.[4] Nevertheless, the rejection of holistic theories and the intense reaction against any imputation of primacy to ideas in history certainly punctured the more grandiose pretensions of intellectual historians. In the 1950s intellectual history had seemed to offer the master key that could unlock the deepest secrets of the American past. By the late 1960s all claims issued in the name of an "American mind," a national "myth," a "climate of opinion," or a "liberal tradition" were subject to drastic skepticism.

Why so strong and abrupt a reaction? Clearly, the sociocultural upheaval of the sixties created the occasion. It deflated "consensus" history by dramatizing conflict and making power more vivid than consent. It commonly discouraged any special interest in the role of intellectuals in history by glorifying action and attributing primary importance to the "inarticulate" masses. So much is obvious, but this does not fully explain the undeniable persuasiveness of the new scholarly initiatives that rather suddenly emerged. The reaction against intellectual history would surely have been less severe had the occasion not precipitated a long overdue change in priorities within the historical profession. Social history came into its own.

After a vigorous development in the early decades of the twentieth century, the progress of social history was retarded in the 1940s and 1950s. When the political historians' dominance of the historical profession had first been challenged, the mavericks had not distinguished between social and intellectual history. They had cultivated an eclectic mélange they sometimes called social history, sometimes "social and intellectual history." In works such as *The History of American Life*, a thirteen-volume series that Arthur M. Schlesinger and Dixon Ryan Fox

INTRODUCTION

inaugurated in 1927, the early social historians came very much to the fore. Then, after their achievements had prepared the way, intellectual history separated itself from the older amalgam, and seized the initiative.[5] The mounting fascination with ideas and mentalities captured the imagination of young historians who might otherwise have studied the tangible, external dimensions of society. The study of social history was eclipsed for a generation.

Thus what happened in the 1960s was like the bursting of a dam. Social history had accumulated over the decades, but it had been contained. It had never seemed powerful. Now an earthquake split the dam and released a flood of waters across the entire terrain of scholarship. Accordingly the sixties did for the academic status of social history what the forties had done for intellectual history. It was now the social historians' turn to bask in the limelight, rallying throngs of students, mounting lavishly funded projects, and issuing brave pronunciamentos on their generalizing mission.[6]

The shift in priorities proved not entirely disadvantageous to intellectual historians. Above all, it relieved them from overextended commitments. Whether or not intellectual history has any intrinsic advantage as a medium of generalization may remain an open question; but it can hardly be doubted that the generalizations of the 1950s and 1960s needed a deepening and a complicating intellectual historians were unprepared to supply. Moreover, the "new" social history, far from discarding the entire agenda of the intellectual historians, has actually adopted some of their interests and has pursued them with fresh sophistication and precision. Studies of consciousness within specific groups or institutions (blacks, women, professions, mobs) have most especially gained from the impetus of social history, though such studies belong just as comfortably in the repertoire of many intellectual historians.

Still, a good many who persisted in calling themselves intellectual historians felt a loss of momentum. I noted something of the kind in an address I gave in 1968, but the full force of the shift did not come home to me until 1973, when I was president of the Organization of American Historians. The planning for the annual meeting was nearly completed before the able program chairman, Robert Kelley, and I became aware that only a couple of sessions out of a total of almost sixty might be labeled as intellectual history, and both of them concerned early periods. An additional session, which we speedily set up, turned out to involve a somewhat severe assessment of what the speaker called "The Contemporary Crisis in Intellectual History Studies."[7] That was when I started thinking about the need for a conference to take stock of the field and most especially to identify its assets and possibilities.

If I had had any doubts that intellectual history was in trouble, they

INTRODUCTION

would have been removed by the first reactions I received to the idea of a conference. One very distinguished scholar wrote: "I've been drifting away from intellectual history and doubt whether I personally could contribute anything of value." Another said he was pessimistic about the usefulness of a conference because the field seemed to lack a sense of direction. A third never answered my query at all. When Paul Conkin and I nevertheless joined forces and applied to a funding agency for support for a conference on the tasks and opportunities of American intellectual history, the anonymous reviewers—presumably experts in the field—vetoed our proposal. Among their various objections, we later learned, were a feeling that our plan lacked positive focus and a suspicion that we would not call upon the best authorities.

Conkin and I got a dramatically different reaction from the younger intellectual historians we approached. They responded with unbridled enthusiasm. Some of them felt not only a concern about the status of the field but also a certain isolation from other intellectual historians. The field had no organized structure and therefore no effective means for communication and self-appraisal. (The American Studies Association and its journal, the *American Quarterly*, had long offered a stimulating forum for academic discourse, since intellectual history and American Studies had grown up together in the 1940s and had flourished symbiotically. But the interests of the ASA had expanded beyond the scope of intellectual history, and the methodological preoccupations of American Studies had always been more diffuse.) Thus two acute needs seemed to beg for an organized response: first, a need to assess what is new and vital and heuristically significant in the study of American intellectual history, and second, a need to activate critical dialogue, especially among younger scholars in the field. A conference responding to this second need might, we hoped, create a continuing mode of association.

The mixed reactions to our first initiatives affected subsequent planning. Indifference from older professors and fervent support from younger ones indicated, we thought, the desirability of a conference deliberately tilted toward the emerging scholars in the field. We would of course endeavor to draw broadly and fairly on the widest possible variety of perspectives. Well-established people would be indispensable. But we would make a particular effort to provide a platform for the rising generation.

To allow new voices to speak to their own concerns, we avoided imposing an agenda. We left to the invitees the choice of their subjects, except for three or four topics we knew would have to be treated and for which we therefore actively solicited speakers. From the other participants we asked only for the most important thing he or she might have to say. We indicated that we were seeking clarification of basic issues

INTRODUCTION

and hoped the resulting book would constitute a showcase of what intellectual historians can do and are doing.

Early in 1977 funding was finally assured for a conference of twenty-four intellectual historians of the United States. We then had to choose among several hundred possible participants, many of them personally unknown to either of us. Several guiding principles simplified the selection. With one exception, we invited no more than a single scholar from any campus. Where we knew of two or more intellectual historians at the same institution, it seemed easiest to ask the senior one (diverging here from the youth principle). We admitted a maximum of two historians trained by any single professor. We sought a reasonable geographical distribution, which included one scholar from Canada and one from England. And we insisted that every participant submit an original paper in advance of the meeting.

A certain arbitrariness entered into the mix of authors and topics. Nearly everyone we asked accepted, even one eminent historian who had told me earlier he did not think such gatherings accomplished anything. Though three who accepted later withdrew, the conference spaces filled up before we could invite some of the very best people. Still, the papers our rough-and-ready procedures elicited probably tapped the intellectual energies at work in the field more fully than any exclusive roster of leading authorities could have done.

The conference met from 1 December to 3 December 1977, at Wingspread, a great house designed by Frank Lloyd Wright and located near Racine, Wisconsin. Every session was intense and stimulating. Instead of publishing the full proceedings, valuable as they would be, we have limited this book to the papers that seemed to offer a special methodological insight or a conceptual innovation of more than ordinary significance. Some of these essays have been extensively revised, even, in one case, entirely redesigned. Yet they still reflect several striking features of the original conference.

It was no surprise that two contrasting tendencies, which have shaped the study of intellectual history throughout the twentieth century, ran through every session. The essential difference, as Laurence Veysey makes abundantly clear in his chapter, has to do with the level of consciousness a historian chooses to highlight. Some historians concentrate on clearly articulated beliefs that are amenable to formal exegesis. Others are strongly drawn to examining the less refined level of consciousness the French have taught us to call collective mentalities.[8] We have followed that distinction in organizing this book. The essays relating primarily to the first tendency are grouped in part 2 under the rubric History of Ideas. Essays exhibiting the second tendency appear in part 3, History of Culture. The division, however, is far from clear cut. A number of essays, especially those we have placed in part 1, address the field as a whole. Each of those essays may be read as a particular conception of how the two tendencies can or should relate to one another; but the final impression they leave is of interdependence.

In contrast to the earlier fissions that aligned social historians against political historians, and then split intellectual historians away from social historians, one senses in the Wingspread group no susceptibility to further bifurcation. On the contrary, among the present company those who take the high road into the history of consciousness and those who take the low road seem less sharply opposed than their predecessors used to be.[9] The only previous conference on American intellectual history, a gathering at Arden House, New York, in 1960, discussed at length the relative desirability of the two tendencies.[10] The Wingspread conferees behaved quite differently. Throughout, they accepted without question the legitimacy of both tendencies. They argued about the fruitfulness of various methods for specific purposes, not about the proper domain of inquiry. What stands out in the work represented here is the interplay of approaches to intellectual history that used to stand in starker opposition.

By refusing to argue about boundaries and jurisdictions, the authors of this book have left their common terrain undefined. None tries to make authoritative a distinct conception of intellectual history, history of ideas, or cultural history. While various contributors employ these terms in diverse ways, a general disinclination to formulate exclusive claims permits a many-sided discourse to flourish.

Another feature of the Wingspread Conference was the special interest many of its participants showed in studying communities. Thomas Kuhn's interpretation of scientific communities has influenced several of our contributors. Taking off from Kuhn's stress on the control a scientific community exercises over the work of its members, Thomas Haskell suggests that "paradigmatic" assumptions may dominate all human communities so powerfully as to give intellectual history a highly deterministic cast. David Hollinger, moving in a more voluntaristic direction, uses the process of inquiry within scientific communities as a model for "communities of discourse" in many other domains of thought. In Hollinger's terms, intellectual history becomes a history of communities pursuing complex answers to their focal concerns. Thomas Bender also writes about a community-structured intellectual life. His special contribution is to bring out the importance of a transition in nineteenth-century America from one kind of community of discourse to another.

The fascination with community is reinforced in these pages by the influence of anthropology. Our contributors' acknowledgments in footnotes to Clifford Geertz (virtually the patron saint of the conference), to

INTRODUCTION

Anthony F. C. Wallace, to Mary Douglas, Victor Turner, Marvin Harris, and E. E. Evans-Pritchard are inescapable evidence of the increasing affinity intellectual historians have recently felt for the social science that shares most fully their own engagement with community and with culture—a science, moreover, that has in recent years notably enriched our grasp of the meanings expressed in symbol, ritual, and language.

A decade or two ago a gathering of intellectual historians would have talked a good deal about the heuristic insights of literary critics like Lionel Trilling and of psychologists in the Freudian tradition. Why the psychologists are represented in this collection only in Warren Susman's essay I do not know. Their absence otherwise may have been an accident of selection. But the shift of attention away from literary criticism, and in a larger sense from the whole realm of literature, is unmistakable. Through the middle decades of the twentieth century intellectual history, together with American Studies, did much to maintain traditional ties between history and literature. Sacvan Bercovitch's paper is cheering evidence that the connection is not entirely broken. Yet Bercovitch, the only Wingspread participant who is located in a Department of English, pays homage in his footnotes not to theories of literature but to the symbolic anthropology of Victor Turner.

Along with their relative indifference to literature, the Wingspread historians displayed a skepticism about the importance of individuals in history. Here we see the reverse side of the new attraction of communities and anthropological points of view. A generation or more ago intellectual history flourished in partnership with biography, since both seemed to assert a dimension of subjectivity and freedom in human affairs.[11] At the Wingspread Conference an interest in the creative individual—and thus ultimately in man's freedom—was far from absent. Yet that concern surfaced chiefly in papers that sharply circumscribed the role of individuals in history. These papers, by Thomas Haskell and Gordon Wood, approach ideas not as motives but as massive constraints on individual intention and will. Wood, it is true, ultimately grants a crucial significance to the "great thinkers." Even as it is made, however, the concession is partially withdrawn. Intellectual history, as represented in the present volume, does little to encourage the study of distinctive individuals.[12]

Finally, in placing this book in historical perspective, one should notice the insistent demand for rigor and precision, a demand made even more strongly in the conference discussions than in the papers themselves. "Generalizations," Laurence Veysey warns us in the paper that turned out to be the keynote address, "must be extremely hard earned." Veysey's essay makes quite explicit how much his severe admonitions are a reaction against the "pretentiously grandiose" interpretations of leading

INTRODUCTION

intellectual historians of the 1950s. Even Rush Welter, writing after the conference ended and arguing for the necessity and possibility of sound, nationwide generalizations, rejects the concept of national character. Welter's essay offers a prescription for generalizing about large, internally differentiated populations without sacrificing the rigor the conferees typically required. Intellectual history seems to have met the setbacks of the 1960s by honing its critical and analytical techniques.

However, there is no unanimity in this lively dialogue. Sacvan Bercovitch, Warren Susman, and in a more tentative way Dorothy Ross have given us broadly conceived papers that do not altogether conform to Welter's rules for studying the national mind. Nor do they submit to Veysey's insistence on studying identifiable social aggregates. In these papers the pursuit of wider schemes of thought, extending beyond discernible networks or social categories, continues in various ways. Remembering the Wingspread Conference and reading this book, one may conclude that the division between historians of ideas and cultural historians may be less important than a cross-cutting division of purposes: a predominant desire in both camps to assure the integrity of intellectual history as specialized knowledge, and a countervailing determination among a few to carry the intellectual historian's quest for meanings beyond the safety of all specialized communities.

Notes

1. In 1951 John Caughey polled "an approximate cross section" of academic historians of America, including all ages and specialists in all phases and periods, on the best works in American history published since 1920. Parrington's *Main Currents* led the list so commandingly that nothing else even came close except Frederick Jackson Turner's *The Frontier in American History* (1920). Among the more recent books on Caughey's list—those published from 1936 to 1950—the top scorer was Merle Curti's *The Growth of American Thought* (1943). John Walton Caughey, "Historians' Choice: Results of a Poll on Recently Published American History and Biography," *Mississippi Valley Historical Review* 39 (September 1952): 289–302. For an account of this early period see my own starry-eyed survey, "The Rise of American Intellectual History," *American Historical Review* 56 (April 1951): 453–71, and Robert Allen Skotheim's *American Intellectual Histories and Historians* (Princeton, N.J.: Princeton University Press, 1966).

2. H. Stuart Hughes, *History as Art and as Science: Twin Vistas on the Past* (New York: Harper & Row, 1964), p. 107.

3. Robert F. Berkhofer, Jr., "Clio and the Culture Concept: Some Impressions of a Changing Relationship in American Historiography," in *The Idea of Culture in the Social Sciences*, ed. Louis Schneider and Charles M. Bonjean (Cambridge: At the University Press, 1973), pp. 77–100.

4. John Higham, "The Cult of the 'American Consensus'," *Commentary* 27 (February 1959): 93–100; John P. Diggins, "Consciousness and Ideology in American

INTRODUCTION

History: The Burden of Daniel J. Boorstin," *American Historical Review* 76 (February 1971): 99–118.

5. Felix Gilbert, "Intellectual History: Its Aims and Methods," *Daedalus* 100 (Winter 1971): 89–93. This is the first of two issues of *Daedalus* devoted entirely to the state of historical studies at the beginning of the present decade.

6. Samuel P. Hays, "A Systematic Social History," in *American History: Retrospect and Prospect*, ed. George Athan Billias and Gerald N. Grob (New York: Free Press, 1971), pp. 315–66. See also Gene Wise, "The Contemporary Crisis in Intellectual History Studies," *Clio* 5 (1975): 55–69.

7. Wise, "Contemporary Crisis."

8. In France the history of mentalities has become a somewhat distinct genre, which is contrasted with the history of ideas and which has concerned itself especially with popular fantasies and delusions. (See Jacques le Goff, "Les mentalités: Une histoire ambiguë," in *Faire de l'histoire: Nouveaux objets* [Paris: Éditions Gallimard, 1974], pp. 76–94.) In this book we have retained the older, looser, and more capacious term, "cultural history," while recognizing that the American historians who use it to describe their work are usually most interested in mentalities.

9. The interplay between these tendencies is traced over time in John Higham, *Writing American History: Essays on Modern Scholarship* (Bloomington: Indiana University Press, 1970), pp. 41–72, and is analyzed on a larger scale in Leonard Krieger, "The Autonomy of Intellectual History," *Journal of the History of Ideas* 34 (October–December 1973): 499–516.

10. Charles Barker to Frederick Burkhardt, American Council of Learned Societies, 10 November 1960, and accompanying documents in the author's files.

11. John Higham with Leonard Krieger and Felix Gilbert, *History* (Englewood Cliffs, N.J.: Prentice-Hall, 1965), pp. 204–10.

12. A qualification may be in order. Two of the original group of Wingspread papers did focus on the ideas of a single intellectual, with the object of demonstrating the historical significance of those ideas. The editors have chosen not to include these papers, since neither seemed altogether to serve the exemplary purposes of the present book. Thus our own criteria are partly responsible for the absence of studies of individuals.

DEFINITIONS

INTELLECTUAL HISTORY
AND THE NEW SOCIAL HISTORY

LAURENCE VEYSEY

Writers of intellectual history, like the members of any group, may sometimes be tempted to put a cheerful face on things, to minimize the difficulties they confront when their claims are measured on a broader stage, for instance by other kinds of historians. The ethos of specialization allows us to do our own work, looking toward our closest intellectual neighbors for reassurance, enjoying our undeniable successes, and regarding outside criticism as based largely on lack of comprehension of what we are about.

Because such tendencies can be so powerful, and because my own loyalties are genuinely divided between social and intellectual history, I deliberately want to emphasize rather than downplay the sense of threat that has lately arisen as to the viability of our enterprise as intellectual historians. I shall ultimately defend intellectual history, but only after making some rather large concessions to its critics, perhaps thereby leaving a number of its practitioners uneasy. I do hope that the spirit of unflinching self-examination once thought appropriate in Massachusetts Bay has not yet entirely gone out of fashion.

Intellectual history has never been altogether admired by historians of other persuasions. When it was an upstart field in the 1940s and early 1950s, those who wrote political history sometimes regarded it with disdain.[1] Perhaps they felt threatened. Intellectual historians often treated subject matter with a new subtlety; between the lines they implied that the scholar was to be more like an intellectual himself. Yet, while it unleashed these sometimes quite hostile reactions, intellectual history gained ground rapidly in the 1950s. It had the sense of fresh excitement, of avant-gardism within the discipline that now attaches itself to social history. Moreover, in political terms it was uncontroversially nationalist; it contributed to, rather than challenged, the basic ideological mood of the decade. It reenforced the sense of a distinctive American national culture and of the power and dignity of leading ideas or "myths" that were attributed to it. And it did this despite the germ it contained of a conservative or aristocratic critique of America, along lines laid down by Tocqueville and Henry James.[2]

3

LAURENCE VEYSEY

More recently the claims of intellectual history, insofar as they involve the autonomy and the influence of formal ideas or systems or belief, have been challenged simultaneously on several distinct fronts. Marx and Freud have divided much of the intellectual authority of the Western world between them during the twentieth century; though their vogue might in itself serve to illustrate the potency of certain ideas, their explicit messages helped to undercut belief in the explanatory significance of thought, considered as the surface level of intellectual discourse. (In this respect, unlike others, their effect paralleled the rise of skeptical relativism.) Thought on its literal face has come to be regarded as a "front," either for class interests or for deeper emotional desires.

Yet, insofar as the climate of American scholarship remained antitheoretical and hence unreceptive to Freudian or Marxist interpretations, it again fostered skepticism toward nonutilitarian motives and bred a disposition to counter the "fanciness" of intellectual history in the style of the older political historians. Meanwhile, colleagues in such adjacent fields as literature and philosophy could often justly regard intellectual historians either as dilettantes, engaged in rapid, superficial forays over their own best-loved terrain, or else as dangerous relativists simply because they were historians—never concerned with the truth of anything, only with the endless spectacle of rising and declining fashions.

Faced with such diverse pressures, many intellectual historians retreated into the rather safe and limited arena of political and social thought; their courses became no more than background for the study of standard topics in American politics. If they justified their labors in terms of cultural holism (the "Americanness" of this or that), they found themselves under further fire from opposite directions as the 1960s wore on—there was pressure either to expand to a more cosmopolitan frame of reference, beyond the provincialism of the United States, or to pay newly serious heed to the difficulties of generalization about American attitudes or beliefs as distinct from those of specific classes, regions, sexes, and ethnic groups.

Intellectual historians thus emerged with few friends. Alone among all academics they operated (if they thought carefully about what they were doing) under the paradoxical working assumption that all ideas are false but important.

First, false, in the sense that nothing can be flatly or eternally true, for every form of belief will no doubt peak and then decline, or at any rate go through changes that make it all but unrecognizable—as Christianity did in the early nineteenth century and natural science in the early twentieth. (It seems scarcely necessary, in the post-Kuhnian climate, to argue that ideas that claim to be scientific are no less "false" in this sense than any others. The only difference between scientific and other ideas, for example, concerning the nature of the universe, which probably withstands current insights into the temporality and ultimate fallibility of beliefs, is the more than coincidentally close relationship between the scientific ideas of the last few hundred years and the technological transformation of the physical appearance of the planet.) As historians, our task is to relate phenomena, whether events or ideas, to specific points in time. This in itself casts doubt upon the idea of ultimate truth. Further, the effort to seek historical objectivity requires us to write about all ideas as if they were equally credible or incredible, except as judged by particular temporal or cultural biases from which we must try to stand apart. We often rather harmlessly violate this injunction by indulging in clever asides. But when we go beyond this to allow our preferences among ideas to affect our basic account of the reasons for the rise or decline of particular ideas over time, we become vulnerable to the criticism that we have lost sight of the main point of what we are doing and have instead become amateur cosmologists or moral philosophers. The histories of such topics as witchcraft or Pentecostalism have not been advanced by writing as if such beliefs were "bound" to disappear in the sunlight of reason, nor by the claim that these creeds offer true knowledge. A posture of distance from them and from the Enlightenment is required.

If intellectual historians do well to adopt the working assumption that ideas of all kinds tend to be false, they nonetheless retain commitment to a second proposition that ideas are important as historical agents, and are not to be subsumed under economic, psychological, or other categories lying beyond them. Generally, other humanists would not treat ideas as if they were all timebound, while other social scientists would not usually subscribe—at least so wholeheartedly—to their causal importance. Only intellectual history, if I read these comparisons right, has as its very core an extreme juxtaposition of intellectual skepticism with meticulousness in the handling of ideas. Out of such austere requirements issues a form of historical writing with very rich potential, yet (when well done) drastically unlike the kind of history a layman—or an economic historian—can easily connect with. Moreover, it is a kind of history that in today's climate almost seems to invite attacks of great cogency and force, asking whether such an approach has any right to command attention as more than an arcane curiosity.

During the 1960s and early 1970s social history rapidly came to eclipse intellectual history as the major source of excitement within our discipline. Whether it was a truly "new" social history I shall not try to argue here, though the high value it places on the quantification of evidence, as well as its thoroughgoing insistence on elevating the history of anonymous masses of people above that of cultivated elites, at the very least

LAURENCE VEYSEY

gives it emphases that challenge most earlier political as well as intellectual history.[3] Social historians have behaved aggressively toward other kinds of historians. Though they will sometimes offer polite gestures about the continuing need to make use of literary evidence,[4] they frequently take pride in advancing a behavioralist conception of human nature that leaves no room for the autonomy or significance of nonutilitarian ideas. Much of the earlier political historians' animus against intellectual history has infected the younger social historians.[5]

At stake in this controversy is not only the relative worth of studying "ordinary" as compared with exceptional people but drastically different notions of the human mind itself. In effect, behavioralists put forward an uncomplicated, utilitarian conception of motivation, not trying to deny consciousness in the exact spirit of John B. Watson, but applying common-sense notions of the "realistic" pursuit of self-interest, such as in upward social mobility, and tending to dismiss all else as insubstantial. (It must be said that certain intellectual historians, for instance Daniel J. Boorstin and also to a degree some of the older "progressives" under the spell of Deweyan pragmatism, were guilty of going rather far in the same direction.) Behind slogans cast in the archaic shorthand of "ideas" versus "social forces," there lurks the more genuine question of the relative weight to be given deep-seated cultural predispositions as against immediate calculations of gain in affecting actions. In India, where cows go unconsumed during famines, the answer would seem given. But in America, where the affluent eat fats their long-range self-interest would spurn, and where utility is said at the same time to have become a cultural predisposition, a rather complicated argument along these lines emerges.

In substantive terms, social and intellectual history have lately offered versions of American history that are ever more distant from each other. Insofar as intellectual historians still claim to be accounting for the whole of America,[6] these dissimilar renditions of American history have become clear-cut rivals. Social history portrays a deeply segmented society, split by race, sex, and social class. Intellectual history either suggests a single culture or dwells on subworlds within the Protestant and Jewish elites. Social history dwells upon blacks, immigrants, women, the poor, New Yorkers, Pennsylvanians, Marylanders. Intellectual history emphasizes ministers, lawyers, radicals, writers, professors, New Englanders, a few whites from the deep South, and (by an odd quirk) the more articulate politicians. For social historians the central institution of the past century is the factory; for intellectual historians, the university. Social history, finally, studies census returns and city directories, sources that offer representative evidence about populations. Intellectual history

INTELLECTUAL HISTORY AND THE NEW SOCIAL HISTORY

unashamedly studies some of the most unrepresentative evidence conceivable.

⊂══════⊃ ⊙ ⊙ ⊂══════⊃

Let us move from this attempt at a descriptive and historical summary to the analytical and prescriptive question of what the relations between intellectual and social history should be. Or, to phrase this more pointedly, should intellectual historians change their methods and approach to respond to the kinds of challenges recently posed by the younger social historians?

In order to make my suggestions comprehensible, I shall briefly put forth a larger conception of the historical enterprise, so that we may locate social and intellectual history (and various versions thereof) within it.

An overriding concern for temporality distinguishes the historian from academics of all other persuasions—except astronomers, earth scientists, and some biologists, who might be called the historians of nature.[7] In one way or another, this has long been said.[8] I think it is possible to be still more specific. Historians are primarily concerned with trying to understand unevenness in rates of change—that is, why relative continuity and stability (a slow rate of change) exist in some times and places, and extremely rapid rates of change (often called "revolutions") exist in others. In graphic terms, our eyes are attracted to kinks in the curve of change—in politics, such years as 1776, 1861 to 1865, 1917 to 1919. We want to know why change fails to arrive in the quiet periods, why it occurs so rapidly when it does come. Now, this fundamental notion of studying changes in the rate of change may be applied to any subject matter whatever, whether it is a solar system, an entire society, or, in a biography, the trajectory of a single individual's career. A definition of historical inquiry along these lines emphasizes that all subject matter is equally legitimate (hence, certainly, both social and intellectual history). What is historical about any study is the attempt to contribute to an understanding of the reasons for relative change or continuity over time of the entity one is addressing. Some books, of course, attempt only to describe a given society, or a portion of one, at a particular point in time. But they are really part of this same undertaking, for they help establish chronological landmarks with greater precision and usually offer a portrait of a "plateau" period (one with relatively slow change), thus furnishing important counterweights to the study of revolution. Historians, in one way or another, usually tell us, "Something happened, or failed to happen (like socialism), and this is why."

LAURENCE VEYSEY

The use of the words *reasons* and *why* in the above definition calls for a brief aside. The concept of causality is currently in rather bad form among philosophers and social scientists; the latter often substitute the word "significance" to describe correlations, yet when they do so the idea of "cause" continues to lurk in the mind. Such devices amount to over-protections against Humean arguments. It seems to me that, despite all the difficulties that adhere to the notion of causality, historians must surely continue, with whatever vocabulary, to regard as central the effort to answer "why" questions about the past—why a given outcome and not another one, occurred. A purely narrative history, or a merely evoca-tive history, can evade these issues. But then it wraps its subject in an unexamined assumption of inevitability. Forthrightly to analyze alter-native outcomes gives us a historical universe far livelier than narrow accounts of particular battles from the inside, though the feeling of what it was like to be alive inside such a battle may crucially convey what was at stake.

The subject of history, to return, may be anything—planets, cows, or ideas, as well as men—so long as a reasonably convincing explanation of important turning points in that history can be attempted. Therefore, in practice, a history of cows (or indeed of nearby planets during the present century) would have to include some aspects of the history of men. Whether this is also true about the history of ideas is a central bone of contention between some intellectual and social historians. That is, can ideas be treated autonomously, as if they were unlikely to be affected by any potential solar catastrophe? Do they form disembodied abstractions apart from any origin in or consequence for the broader lives of men, including their own creators? A substantial fraction of current writing in intellectual history proceeds, at least in practice, as if this might be so.

The history of men and women, I would argue, is social history before it is anything else. A broad tradition in social science, exemplified by such figures as Durkheim, Cooley, and Mead, tells us that man is at bottom a social being, that membership in collectivities is his most fun-damental attribute, and that individual distinction of all kinds, including intellectual, represents variations from this norm. The fact that single persons have a shorter life expectancy than the married lends possible biological weight to this line of reasoning, though American society cur-rently attempts to equalize the moral value of these respective possibil-ities.

Mankind—or any particular nation-state or city—may be thought of as a mosaic of social groups. These groups, or aggregates, are the basic building blocks of social history. All people are members simultaneously of more than one such aggregate (for example, family, workgroup, na-

INTELLECTUAL HISTORY AND THE NEW SOCIAL HISTORY

tion), and each aggregate imposes its own quite distinct demands and expectations upon us, often called social roles. Certain social aggregates —generally of small size—have peculiar relevance to intellectual history ("serious" novelists, Cannonite Trotskyists, Presbyterian theologians, and so on). So another way of stating the problem of the relationship between social and intellectual history is to ask whether a person's role as an intellectual may be sufficiently self-contained to make it unimportant to look for links between it and the same person's other roles. Beyond this, are some thinkers so very sufficient entirely as individuals ("geniuses," in the vocabulary of romanticism) that their thought, aside from its later influence, requires no aggregate context at all? I wonder if anyone, pondering the lives of a dozen or so familiar intellectual figures, would feel entitled to give a categorical "yes" or "no" answer to these questions. We think of the absurdity of trying to understand Charles Ives in the context of the insurance business, but then we recall his relationship to the Fourth of July. We are led to review the intricacies of selectivity in the encounter of such men with the world, the degree of compartmentalization that some persons, perhaps especially intellectuals, experience for long periods in their lives. The degree of autonomy in one's intellectual life—both from the nonintellectual and from other intellectuals—would seem to be one of the variable conditions of such an existence. At one end of this spectrum stands Immanuel Kant, apparently troubled only by the ghost of David Hume; at the other, perhaps someone like Mike Gold, affirming that the only valid literature is written by steelworkers in their spare moments. (But what unknown experiences of isolation did he have to endure in order to reach such an emphatic conclusion?)

Most of the time, even in intellectual history, one is dealing with social aggregates. One is trying to explain changes or failures to change within such collectivities. Is there anything special about the kinds of social aggregates the intellectual historian studies? Some would in fact define intellectual history on this basis, as the history of those small groups of people who, in modern parlance, we term "intellectuals."[9] The virtue of this definition is that it provides a clear-cut (if extremely modest) role for intellectual history within the overall context of social history. Questions of the broader influence of intellectuals are avoided; intellectuals become a self-contained group engaged in mutual discourse. Of course such a modesty of definition is from the numerical standpoint of a broader social history; it may in fact free the historian to pursue, without guilt or restraint, the most arcane thought processes of exceptional individuals.

It is not likely that a majority of intellectual historians will even now take this way out. They would prefer to picture themselves as competent to deal with the history of larger social aggregates, even if not such truly major ones as the United States. They would define their role as putting forward a particular kind of explanation, or understanding, of human motivation with regard to historical outcomes in groups. At its crudest, this has sometimes been formulated as "the power of ideas" to control the lives and actions of men. Intellectual historians, from this perspective, are specialists in an antimaterialist, or anti-Marxist, view of history as a whole.

It was no doubt such a propensity among intellectual historians, stronger in the 1950s than it is today, that gave them so much persistent trouble with political and social historians. The collision of intellectual history with Marxism was no doubt less important, among the wider audience of historians, than its affront to a native (or Anglo-American) tradition of skeptical empiricism. Intellectual history became widely identified with claims that the ideas of Puritan ministers, and later of Woodrow Wilson, were broadly influential (for good or for ill) in shaping the outcome of American history. Political and social historians, meanwhile, put forward a much more "realistic," or cynical, view of human nature. Our earlier discussion showed that the weighing of utilitarian and nonutilitarian motives in American culture is in fact an intricate question, possessing much potential interest. But in its simplified form, the debate that long went on over the matter of American "idealism" or its absence became exceedingly tedious. On the sweeping level in which the issue was put, the answer was never resolvable so long as both "idealistic" and material forces were pushing the United States in the same direction, toward wealth and power.

Nowadays we can review the broad picture of human motivation, and the kinds of pigeonholes we commonly construct to account for it, in a far more complex way than in that older, two-sided juxtaposition of "ideas" and "material forces." In the accompanying table, I have tried to do no more than make explicit the classification of motives that I believe historians of the present time routinely follow in their work. Needless to say, I scarcely regard the categories in this table as in any sense final or absolute, even at the level of sheer description; the table is only a working attempt to list the kinds of explanations historians most frequently advance. The approach taken in coming up with these various categories and labels was simply to ask this question: If all important historical writings by Americans of the past century were to be visualized as a series of maneuvers on a gameboard, what might that gameboard look like? The game would be called "I've Got a Causal Explanation for Change or Failure to Change in a Social Aggregate!"[10] In the table, the vertical columns (I, II, and III) present characterizations of thought or

CATEGORIZATION OF EXPLANATIONS FOR CHANGE OR FAILURE TO CHANGE IN SOCIAL AGGREGATES
(THE GAME HISTORIANS ACTUALLY PLAY)

Stages of Inquiry

1. Identification and definition of a social aggregate (or two or more in temporal, comparative, or conflictual relationship), a universe of intended generalization.

2. Advancement of a causal explanation for change or failure to change in some area(s) of the members' lives, or for the outcome of their interaction with other aggregates, in a given period of time, roughly along the lines of the chart below, selecting one of the boxes that has been neglected or minimized by previous historians, or according to one's cognitive or political bias:

I. Social Realities (perceived by observer)	II. Collective Mentalities (expectations, self-perceptions)	III. Formal Systems of Thought
A. Economic. Conditions of physical subsistence; goods; living standards; distribution.	A. Economic. Degree of desire for betterment or fear of deprivation; degree of rationality in Weber's sense.	A. Economic. Philosophies of ideal distribution of resources.
B. Status oriented. Stratification systems; organizational hierarchies; degree of mobility, fluidity, dignity.	B. Status oriented. Perceptions and expectations of rising, or of equal treatment, or of discrimination, or of failing.	B. Status oriented. Philosophies of social equality or inequality, for example, of social democracy.
C. Political. Degree of domination of or by others; actual power networks.	C. Political. Expectations as to rights to freedom from domination or to dominate others.	C. Political. Theories of government.
D. Collectivity oriented. Loyalties to group, solidarity, "consciousness" as versus isolation, secession, competitiveness. Rituals, ceremonies. Levels of participation.	D. Collectivity oriented. Norms of solidarity as versus permissiveness toward deviance, originality, competitive struggle, indifference, apathy.	D. Collectivity oriented. Much moral and religious philosophy belongs here, as well as general social philosophy.
E. Sexual. Rates, forms, varieties of sexual contact.	E. Sexual. Sexual norms.	E. Sexual. Sexual philosophies (for example, Freudianism).
F. Aesthetic. Level of complexity, balance, ingenuity in decoration. Works of art.	F. Aesthetic. Attitudes toward beauty, nature, art; literary criticism.	F. Aesthetic. Aesthetic philosophies.
G. Cognitive. Level of awareness of outside world; level of abstractions and of realism in ordering them.	G. Cognitive. Definitions of the universe, moving forces in it, etc. Popular religious beliefs.	G. Cognitive. Epistemological systems (scientific or theological).
H. Affective. Intensity of passion as against quiescent resignation or acceptance of one's lot (emotion as ordinarily understood).	H. Affective. Beliefs, moral codes regarding whether to express or hold in one's desires, discontents, of particular kinds.	H. Affective. Aspects of philosophies that relate to abstinence or indulgence in gratification.

2a. At some point, to explain change or failure to change (action or inaction), the historian may also introduce the following factors on the level of catalyst or immediate agent:

3. Application of the explanation to the existence of an unusually slow or rapid, deceptive or genuine, rate or kind of change in the social aggregate, preferably with implications for other social aggregates.

4. Embellishment of the argument, through use of impressionistic sources and the historian's own wit and literary talent, to add vividness, nuance, immediacy, and suggestive width of range to the causal explanation that forms the skeleton of the work.

LAURENCE VEYSEY

behavior, which are grossly defined according to their degree and kind of consciousness; the horizontal columns (lettered A through H) refer to specific areas of human life that have long seemed to form semi-autonomous zones of behavior, feeling, and thought, often, in recent decades, with entire academic disciplines built around them, such as economics, political science, sociology, art, literature, and philosophy.[11] This basic distinction tries to account for the fact that as historians we simultaneously employ both modes of ordering the raw material of existence in our minds and that confusion in this respect has been central to earlier oversimplified formulations of a clash between "ideas" and more down-to-earth historical subjects and motives.

The three vertical columns on the chart deserve our attention first. Social historians like to stick close to what they informally think of as "social reality"—institutional structures or behavioral patterns that require only a utilitarian conception of mental processes.[12] At the extreme they wish to omit, or only grudgingly refer to, deeply implanted cultural norms that might affect historical results—for instance, the relative speed with which particular immigrant groups have attained middle-class status in the United States.[13] Less rationalistic explanations, such as that Jews succeeded better than other groups because of inherited cultural norms rather than because of their higher degree of urbanization in Europe (a purely structural reason), are avoided almost as if they smacked of biological racism. Some economic historians would like to picture slaves on Southern plantations as highly rational would-be capitalists. Demographers and historians of disease may speak at times as if human life were only a matter of birth and death, bypassing the in-between cultural content as inessential.

These are excesses of attitude that have occurred during the recent offensive by social historians. Usually in theory, and often in practice, such historians do indeed grant some place to the study of mental norms and expectations—for instance, to the myth of America as a land of economic opportunity—operating beyond the degree of actual social mobility in the society. For even the *Annales* school, that great source of inspiration to American social historians, assigns an important role to the study of *mentalité*, or collective states of mind. What we have been calling social history in fact divides itself between vertical columns I and II on the chart. Indeed, some of its most acclaimed results center on discrepancies between group expectation or self-perception and structural reality, a classic instance being the contrast between rainfall patterns and beliefs about the American West long ago revealed by Henry Nash Smith. More recently, the historical energy focused upon women and sexuality in the nineteenth century gains impetus from a sense of appalling disjuncture between cultural inhibitions and what are now assumed to be more natural, or structurally given, inclinations.

If we turn to the relations between vertical columns II and III on the chart, we encounter another range of issues highly familiar to us as intellectual historians. On the one hand, we have collective mentalities again (which, we should remind ourselves, can refer to social aggregates of any size, including bands of intellectuals). On the other, we have what are here termed formal systems of thought. Social historians, with rare exceptions, do not like to wander over at all into column III, but for some intellectual historians, the historical evidence to be assigned to this column comprises the whole of their lifelong scholarly undertaking. These historians of ideas form a counterpart, at an opposite extreme, to those social or economic historians who rigorously confine themselves to column I. They, along with some devotees of column II, may even seek to minimize or deny the independent existence of social realities in the time-honored fashion of philosophical idealism, warming to Collingwood's notorious dictum that "all history is the history of thought." In this respect they commit excesses of their own. Admittedly, the kinds of information so crudely lumped together in vertical column I are extremely diverse in their character, including everything from what one man ate for dinner in 1810 to national population figures. There is probably no ultimate arbiter between someone who refuses to use a term like "realities" for all such information and someone (like myself) who is willing to do so. Most history today is written as if one could speak about such "realities." Still to reject them on the basis of their insubstantiality is, to my mind, dangerously to approach the ostrichlike posture often associated with Christian Science.

We may still wonder about the relations between columns II and III. What are formal systems of thought, and why should they be singled out from other mental states? Formal thought may be identified by either of two criteria: first, by its degree of explicitness, or, second, by its self-conscious aspiration to be comprehensive or systematic in treating whatever realm of discourse it addresses. The first criterion was enunciated by Charles Peirce when he stated, "It is the belief men *betray* and not that which they *parade* which has to be studied."[14] This has remained a beguiling distinction, central to the understanding of many intellectual historians who treat material on both sides of its dividing line.[15] Yet, on reflection, one may be impressed by the many degrees of explicitness contained in any piece of writing. Much intellectual history depends for its method upon assigning meaning to rhetoric in ways that would not fully have occurred to its author, yet of which he would not have been entirely unaware. Semiconsciousness may be a more frequent mental

LAURENCE VEYSEY

state, whether or not one is writing down one's thoughts, than either full consciousness—whatever it may mean—or unconsciousness. Explicitness may be a frail reed on which to hang a working definition of formal thought.

Not all thought that is explicitly paraded aspires to be systematic. If formal thought, the material for investigation in column III, is defined instead as systematic thought, this admittedly produces its own problems. System implies logic and coherence, as well as the effort to relate one's efforts to a given world of discourse, often to try to comprehend such a world as a whole. It places a high value upon inner consistency. Yet another of our favorite pastimes as intellectual historians is to lay bare inconsistencies and illogicalities in the writings of even the most eminent philosophers, social thinkers, and theologians. Were we to demand a truly rigorous standard of this kind, the subject matter in column III might soon shrink away to almost nothing. If we want to retain column III, we must be more generous. It is better for it to refer, then, to an author's intentions or aspirations, than to our judgment of his or her product. Henry George, for example, ought to be accepted as fit material for this kind of history, because he clearly attempted to produce systematic thought, however much we might debate its quality. This returns us, to be sure, to the sometimes elusive issue of a writer's consciousness, but with only one concrete question in mind—no longer his degree of consciousness in general, but only his conscious desire to produce something within a recognized genre of discourse commonly tied to an established realm of human knowledge. The very appearance of a certain kind of work—bearing in mind the injunction to be generous as to matters of quality—should in most cases suffice to answer such a question. The Bible, as arranged by the early church fathers, carries with it the pretension to be an inclusive and in that sense a systematic exposition of God in his relations to men, despite its frequent internal incoherence; *Progress and Poverty* clearly aspires to similar inclusiveness in its address to American social problems. On the other hand, the output of literary circles in nineteenth-century New England would qualify only to the degree that the authors saw their essays and novels as vehicles for contributing to an aesthetic, philosophical, political, or social paradigm of understanding, and not merely as reverie, psychological insight, or random commentary. I hope these examples help to clarify a possible boundary line between columns II and III on the chart.

Yet what after all really justifies the separate existence of column III? It is possible, of course, for a historian to cling to column II as exclusively as to column I, and from that perspective to deny that formal systems of thought have any historical importance, at least in our own society. To judge this issue is partly to evaluate the achievement of

INTELLECTUAL HISTORY AND THE NEW SOCIAL HISTORY

Daniel J. Boorstin's three-volume history of the United States, *The Americans*. For Boorstin devoted his whole career to nothing less than the effort to write history as if collective mentality were the only thing that mattered, while discounting the role of ideologies. Such boldness on his part drew great excitement in the 1950s. Yet John Higham, John P. Diggins, and others have done much to deflate his credibility on precisely this score. It would be highly partisan, at this point in time, to maintain that formal systems of thought, and the discourse that surrounds them, have no recognizable place in the history of ideas in this country. Moreover, to do this would deny the legitimacy of major recent works in American intellectual history, such as Elizabeth Flower's and Murray G. Murphey's *A History of Philosophy in America*,[16] that offer us the inner workings of a highly developed tradition of mental activity confined to very small numbers and clearly distinct from larger collective mental states in the main, if not in every detail. Even if such rarefied ideas had no wide influence (and many of them clearly did not), their history would deserve to be studied simply for its own sake, in the same way that paleontologists come to admire strikingly absurd forms of life that no longer exist.

We can by now see how clearly the older debate within our discipline between advocates of an emphasis on "ideas" and those stressing material forces has been transcended. At the very least, such a debate has become three sided. A middle zone, involving the study of collective mentalities, is occupied by persons variously calling themselves social, cultural, or intellectual historians. At the same time, it is possible for a scholar to spend an entire lifetime happily and fruitfully confined within any one of the three vertical columns on the chart. Indeed, in this connection many distinguished names come easily to mind. My aim in presenting this chart has been, first of all, to help foster respect for widely varying kinds of excellence and, by laying out this entire landscape, to plead that we think of ourselves as historians foremost, rather than in terms of any narrower classification. History may be unique as a discipline in allowing its practitioners to study any area of human interest and motivation whatsoever, and openmindedly to compare one area with another in their relation to a given event or situation. Most other academics have their salaries paid by hierarchies loyal to one such zone (be it art or economics); in a sense, no matter how restless they become, they are forced to emphasize a single parochial region in everything they say and write. But historians throw away their inestimable advantage when they voluntarily confine themselves to explicating some particular motive.

The addition of the chart's second dimension, the subject-matter specialties defined in horizontal columns A through H, breaks down the

LAURENCE VEYSEY

stark distinction between ideas and economics still further. The area of our lives we label as economic has both its tangible and its mentally defined aspects; so indeed do the areas having to do with aesthetics and cognitive philosophies. The economy is an entity, among others, that one may have an idea about, and a theory of historical materialism is an idea. At the same time the economy is only one portion of what we term social reality, no doubt always prominent, but at some moments less so than the emotional "boiling point" of a crowd. (I.H on the chart). Perhaps by now we can see how many important distinctions must be made among the kinds of evidence and assertion that are still too often crudely lumped together as "economic."

An instance of trying to play an actual game on this historian's game-board will further show the obsolescence of simplistic confrontations between ideas and economics. No more hallowed chestnut of this kind can be found than the question of the relations between Puritanism and the rise of wealth in America. (Indeed, here lies the heartland of what I earlier described as an exceedingly tedious debate over the influence of "idealism," in the popular sense, in our society.) A brief analysis of this debate may at least put some of the issues to rest. Intellectual historians have tended to argue that Puritan theology (III.G on the chart) translated itself into a burning desire for material betterment (II.A), and thereupon into an actual sharp rise of income (I.A). Contrastingly, social historians have claimed that frontier conditions, such as an abundance of land (I.A), broke down traditional religious inhibitions (III.G and III.A) to lead to rising wealth (I.A again, without need to resort to some explanation beyond social reality), producing eventual effects on the collective state of mind (II.A). First of all, these interpretations are notable for their opposite readings of the Puritan message on wealth-seeking. And, after decades of debate, if the factual matter remains unclear, little hope would seem to remain for a resolution of the essentials of the argument when it is cast in these terms. Further, if two disputed causes (I.A and III.G) both feed into a given result (wealth), in purely logical terms it will never be possible to weigh their relative effects. It may be high time to recast the issue according to a more complicated model of the human mind, which the very distinction on the chart between vertical columns II and III enables us to suggest.

Let us suppose (though historians are only beginning to talk about it) that early New England merchants and farmers were perfectly able to compartmentalize their thinking—that is, to be pious and thus conversant with some of the particulars of Puritan theology (III.G), and yet to do their work in the world in accordance with quite separate, non-religious, largely unarticulated norms (of thrift, diligence, etc.), whose origin in English history is for all practical purposes simply a mystery.

INTELLECTUAL HISTORY AND THE NEW SOCIAL HISTORY

Then we might find in Massachusetts the simultaneous operation of two distinct levels of thought, one of them formal and systematic, the other a matter of broad collective mentality, the first probably somewhat less widespread in its actual penetration of the populace than the second, yet more widespread than similar formal systems of thought have been in the twentieth century. If the weight of the explanation is placed on the broad mentality, then the possibly ambiguous posture of Puritan theology toward wealth-seeking becomes more of a side issue.

Meanwhile, with this excess baggage removed, it may be possible more closely to assess the relative importance of social reality and collective mentality in producing material well-being. Non-European tribal societies had utilized the very same terrain and resources for thousands of years before the Englishmen arrived. Their dealings with nature had produced a far more static result. The appearance of a new collective mentality, coming into contact with this physical environment—one not all that favorable by the standards of 1820—drastically and suddenly transformed that environment. The collective mentality (neither a product of Puritanism in any simple sense, nor of some mystical Turnerian impact of the forest) appears to be crucial to the outcome. And thereby a long-standing problem in American history has been moved back into the earlier history of the English middle class.[17] Yet we can continue to relish the intricate inner workings of Puritan theology, and to honor Perry Miller's masterly explorations of them, without any longer feeling compelled to attach them to grandiose explanations of the American character. Instead, they become the earliest chapter in a rarefied form of cognitive speculation conducted by the members of a specially trained elite over many succeeding generations, initially in churches, eventually in colleges and universities.

Of course the distinctions made in the chart offer no magic solutions in themselves, apart from substantive reconsiderations. But they may help to illuminate some characteristic kinds of confusion that have frequently plagued us as historians. We have seen that a historian may choose to operate on any level—social reality, collective mentality, or formal thought—taken in isolation, and with regard to any of several distinct zones of human thought and activity. But, as we have already noted in connection with the gap between structural reality and mental belief or expectation, the attempts to move between levels are frequently the most interesting of all, and the Puritan example should not discourage us from cheering on such efforts. The most venturesome kind of study crosses levels to try to establish, for instance, the broader influence on a collective mentality of a formal system of thought, taking infinite pains to cover the same ground that, alas, someone like Perry Miller too often tried to encompass by a kind of fiat.[18] The older progressive historians,

LAURENCE VEYSEY

perhaps tediously at times, often did the reverse, trying to show the effect of a broadly collective state of mind in America ("democracy") on formal theorizing (for example, among social reformers, such as in the endlessly trumpeted case of John Dewey).

Indeed, the game historians play usually consists of the effort to invoke some striking but hitherto neglected explanation for a well-known phenomenon, reaching for evidence into an unexpected box on the chart. (Often their choice of a box is also dictated by some particular political or cognitive bias on their part, but we should not worry unduly about this, as any finished work will have to earn its reputation from an audience composed not just of the similarly committed but also of historians with a wide variety of such biases.) On the one hand, one wants to avoid the blandness of simplistic multicausality—listing a variety of explanatory factors without trying to assess their weight—but on the other to avoid overreaching oneself and falling vulnerable to the accusation of a blatant onesidedness in one's account. This is the true balancing act that historians, intellectual or social, maintain on a continuing basis in their writing, if they have tackled subject matter more ambitious than some mere isolated bit of a social or intellectual mosaic. Far from abandoning all efforts to claim that some things are more important than others in advancing a particular explanation, the historian needs to be sure that his claim can be defended from counterattack on the basis of evidence and logic, rather than simply launched in the form of rhetoric. Intellectual historians, more than others, are probably too much swayed by rhetoric in and for itself, as contrasted with the logical backbone of an argument.

Historical explanations thus tend to be attempts to assert convincingly the influence of one category and level upon another, for instance, that Henry David Thoreau's attitude toward nature (II.F on the chart) is explained by his sexual repression (II.E), or that Progressivism is explained by the status orientation of Progressives (II.C by II.B), or that no "real" revolution has ever occurred in America because of consensus (I.D by II.D), or that the family changed its functions in nineteenth-century America as a result of the industrialization of work (I.B by I.A), or that Americans failed to turn radical in large numbers in the depression of the 1930s thanks to the continuing influence of laissez-faire individualism in their minds (II.D by II.A and B, or possibly even III.A and B).

Ingenuity accompanied by plausibility in such explanations is highly prized. But what determines plausibility? Does some kind of a further logic exist that can reveal which of these boxes on a chart like this can conceivably influence a given set of other boxes? If so—and I certainly have not found it yet—one might be able to say something on a more

INTELLECTUAL HISTORY AND THE NEW SOCIAL HISTORY

general level about the place of various kinds of intellectual history within the larger array of possibilities for historical explanation. One can only note that inquiry in the areas labeled economic, sexual, aesthetic, and cognitive (A, E, F, and G on the chart) has often tended to proceed in relative isolation, as if these were each extremely self-contained areas of existence, while the topics that historians most commonly write about tend to involve some intermingling of the political, the status oriented, and the collectivity oriented (B, C, and D on the chart). One wonders whether this tendency mirrors only the inherited bias of the discipline, or whether it might be present in some way in the nature of our civilization in the West.

As historians, whether social, cultural, political, or intellectual, we shall go on choosing our emphases within both the vertical and the horizontal dimensions of this chart, and we should recognize that excellence does not so much stem from our initial choice of subject, as if there were somehow an intrinsic, epistemologically given hierarchy of themes, as it does from the clarity, the ingenuity, and the soundness and spread of documentation with which the argument is advanced.

If we conceptualize the whole endeavor to write history along lines somewhat resembling those I have here laid out, then it should be clear that intellectual history, in more than one version, has its own integrity. Its own defined possibilities are every bit as distinct as those of social history. Thus, for those intellectual historians who will not see their field simply as the study of intellectuals taken as a social group, several further choices have emerged. Intellectual history may be defined in terms of the history of collective mentalities or in terms of the history of formal systems of thought (the discourse within a given genre), or in terms of either the cognitive or the aesthetic realms of existence for all people (including relevant behavioral data such as planetarium attendance figures). A social historian may insist that the entire content of the earlier table equals social history, but such a statement is fairly unimportant one way or the other as soon as one recognizes the legitimacy of any sort of specialization within the historical enterprise.

However, there are—in my view—some important lessons intellectual history should learn from social history. Largely in connection with the rise of social history, over the last fifteen years there has been a quiet but definite upgrading of standards of rigor in historical argument. It is in this connection that much traditional intellectual history now appears deficient.

Consciousness of the need for rigor has advanced on two major fronts:

LAURENCE VEYSEY

in a demand for greater precision in defining the social aggregate one selects to discuss, and in an expectation of greater precision in the inferences one makes from the varying kinds of historical evidence. Much of the clamor over social history has revolved around its shift toward quantification, but that is a relatively superficial issue that has distracted attention from more basic matters of logic concerning all types of evidence which, indeed, a high regard for numerical accuracy, especially for percentages, brings increasingly to our awareness.[19]

The lessons from social history in these respects might be condensed into two axioms: (1) a historian should not claim to be writing about a social aggregate broader than the one reflected in the evidence collected; (2) by some means, whether quantitative or intuitive, a historian should do everything possible to maximize the representativeness of the evidence used to describe either the behavior or the mental states of any given social aggregate.

The first axiom, unfortunately, judges a very large share of earlier intellectual history written in this country to have been of poor quality. It says that one cannot claim to write about "America" or "American thought" on the basis of its ministers, novelists, or political pamphleteers. If Fourth of July orations are one's principal source, one is entitled to talk about the views of the speakers as a collective entity, not about Americans as a whole. If school textbooks are used, one may discuss the views of their overwhelmingly Whiggish New England authors, not those of Americans at large. In the first instance, it is relevant to remember that, despite our great interest in the issue, we know today almost nothing about the effects of audience exposure to the media in any precise fashion. Similarly, we do not know the reason crowds then gathered to hear the Fourth of July speakers; it may have been mere hunger for entertainment. Though such speakers might want only to utter sentiments that would not offend a representative crowd, this tells us too little about the relative weight of such sentiments, compared to others, in the minds of the audience.[20] In the second case, we do know, or can guess, something about why the children were in school. But, especially taking into account their unruly, defiant behavior in nineteenth-century schoolrooms, we are entitled to infer little about the penetration of specific values or attitudes into their minds on a mass basis simply from examining their textbooks.[21]

Major works of intellectual history have suffered greatly from lack of clarity as to the social aggregate they are purporting to describe. Perry Miller's work, as we have already seen, created immense problems by its constant evocation of a massive social unit, New England, instead of adopting the far more credible and specialized posture of a study of the ideas of a ministerial elite. When Miller was challenged by social his-

INTELLECTUAL HISTORY AND THE NEW SOCIAL HISTORY

torians as to whether his kind of literary evidence could really speak for the entire social aggregate, he took on an aggressive-defensive stance that, when looked at closely, seems merely confusing.[22] Another classic instance of this lack of precision is found in Henry Nash Smith's *Virgin Land*, where for long stretches we are not sure whether given thought patterns are being attributed to all Americans, to Westerners, to Easterners thinking about the West (as Smith insisted was the case in a letter to me many years ago), or, what is more believable, to second-rate novelists and poets.

A related, though distinct, problem affecting intellectual historians has been the temptation to upgrade inappropriately the degree of coherence to be found in thought, especially when it is on a semipopular level, so as to invest it with the greater dignity of formal thought. The confusing term "myth," which Smith invoked to describe the collective mental constructs he had unearthed, may have stemmed from just such an impulse. A major danger lies in trying to posit a far more systematic character to the thinking of ordinary people—or even of members of an elite—than there really was. Codification of ideas can easily slide over into their reification. The notion that all people think in terms of systems, rather than that the degree of system in their thinking is a variable condition to be empirically discerned, rests on a naive conception of the human mind (unfortunately shared by Claude Lévi-Strauss, among others) that transfers one's own hunger, not only for rational clarity but also for aesthetically satisfying intellectual intricacy, onto the entire human race. For intellectual historians to go too far beyond their subjects in construing the systematic aspects of their thought is to hazard creating a kind of history that freezes and distorts reality into a sterile and misleading scholasticism. Yet this is obviously a delicate matter, for it is a central and legitimate aspect of the intellectual historian's labors to explicate, or bring out, the implications in a line of thought that a writer could not himself fully discern at the time. One can only say that it ought to be done with painstaking respect for the surrounding social and intellectual context, closer to the model of delimiting and carefully describing a natural preserve than to creating a zoo where the species are displayed in artificially arranged cages.

Care with regard to the definition of the social aggregate being discussed offers one important means of checking such excesses. The healthiest trend in the writing of intellectual history during the past two decades has been the move toward greater modesty in defining social aggregates. We look back upon the earlier masters of our subdiscipline, men like Vernon L. Parrington and Ralph H. Gabriel, with mingled reverence and misgivings. Their claim to be writing comprehensively about "American thought" now strikes a great many of us as impossibly

LAURENCE VEYSEY

pretentious. As we reread their works, we find them really amounting to
the history of American intellectuals—ministers, literary figures, social
philosophers—but written with a startling, unconscious selectivity in the
choice of emphasis within the group; in other words, often badly done
even within those narrower limits. The writings of these intellectual
historians now assume the stature of fascinating primary sources, reflecting, often poignantly, the beliefs and attitudes of some early twentieth-
century American academics. We no longer take them seriously on their
own terms because we have since learned so much about the complexity,
indeed the jarring discordance, of the thought patterns that have prevailed among large fractions of the population in America.[23] Segmenta-
tion of the many kinds that social historians have been exploring, along
lines of ethnicity, social standing, and sex role, has come to seem not
only the basic structural reality in American history but the cultural one
as well. It is scarcely necessary to argue any longer that the elite figures
taken to be representative of "American thought" in the generation of
Parrington and Gabriel were not spokesmen for a true majority of the
population, quite apart from the claims of minorities to deserve exemp-
tion from being subsumed automatically under blanketing outside labels
for their thinking and behavior.

I do not mean here to contend that holistic statements about America
are always wrong, only that, by the canons of evidence that now increasingly prevail, they must emerge as a result of empirical research within
all significant sectors of the population. I hope we shall some day be able
to return to a grander level of synthesis, after having absorbed more
fully the implications of the life of the mind within each of the various
fragments. But such endeavors will be extremely difficult, since (as
social historians again emphasize) little surviving evidence exists with
which to reconstruct the mental patterns of large portions of the society.
Remarkably ingenious efforts have indeed been made to perform this act
of recovery (one need only think of the work of Lawrence Levine and
others on slave culture), but a mood of cautionary tentativeness, to say
the least, is apt to prevail on this score for quite some time. The study of
collective mentalities now proceeds with an explicit modesty that shares
with the reader a sharply developed sense of the limitations upon
sources in relation to a given social aggregate.[24]

Recognition of the need constantly to match breadth of statements
with breadth of sources is the most important maxim that intellectual
historians should take to heart. This should not be misunderstood as a
call with great fanfare for quantitative methods in intellectual history.
Such an issue does not raise itself to a major degree, because historians
of ideas usually ask questions that are too finely shaped for capture in
the net of a purely quantitative classification, least of all the extremely

INTELLECTUAL HISTORY AND THE NEW SOCIAL HISTORY

crude one furnished by mechanical content analysis. However, there is a sense in which any historian should be concerned with the representativeness of the evidence being used to make statements about the thought or actions of some group of people (whether Americans, blacks, women, New Englanders, intellectuals themselves, or indeed of a single individual over his lifetime). Mastery of the surviving literary sources may provide a historian of a narrow social aggregate with such a highly developed intuitive command of the relevant terrain as to assure far greater respect for the generalizations he makes than for those derived by mechanically quantitative methods. In his own way, such a historian has truly been concerned with representativeness.[25] But to fully satisfy us, any historian must openly share his awareness of the need to define contours between his subject and what lies outside it, recognizing in particular the usual inadequacy of purely geographical boundary lines in this respect.

As I think most of us look back on it, there was something far too pretentiously grandiose about much writing in American intellectual history, and in so-called American Studies, in the 1950s.[26] The scope of intellectual history, on the basis of surviving literary evidence, is bound long to remain more modest if the axioms to be learned from social history are heeded. We should welcome a more honest, if humbler, redefinition of our tasks. Enormously challenging work remains to be done, in the realms of both wider collective mentalities and narrower intellectual circles. Dropping the larger social labels (perhaps most especially "American") from our vocabularies while we explore the particulars that might eventually enable us to use such words again from a more informed standpoint detracts nothing from the fascination of our subject matter or from the subtlety we can employ in trying to write about it. And it is less misleading to innocent undergraduates and other outsiders.

Generalizations, in other words, to be credible, must be extremely hard earned. They require far more arduous preparation, far more careful spadework, far closer attention to logic, than many of our predecessors a generation ago were aware. Here lies the central shift in the writing of history in the meantime, I believe. And if intellectual or cultural historians have lagged behind some other historians in accepting this change in standards, then they should resolve to "tone down" what they do in order to catch up. It may no longer stir disagreement at this point in time to suggest that we stop using Henry James as a routinely acceptable window into an understanding of nineteenth-century America,[27] while we go right on speaking of him either as a remarkable example of reversal of attitudes among sons of Transcendentalists or as an important international figure in the history of the novel as a genre.

LAURENCE VEYSEY

Let the memory of the giants of thought survive on a proper, if somewhat reduced, basis.

Notes

1. Few of these expressions of contempt probably reached print. Yet, especially in the Midwest and Far West, for instance at the University of Wisconsin and (for a briefer time) the University of California at Berkeley, oral tradition convinces me of their reality.
2. Admittedly this generalized picture of American intellectual history in the 1950s leans more toward such figures as R. W. B. Lewis, Stanley Elkins, Ralph H. Gabriel, Daniel J. Boorstin (in whom the right-wing critique emerged only tardily), and Louis Hartz (in effect rather than according to his own protestations) than toward Henry May, Henry Nash Smith, Merle Curti, or John Higham, all of whom wrote history in a less holistic fashion.
3. For an attempt to compare older and newer works in American social history in order to discern more precisely what is new in the social history of the years since about 1965, see my essay, "The 'New' Social History in the Context of American Historical Writing," *Reviews in American History* 7 (March 1979), which in a different form will also appear in Georg G. Iggers and Harold T. Parker, eds., *Contemporary Developments in Historical Studies* (Westport, Conn.: Greenwood Press, 1979). The "new" history of James Harvey Robinson and others writing around 1910 used rhetoric quite similar to that of social historians in the 1960s, but it showed neither the same awareness of the true bottom layer of the society nor anything like the methodological ingenuity of the recent social historians.
4. For example, Stephan Thernstrom and Peter R. Knights, "Men in Motion," in *Anonymous Americans*, ed. Tamara K. Hareven (Englewood Cliffs, N.J.: Prentice-Hall, 1971), p. 40.
5. These observations come from contacts with younger social historians on my own campus, at the Charles Warren Center at Harvard, and elsewhere. In addition, a newly arriving intellectual historian at a major university told me that he has felt socially ostracized by the many social historians in his department simply because he is in intellectual history. Though this mood obviously varies a great deal from campus to campus, its depth should not be underestimated.
6. At least one recent major book, Rush Welter's *The Mind of America, 1820–1860* (New York: Columbia University Press, 1975), continues to deal holistically with America on the basis of traditional types of literary evidence.
7. I shall not try to argue the special case of anthropology here; prehistory forms an important but subsidiary theme in that discipline, which is largely devoted to the static analysis of the content of tribal cultures.
8. For example, by Leonard Krieger in "The Horizons of History," *American Historical Review* 63 (1957): 69–72, focusing on the idea of change; and by Robert F. Berkhofer, Jr., in *A Behavioral Approach to Historical Analysis* (New York: Free Press, 1969), p. 267. My thinking in what follows has been influenced by Krieger and and also by Alexander Gerschenkron, "On the Concept of Continuity in History," in *Continuity in History and Other Essays* (Cambridge: Harvard University Press, 1968), pp. 11–39.
9. For example, see David A. Hollinger, "Historians and the Discourse of Intellectuals," chapter 3 of this volume.
10. For fascinating illustrations of unfamiliar gameboards from the nineteenth century, which may help to unlimber one's imagination in this overall respect, see David Wallace Adams and Victor Edmonds, "Making Your Move: The Educa-

INTELLECTUAL HISTORY AND THE NEW SOCIAL HISTORY

tional Significance of the American Board Game, 1832 to 1904," *History of Education Quarterly* 17 (1977): 359–83.

11. The only major liberty I have taken is to subdivide what is more often called the "social" realm into status-oriented and collectivity-oriented subsectors (B and D), hoping thus to reduce the nebulousness of the customary phrase "social forces" in a way that is now widely accepted.

12. A synthetic work that goes far in this direction and that has received much highly favorable attention is James A. Henretta's *The Evolution of American Society, 1700–1815* (Lexington, Mass.: D. C. Heath, 1973). But Stephan Thernstrom's *The Other Bostonians* (Cambridge: Harvard University Press, 1973) goes still farther, as do other works in the mode of the "new" social history which makes the entire text a running commentary on statistical tables. Like economists, such historians simply do not care to make explicit their view of human nature, or to allow for cultural variables.

13. In one of the very few places where Thernstrom introduces a possible cultural explanation for his data, he does so apologetically (*Other Bostonians*, p. 168), remarking on how unsatisfyingly vague such explanations tend to be.

14. Charles Peirce, *Collected Papers* 5: 297 n., quoted in Fred Somkin, *Unquiet Eagle* (Ithaca, N.Y.: Cornell University Press, 1967), p. 8. (Italics in original.)

15. For example, it becomes the prominent focus of the definition of intellectual history advanced by Thomas Haskell in "Deterministic Implications of Intellectual History," chapter 8 of this volume.

16. 2 vols. (New York: G. P. Putnam's Sons, 1977).

17. See Michael Zuckerman, "The Fabrication of Identity in Early America," *William and Mary Quarterly* 34 (1977): 183–214.

18. Here a recent example is Nathan G. Hale, Jr., *Freud and the Americans* (New York: Oxford University Press, 1971), though only subsequent volumes will reach the era of Freud's really wide popular influence. Of course, in fairness to Miller, far less evidence is available for a study of similar dimensions in early New England. But Miller, who was magnificent in so many ways, was a victim of his intermittent arrogance as it sometimes affected his claims about the causal importance of ideas and also some statements of his about the internal course of the history of ideas. For example, see "From Edwards to Emerson," *Errand into the Wilderness* (Cambridge: Harvard University Press, 1956), especially p. 184.

19. David H. Fischer's *Historian's Fallacies* (New York: Harper & Row, 1970), though sometimes irritating, is a sign of the kind of upgrading of standards in historical reasoning that I am here talking about.

20. For an example of intellectual history attempting to make use of Fourth of July speeches, see Somkin, *Unquiet Eagle.*

21. For a nonetheless attractive example of intellectual history using this source, see Ruth Miller Elson, *Guardians of Tradition* (Lincoln: University of Nebraska Press, 1964).

22. See his preface to *The New England Mind: From Colony to Province* (Boston: Beacon Press, 1961).

23. The long way we have come in intellectual history in terms of respect for diversity of flavor and use of firsthand sources may be shown by the fact that Ralph H. Gabriel's course in American intellectual history at Yale, when I took it in 1952, had as its entire reading list for the year: (1) his own textbook, (2) Parrington, and (3) Harvey Wish, *Society and Thought in Modern America* (New York: Longmans, Green, 1952).

24. Among many examples, see Nancy F. Cott, *The Bonds of Womanhood: 'Woman's Sphere' in New England, 1780–1835* (New Haven: Yale University Press, 1977). Cott carefully tells readers at the outset that she is only claiming to discuss middle-class women, the kind who kept diaries, and emphasizes the number of different diaries that she read, though she cannot pretend they represent a fair sample even of middle-class New England women at that time.

25. Certainly in my mind the work of Henry F. May forms a model of this kind.

LAURENCE VEYSEY

And in *The Enlightenment in America* (New York: Oxford University Press, 1976), May additionally does quantitative checking of libraries to verify intuitive impressions.

26. For a further argument along these lines, see Cecil F. Tate, *The Search for a Method in American Studies* (Minneapolis: University of Minnesota Press, 1973), especially pp. 3–16 and 105–26.

27. As, for example, in such highly creditable books as Yehoshua Arieli's *Individualism and Nationalism in American Ideology* ([Cambridge: Harvard University Press, 1964], pp. 272–73); Stanley M. Elkins's *Slavery* ([Chicago: University of Chicago Press, 1959], p. 143); and Leo Marx's *The Machine in the Garden* [New York: Oxford University Press, 1964], pp. 239–40, 350–53).

INTELLECTUAL HISTORY
AND THE SOCIAL SCIENCES

$\Longleftrightarrow \Box \odot \Longleftrightarrow$

GORDON S. WOOD

There can be no doubt now of the influence of the social sciences on history. Although the penetration of the social sciences into history has been going on for a long time in America and has been talked about since the "new history" arose at the beginning of the twentieth century, only in recent years has it reached the inner and outer limits of the discipline. What began as a trickle is now a torrent, and there is scarcely a historian who has not been affected either consciously or unconsciously by at least one of the social sciences. Quantification, only the most visible manifestation of the influence of the social sciences, promises to transform not only the procedures and the sources of historical research, but even our traditional understanding of the historical process. Older fields like political and economic history have been turned over and refreshed, and new fields like demographic and family history have been opened up. Everywhere social science has enlarged and lent vigor to our study of the past. New subjects are being investigated and new kinds of historical data are actually being created. We are experiencing nothing less than a revolution in our history-writing.[1]

Many intellectual historians cannot help being suspicious of this historiographical revolution. Most of us who are concerned with ideas and beliefs can see little place for counting in what we do, and we are understandably afraid of the implications of science in assessing the role of ideas in behavior. Social scientists too often seem to treat human behavior as a series of events similar to events in the physical world, and thus they appear to be inherently hostile to thought and conscious will. They seem unconcerned with the personal intentions, the distinctive ideas, the concrete beliefs of specific individuals—the particularity that is the stock in trade of historians. They threaten to bleed consciousness out of the past and to make individual ideas irrelevant.

In the large-scale aggregate behavior that most social science is concerned with, the reason and moral purpose of a particular individual simply do not seem to matter. The serial rhythms and cycles that "social science" historians are revealing from the impersonal data of parish registers, tax and price lists, and census returns were not products of the

GORDON S. WOOD

conscious intention of the historical participants. Of course, individuals created these historical patterns, but they did so without knowing what they were doing. "History," as Engels said in 1890, "is made in such a way that the final result always arises from conflicts between many individual wills. . . . [It] works as a whole *unconsciously* and without volition. For what each individual wills is obstructed by everyone else, and what emerges is something that no one willed."[2] The sheer multiplicity or number of purposes renders an individual's purpose meaningless. No wonder then that many of the new social historians interested in these aggregate patterns have expressed such contempt for traditional intellectual history and its "ideational" materials. Literary evidence, they believe, can only be anecdotal in value, and the particular intentions and ideas of individuals by themselves can never tell historians much about the uniformities and regularities that all science is after.

The social sciences, like all science, are after all inherently concerned with recurring events, with the regularities and uniformities of human action out of which theories of behavior can be formulated. That is what makes them scientific. They can never be much bothered with the particular and the unique and still remain scientific.[3] The behavior of the particular and the individual is chaotic, uncertain, and indeterminate, and cannot be the basis of any theory. Only repetitive, replicated actions can form the series and regularities that underlie all science. Hence all would-be scientists are inevitably led into studying objects in large numbers, which is why quantification is such an integral part of the scientific method. In this respect the social scientists are no different from the natural scientists. No physicist, for example, can determine the behavior of any individual particle, but he can determine the probable behavior of a large number of particles. In a like manner, the demographic historian cannot be interested exclusively in the behavior of one person. That individual's behavior appears random and meaningless; it cannot tell the historian what the society was doing. Only in a series or in aggregate do individual actions—births, marriages, deaths—add up to a pattern that the demographic historian can make sense of. The need of science to deal with large numbers in order to find regularities and uniformities implies that objects can be studied only on a large scale and at a distance. It is not surprising therefore that the new social historians have tended to view the behavior of human beings in the past in much the same way scientists view the behavior of insects in a colony or molecules in a chemical reaction.

Even those social sciences interested in individual attitudes and behavior are ultimately implicated in the search for uniformities and regu-

INTELLECTUAL HISTORY AND THE SOCIAL SCIENCES

larities. Psychology, for example, focuses on individual actions and motives and has had a great influence on history-writing, including the writing of intellectual history. Although it tends to discredit the traditional materials with which intellectual historians work by assuming that nothing said or written can be taken at face value, it has forced us to account for the unconscious and to look at new kinds of evidence in new ways. Psychology has helped teach us that all sorts of seemingly insignificant things can be the visible traces or expressions of emotions or feelings that lurk beneath the surface of consciousness. Some such notions inform much of our social analyses of culture and generally underlie a good deal of the work in the American Studies movement. Indeed, so many of the perceptions of psychology have insinuated themselves into our orthodox history-writing that we are hardly aware that we are often writing interdisciplinary history.[4]

Yet in the end psychology, like all the sciences, only gains its force and meaning by resting its theories of behavior on regularity and recurrence. Philip Greven's psychological categorization of the Protestant temperament in early America assumes constancies of behavior over centuries, and it is Greven's scientific assumption of regularity that allows him to apply theories of human behavior based on present clinical data to different times and places and juxtapose evidence drawn from 1630 alongside that from 1830.[5] Insofar as would-be psychohistorians ignore these uniformities in their applications of psychology to past behavior they are not being scientific at all, and thus are really no different from all those ordinary historians who improvise their notions of motivation and behavior from "common sense."[6]

In a like manner, the other social sciences are ultimately concerned with the classifiable aspects, the regularities and uniformities, of man's behavior. None of them has recently had a more potent influence on history-writing than anthropology. Of all the social sciences anthropology seems to have the greatest kinship with history because it treats the people it studies on their own terms and begins with the assumption that such people do things differently. With its central concern with culture, it has spoken directly to the interests of intellectual historians and has introduced them to new subjects for study and new sources for research. Anthropology has demonstrated the importance of interpreting the thought of past societies in more than just the literary terms expressed by a few supposedly representative thinkers, and has helped historians create new kinds of documents in order to get at the beliefs and attitudes of the masses of people in the past who left no written record. Borrowing from ethnography, historians have begun examining the rituals, iconography, and popular "languages" and signs of past cultures and are now

GORDON S. WOOD

reconstructing mental worlds we scarcely knew existed. Histories of ideas can now include conceptions of childrearing, beliefs in magic and witchcraft, and attitudes toward aging and death in past societies.[7]

Yet despite all of its affinities with history and its recent enrichment of history-writing, anthropology remains a human science. Its aim in the end is to find regularities and correlations in various classes of human behavior. "Events," wrote the social anthropologist E. E. Evans-Pritchard, "lose much, even all, of their meaning if they are not seen as having some degree of regularity and constancy, as belonging to a certain type of event, all instances of which have many features in common." Hence most anthropologists who study dated events are necessarily interested in structures or patterns—those "temporal, repetitive, replicated series of actions, operations or motions, involved in the accomplishment of an end, either natural, artificial, or cultural."[8]

The inevitable pull of science toward the large scale in which uniformities and replicated series of actions are possible can be most vividly seen in the intellectual history written by the most social science–oriented historians now at work—those influenced by the *Annales* school of French historiography. These French historians have fully accepted the necessary interest of science in the long range and in aggregate numbers. The particular ideas of a Locke or a Rousseau are less important for these historians than the accumulated thoughts and feelings of great masses of people. What counts (and is countable) are not the particular creations by a few thinkers working on the conscious surface of life, but the replicated series and rhythms of thoughts—regularities and patterns—that lie beneath that surface and over long periods of time give form to the symbols and myths of social life—what the French call *mentalités*. Man has a consciousness of sorts, but it is a collective one of long duration; particular reason, momentary purpose, and individual volition count no more in its formation than they do in the formation of a demographic profile or an economic cycle. Unique events are swallowed up in a repetitive series of actions or ideas.

Such a scientific view of the historical process has pessimistic deterministic implications. The *Annales* school's aversion to *histoire evenementielle* does not come from any simple dislike of old-fashioned political history. It is not merely the ephemeral and superficial quality of unique events these French social science historians are rejecting; they are in fact denying any concept of the historical process that concentrates on such particular events. They have abandoned any suggestion of a teleological process in history, any progressive belief, whether liberal or Marxian, that history is going somewhere. For these historians events do not mark any stage in the advent of anything, whether it is liberty, democracy, or the classless society. Without a nineteenth-century sense

INTELLECTUAL HISTORY AND THE SOCIAL SCIENCES

of progressive development toward some end, these historians argue, there is no criterion of significance for the historian's selecting one unique event over another for emphasis. Thus in place of unique and discontinuous events the new social historian can be concerned only with those events replicated in series, only with the enduring continuities of aggregate numbers, in order to get at the long-existing, deep-lying structures beneath the chaotic surface of life.[9] Only this kind of new high-altitude social history can provide the desired late–twentieth-century viewpoint that sees the individual, in Fernand Braudel's melancholy words, "imprisoned within a destiny in which he himself has little hand, fixed in a landscape in which the infinite perspectives of the long term stretch into the distances both behind him and before."[10]

Few American historians as yet share this melancholy but possibly liberating vision, and consequently few of us as yet are prepared to write such large-scale deterministic history. Most Americans still write their history as if they were living in the midst of a teleological process; their interest in the past still flows from an interest in the future. Most of us are not prepared to work only in the long run and with large aggregate numbers. Not only is our history relatively short, but historians writing in the national period particularly tend to specialize in what European historians consider to be only brief intervals of time—sometimes only a couple of decades or so. We are therefore still very much concerned with "events," with their momentary and unique character, with individual intention and action, and with change in the short run. Writing about glacially-moving, age-old habits of mind over which individuals have little control can have a limited appeal for most American intellectual historians. We want to know how particular ideas related to particular individuals over a brief period of time. We are not willing, in other words, to look continually at intellectual life from a high altitude in a fully scientific manner, as determined continuities over long spans of time and on a large scale. We want to see ideas and events close up, in the small world of chaotic and random happenings that science cannot ultimately be concerned with.

Yet fearful as we may be of the distancing and deterministic implications of the social sciences, we cannot shy away from them. To ignore the new social history and to write about ideas as if the social sciences were not fundamentally affecting the discipline of history will relegate intellectual history to the backwaters of the historical profession. Moreover, it now appears clear that the social sciences are not as hostile to consciousness as we first imagined. Indeed, it is increasingly evident that without the help of the social sciences in understanding thought and the way it relates to social behavior we will never be able to persuade the rest of the profession of the significance of ideas and to keep intellectual

GORDON S. WOOD

history in the center of things where we believe it belongs. It is in fact the social scientists themselves, or the best of them at least, who have recently begun granting a dominance and power to ideas in shaping social behavior that few intellectual historians have ever dared claim.

Some social scientists, drawing out the implications of the seminal work of Durkheim and Saussure, have come to realize that they cannot understand man and his society by treating human behavior in quite the same way the behavior of the physical world is treated. Man is not really like a molecule in a chemical reaction or an insect in a colony. His behavior is made up not simply of physical events but events that have meaning. Man gives meaning to everything he does, even to such a simple action as a wink. It cannot be the mere physical twitch of the eye that interests students of human behavior; it has to be the symbolic action, the meaning involved in that twitch. Was the wink an enticement, a sign of complicity, or an act of mockery? Meanings determine actions; all human behavior can only be understood and explained, indeed can only exist, in terms of the meanings it has.[11]

Since many of these symbolic actions, these meanings, are what intellectual historians call ideas, all human behavior is, or ought to be, the province of intellectual history. Such meanings that humans give to their actions, such ideas, can never be incidental to social behavior; they are never epiphenomenal. Intellectual historians need never feel that they are working on the fringe of things. For the meanings of man's actions form the very structure of his social world. They constitute what Durkheim called the "social facts" that make social behavior not just comprehensible but possible.[12] Social history and intellectual history are in truth inseparable.

Because man is a symbol-making, language-using animal who gives meaning to everything he does, culture and society, beliefs and behavior, are really of a piece with one another. The human world cannot be sharply divided between an objective physical reality and man's subjective perception of that reality. Neither positivism nor idealism by itself can explain human behavior. Thus our older assumption about ideas operating in some sort of spatial separation from social circumstances is false. Ideas and symbols do not exist apart from some social reality out there. They are the means by which we perceive, understand, judge, or manipulate that reality; indeed, they create it. Even the physical world may not have an objective reality; some physical scientists know that they "should not ask what light *really* is. Particles and waves are both constructs of the human mind, designed to help us speak about the behaviour of light in different circumstances." We thus have to "give up the naive concept of reality, the idea that the world is made up of things, waiting for us to discover their nature. The world is made up by us, out of our experiences and the concepts we create to link them together."[13]

Once ideas are seen in this way—as "templates for the organization of social and psychological processes"[14]—historians have no business trying to isolate ideas from these social and psychological processes. Their task cannot be, as one historian has asserted, "to unravel the truth of the situation as distinct from the myth that is current about it."[15] Ideas do not mask reality; they define and indeed create it. In the 1760s, for example, the opposition Whigs did not have a more "correct" view of the English constitution than did George III. There was no "real" English constitution in the 1760s; there was only the constitution that men of the time described. Recognition of this by John Brewer has led to his persuasive interpretation of the era of George III that transcends and reconciles the work of both the older Whig historians and the Namierists.[16]

If ideas are not just inseparable parts of the social reality but indeed give that reality its existence, then it makes no sense to treat ideas mechanically as detached "causes" or "effects" of social events and behavior. We no longer have to be locked into the endless see-sawing fluctuations between ideas and the social environment that pervades much of our writing in intellectual history, with ideas in the causal ascendancy at one moment and the social factors at another and with their reciprocal ups and downs somehow accounting for historical change. If we have to decide, for example, that the belief in the principle of "no taxation without representation" was either the "cause" of someone like Samuel Adams's opposing the Stamp Act or a "response" to some underlying real causal emotion or interest, then beliefs and ideas will never carry the weight in the discipline of history that we think they ought to.

To make ideas "causes" of social behavior, historians have tended to treat them as motives. That is to say, individuals acted as they did because they believed, "sincerely" believed, in the ideas or principles they expressed. But in this postpsychological age such an intellectual explanation of behavior—making professed beliefs the springs of action—has never seemed convincing to hardheaded realists or to anyone who knows how people really behave. Explaining the coming of the American Revolution in terms of the deeply held beliefs of the Americans in a conspiracy by British ministers against their liberty can easily be dismissed by tough-minded historians as "rhetoric" that "serious men gave little credence to."[17] In the face of such scoffing, all we tender-minded intellectual historians have done is underline the sincerity with which the ideas were held and double our citations to the documents in which these ideas were expressed. But we have not made many people believe that ideas can "cause" something like a revolution.

Or if we intellectual historians make ideas simply "consequences" of

GORDON S. WOOD

behavior, we are no better off. To be sure, ideas can then be written about, but only as responses or reflections of something else that is inherently more important. In other words, by treating ideas as epiphenomenal consequences of behavior we effectively surrender to the realists' presumption that ideas are only ex post facto rationalizations for actions determined by other forces. "What matters most," wrote Sir Lewis Namier in a concise summary of the tough-minded position, "is the underlying emotion, the music, to which ideas are a mere libretto, often of a very inferior quality."[18]

Only by rejecting the futile dichotomy of ideas or beliefs as causes or effects of social forces can intellectual historians escape from what will always be a losing struggle with the realists and materialists. Instead of asking what ideas were—whether they were rational or not, whether they were the motives for an action or the effects of a hidden emotion or interest—we ought to be asking what the ideas did in a specific situation and why the historical participants used particular ideas in the way they did.[19] We should not, for example, be arguing whether the Americans' belief in a British conspiracy against their liberty "caused" the Americans to revolt; for such a belief, however prevalently or sincerely expressed, can not easily be made a plausible motive for revolution. Rather we should be analyzing why the Americans expressed this idea of conspiracy in the way they did and why, given their eighteenth-century understanding of how events occurred, there was no other explanation for what was happening available for them to use.

Treating ideas functionally and instrumentally will greatly affect the character and scope of our intellectual history-writing. Because ideas are important for what they do rather than for what they are, any idea or symbol that gives meaning to behavior and does something, whatever its nature or source and however irrational or silly it may seem in retrospect, has significance for intellectual historians. Ideas and symbols are forms of expressive action and are more than what is embedded in literary texts; the mob's effigy may have been as meaningful as the learned pamphlet. Since idea- or symbol-making is itself a social process and is such a dynamic, effortful, instrumental, and problem-solving activity, ideas can only be considered in terms of the actors' intentions as historically specific and not as timeless. Although words and concepts may remain outwardly the same for centuries, their particular functions and meanings do not and could not remain static—not as long as individuals attempt to use them to explain new social circumstances and make meaningful new social behavior.[20] Only such a dynamic, instrumental, and actor-oriented view of the thinking and symbol-making process will allow us to deal with the small, close-up world of unique events and intellectual conflict and change and thereby satisfy our tradi-

INTELLECTUAL HISTORY AND THE SOCIAL SCIENCES

tional humanistic desire to write particular history about particular individuals and their diverse intentions, purposes, and beliefs.

Of course, treating ideas in this instrumental and rhetorical way—as mechanisms for perceiving, persuading, manipulating, and ordering the world—may seem to concede too much to the materialists and realists. It may make ideas seem to be merely the reflections and consequences of underlying forces after all. Treated crudely as instruments, ideas become mere propaganda, masks and covers for actions determined elsewhere.[21] But this would be true only if the participants in the past were free to use whatever symbols or ideas in whatever manner they wished, free to make whatever map of the problematic social reality they wanted. But no one was or is free in this way. For ideas are not merely "maps of a problematical social reality," but also "matrices for the creation of collective conscience."[22] It is this collective nature of human thought, its aggregate symbolization in a system of rules and norms, that enables ideas to affect and influence behavior. Ideas affect behavior not by being motives for action, but by giving meaning to that action and defining and delimiting it. They do so because, as philosophers, linguists, and social scientists are now telling us, "the nature of human thought" is "a public and not, or at least not fundamentally, a private activity."[23] Human thought is necessarily rhetorical, a discourse involving communication with others. Men wrestle with ideas and symbols in order to explain, justify, lay blame for, or otherwise make sense of what is happening, not just for themselves but for others. Discourse and communication and ultimately behavior are possible only because they take place within a public system of conventions and values, that is, meanings. As Clifford Geertz says, "Culture is public because meaning is."[24]

We inherit this culture, this structure of thoughts, symbols, and values, and we can control and manipulate it no more easily than we can our inherited social world. This collective cultural system that we have assimilated, consciously or unconsciously, suffuses all parts of our mind and in effect creates our behavior. It does so by forcing us to describe that behavior in its terms. The definitions and meanings that we try to give to our behavior cannot be random or unconstrained. Our actions tend to be circumscribed by the ways we can make them meaningful, and they are meaningful only publicly, only with respect to an inherited system of social rules, conventions, and values. What is "polite" or "rude," "liberal" or "tyrannical," is determined by this structure of meanings. In a sense then we can do only what we can conceive of, legitimate, or persuade other people to accept. What is permissible intellectually or culturally affects what is permissible socially or politically. In this way ideas affect behavior. Therefore, even if we want to write a fully satisfying intellectual history of only a few events occurring over a brief

GORDON S. WOOD

period of time, we will have to know what structure of conventions existed, what choices of ideas were available to the historical participants, in order to know why they selected and used those they did. In the end this means understanding the larger cultural world, the system of values and conventions, in which the historical actors lived—what historians have called "traditions," "climates of opinion," or "habits of thought," but what seem to resemble the very deterministic regularities and patterns that science says we should be concerned with all along.

At this larger scale of intellectual life there is no possibility of our writing about individual intention and conscious will. For such cultural traditions or patterns, like demographic profiles or economic cycles, are the aggregate consequences of so many different perceptions and purposes expressed over such long periods of time that no individual can be said to have created them or to be in control of them. Since these "traditions" or "habits of thought" are not the products of human intention, they are not reducible to or explicable in terms of individual motives or drives. These cultural patterns cannot think or feel, but, like economic or social consequences or nature itself, they do have their own logic and order, their own institutions and structures of collective meanings that transcend the particular aims and purposes of individuals.[25] Past cultures may even have meanings of which many of their participants were unaware; and indeed much of our intellectual history-writing is involved in trying to bring to light these hidden meanings.[26]

From this broadened and distant cultural perspective individuals no longer seem as free as they did close up. They no longer use ideas but are used by them, and they are forced to deal with their inherited collective culture on its terms. If they wish to explain, legitimate, or make sense of new social circumstances or behavior, they must take into account the prevailing conventions and norms of the culture. Like Geertz's example of organized labor's misfired effort to label the Taft-Hartley Act "a slave-labor law," ideas and arguments that do too much violence to the existing vocabulary and conventions of the culture can have little meaning and persuasive force.[27] Without the ability to symbolize and make meaningful new circumstances and behavior, the development of those circumstances and behavior is inhibited. Ideas thus influence behavior, not by being motives for action, but by giving meanings to action and thus publicly prescribing and circumscribing what behavior is legitimate and permissible, indeed, possible.

It is this prescriptive and circumscriptive force of culture and its institutions that E. P. Thompson seems to be getting at in the remarkable conclusion to his book *Whigs and Hunters*. In the end Thompson comes to believe that eighteenth-century English law cannot be passed off as simply the instrument and mask of the ruling gentry in the way a crude reductionist Marxism would have it. To be sure, the Whig gentry tried to use the mystery of the law to confirm and consolidate their dominance. But, Thompson concludes, the gentry were not free to do whatever they wanted with English law. For the law was "something more than . . . a pliant medium to be twisted this way and that by whichever interests already possess effective power." The law existed in its own right, had "its own characteristics, its own independent history and logic of evolution." It was the aggregate product over a long period of time of countless judicial decisions and agrarian practices, backed up by "norms, tenaciously transmitted through the community." The eighteenth-century ruling gentry had to take into account and operate within these inherited norms and conventions. They could not use the law to legitimate their rule without upholding the law's "own logic and criteria of equity." Thus, although the gentry from below in their individual courts, quarter sessions and assizes tried to bend and distort the law to their own interests, the law continuously imposed itself on them from above and restricted and restrained what they could do.[28]

What was true of the gentry and the law in eighteenth-century England is true of all individuals and groups implicated in their culture and its ideas, institutions, and symbols. For example, in 1787 the Federalists wanted to create a new strong national government for particular social and political reasons, but they could explain and justify this new government only in terms of the republican culture that had come out of the Revolution. Given the expanded popular audience that American leaders now had to address, any changes the Federalists wished to make in America's republicanism had to appear to be scarcely changes at all. The vocabulary of "democracy" and "the people" could be reshaped and expanded, but it could not outright be denied or abandoned. The Federalists manipulated this vocabulary but at the same time were themselves manipulated by it.[29]

If we are to write fully satisfying intellectual history we will need a kind of zoom lens that will enable us to move easily back and forth from the small, close-up world of unique events and individual volition where men try to use ideas for their own particular purposes to the larger aggregate and deterministic world of cultural conventions and collective mentalities where ideas control men. Only then will we be able to see how individuals, continuously seeking to mold and manipulate their inherited language, thoughts, and values in order to explain and justify new circumstances or behavior, make small accretive piecemeal changes in the constantly developing cultural aggregates. Usually these cultural changes, these shifts in symbol systems, are slow and subtle—new meanings for old words and ideas; but there can be moments of "revolution," when the manipulative pressures of many individuals have built up over

GORDON S. WOOD

time and become overwhelming, and suddenly long-existing conventions of language and thought, weak and inapplicable to new social circumstances, crumble under severe pressure and are transformed. The "great thinkers" we honor are those who clarify these moments of transformation. And yet, like the manipulations of everyone else, the clarifications these "great thinkers" make in the structures of the culture, the new "paradigms" of understanding they create, quickly become part of the larger developing process, the collective system, that always transcends their particular intentions.[30]

Thus the culture, like an aggregate demographic profile or an economic cycle, is developed and changed over the heads of the historical participants in ways they scarcely anticipated. Although we like to believe that man's culture is under more control than his collective social behavior, this dual perspective, this shifting from the individual to the aggregate, from the particular to the general, tells us differently. Close up we see individuals acting freely, randomly, and purposefully, using ideas and thoughts to justify and make sense of their actions. But at a distance, at a different order of magnitude, the accumulated multitudes of ideas and thoughts transcend the particular intentions and wills of the historical participants and form a collective cultural system that sets limits on what individuals can say and think and hence do at any particular moment.[31] Only by being able and willing to move between these two worlds—the small world of free will, moral purpose, and individual intention and the large world of deterministic aggregate culture—can the historian write an intellectual history that will satisfy both his humanistic instincts and the demands of social science.

Notes

1. See Lawrence Stone, "History and the Social Sciences in the Twentieth Century," in *The Future of History*, ed. Charles F. Delzell (Nashville: Vanderbilt University Press, 1977), pp. 3–42.
2. Friedrich Engels to Joseph Bloch, 21–22 September 1890, in Karl Marx and Friedrich Engels, *Basic Writings on Politics and Philosophy*, ed. L. S. Feuer (Garden City, N.Y.: Doubleday, 1959), p. 399.
3. "There is," says Walker Percy, "a secret about the scientific method which every scientist knows and takes as a matter of course, but which the layman does not know. . . . The secret is this: Science cannot utter a single word about an individual molecule, thing, or creature in so far as it is an individual but only in so far as it is like other individuals." Walker Percy, *The Message in the Bottle* (New York: Farrar, Straus, and Giroux, 1975), p. 22.
4. Frank E. Manuel, "The Use and Abuse of Psychology in History," *Daedalus*, Winter 1971, pp. 187–213.
5. Philip Greven, *The Protestant Temperament: Patterns of Child-Rearing, Re-*

INTELLECTUAL HISTORY AND THE SOCIAL SCIENCES

ligious Experience, and the Self in Early America (New York: Alfred A. Knopf, 1978).

6. Hence Frank Manuel's advice to historians to use psychology eclectically and descriptively rather than scientifically is "modest" indeed, for it undermines the significance of psychology as a science. Manuel, "Use and Abuse of Psychology," p. 208.

7. For examples of the new anthropologically minded history, see Natalie Zemon Davis, *Society and Culture in Early Modern France* (Stanford: Stanford University Press, 1975); Rhys Isaac, "Evangelical Revolt: The Nature of the Baptists' Challenge to the Traditional Order in Virginia, 1765–1775," *William and Mary Quarterly*, 3d ser. 31 (1974); Keith Thomas, *Religion and the Decline of Magic* (New York: Charles Scribner's Sons, 1971); and David Stannard, *The Puritan Way of Death: A Study in Religion, Culture and Social Change* (New York: Oxford University Press, 1977).

8. E. E. Evans-Pritchard, *Anthropology and History* (Manchester, England: Manchester University Press, 1963), p. 4; Margaret T. Hodgen, *Anthropology, History, and Cultural Change* (Tuscon: University of Arizona Press, 1974), p. 68.

9. François Furet, "Quantitative History," *Daedalus*, Winter 1971, pp. 160–61; Fernand Braudel, "History and the Social Sciences," *Economy and Society in Early Modern Europe: Essays from Annales*, ed. Peter Burke (New York: Harper & Row, 1972), pp. 11–42.

10. Fernand Braudel, *The Mediterranean and the Mediterranean World in the Age of Philip II*, 2 vols. (New York: Harper & Row, 1973), 2: 1244.

11. See Peter L. Berger and Thomas Luckman, *The Social Construction of Reality: A Treatise in the Sociology of Knowledge* (Garden City, N.Y.: Doubleday, 1966); and Clifford Geertz, *The Interpretation of Cultures: Selected Essays* (New York: Basic Books, 1973). Following from these assumptions about the social construction of reality, language itself has become as mysterious as the things we try to explain with it. Thus all social science, all knowledge that relies on language, suggests Michel Foucault, is incapable of "representing" and "explaining" human "reality." See his *The Order of Things: Introduction to the Archeology of the Social Sciences* (New York: Pantheon Books, 1970).

12. Emile Durkheim, *The Rules of Sociological Method*, ed. George E. G. Catlin (Glencoe, Ill.: The Free Press, 1938), ch. 1.

13. Otto R. Frisch, *The Nature of Matter* (New York: E. P. Dutton, 1973), p. 105.

14. Geertz, *Interpretation of Cultures*, p. 218.

15. Ian R. Christie, *Myth and Reality in Late-Eighteenth-Century British Politics and Other Papers* (London: Macmillan, 1970), p. 28.

16. John Brewer, *Party Ideology and Popular Politics at the Accession of George III* (Cambridge: At the University Press, 1976).

17. Bernard Bailyn, *The Ideological Origins of the American Revolution* (Cambridge: Harvard University Press, 1967), ch. 4; and Richard B. Morris, *The American Revolution Reconsidered* (New York: Harper & Row, 1967), p. 38. Bailyn himself avoids making any crude argument that the conspiratorial ideas of the revolutionaries constituted motives for their actions, and indeed, in a more recent summary of his interpretation he implies a "semiotic-structuralist" or what he calls an "anthropological" view of the ideology of the Revolution. ("The Central Themes of the American Revolution: An Interpretation," in *Essays on the American Revolution*, ed. Stephen G. Kurtz and James H. Hutson [Chapel Hill: University of North Carolina Press, 1973], pp. 10–12, 23). Yet Bailyn's fleeting suggestions that the ideas of the revolutionaries were revealing of motives and were "really" believed by them—in fact were "a key not only to the thoughts and motivations of the leaders of the revolution but to their actions as well"—have led others to conclude that these ideas by themselves were sufficient springs of action. See Bailyn, *Ideological Origins*, p. vi, and his *Origins of American Politics* (New York: Alfred A. Knopf, 1968), pp. 11, 13.

18. Sir Lewis Namier, *Personalities and Powers* (London: H. Hamilton, 1955), p. 2.

GORDON S. WOOD

19. On this point see especially the articles by Quentin Skinner, "Conventions and the Understanding of Speech Acts," *The Philosophical Quarterly* 20 (1970): 118–38; "On Performing and Explaining Linguistic Actions," *The Philosophical Quarterly* 21 (1971): 1–21; "Some Problems in the Analysis of Political Thought and Action," *Political Theory* 2 (1974): 277–303; and "The Principles and Practice of Opposition: The Case of Bolingbroke versus Walpole," in *Historical Perspectives: Studies in English Thought and Society*, ed. Neil McKendrick (London: Europa Publications, 1974), pp. 93–128. Also see Brewer, *Party Ideology*, pp. 26–38—to all of which this discussion is much indebted.

20. See particularly John Dunn, "The Identity of the History of Ideas," *Philosophy* 43 (1968): 85–104; J. G. A. Pocock, *Politics, Language, and Time: Essays on Political Thought and History* (London: Atheneum, 1971), pp. 3–41.

21. On the Progressive generation's view of the ideas of the American Revolution as propaganda see Gordon S. Wood, "Rhetoric and Reality in the American Revolution," *William and Mary Quarterly* 23 (January 1964): 9–10. It may be that the Progressive historians' assumption that ideas are tools wielded by historical actors is closer to the mark and more helpful than the opposite assumption that ideas are motives for action. For a refined and updated attempt to treat the ideas of the Revolution as rhetoric see Stephen E. Lucas, *Portents of Rebellion: Rhetoric and Revolution in Philadelphia, 1765–1976* (Philadelphia: Temple University Press, 1976).

22. Geertz, *Interpretation of Cultures*, p. 220.

23. Ibid., p. 214.

24. Ibid., p. 12. For one philosopher's reappreciation of this public and collective aspect of the historical process see W. H. Walsh, "Colligatory Concepts in History," in *Studies in the Nature and Teaching of History*, ed. W. H. Burston and D. Thompson (London: Routledge and Kegan Paul, 1967), p. 74.

25. For a lucid explanation of culture similar to that suggested here see F. Allan Hanson, *Meaning in Culture* (London: Routledge and Kegan Paul, 1975). Hanson distinguishes between what he calls "intentional meaning," referring to individual aims and purposes, and "implicational meaning," referring to interrelated customs and cultural institutions. This distinction between subjective, individual motives and objective, social consequences is crucial to social science. See Robert Merton's discussion of this point under the rubric of "manifest" and "latent" functions in *Social Theory and Social Structure* (New York: Free Press, 1957), pp. 19–84.

26. This "structuralist" view of culture does not in any way inhibit the kind of intellectual history that focuses on significant texts. Indeed, it is possible that a single text, say, a Puritan sermon or *Moby Dick*, expresses a unique awareness of the values and conventions, the "implicational" and "latent" meanings, of the culture in which it was written, and thus singlehandedly might be used to explain much of that culture.

27. Geertz, *Interpretation of Cultures*, pp. 209–12. Of course, individual creativity in thought does occur but, like the production of new sentences in a language, such creativity takes place within a structure of rules and conventions.

28. E. P. Thompson, *Whigs and Hunters: The Origin of the Black Act* (New York: Pantheon Books, 1975), pp. 258–69.

29. Gordon S. Wood, *The Creation of the American Republic, 1776–1787* (Chapel Hill: University of North Carolina Press, 1969), chs. 12 and 13.

30. Much of the appeal to historians of Thomas S. Kuhn's *The Structure of Scientific Revolutions* lies in his replacement of the old idealist-materialist dichotomy with just such "a dialogue between traditions and contingent experience" as is suggested here. See David A. Hollinger, "T. S. Kuhn's Theory of Science and Its Implications for History," *American Historical Review* 78 (April 1973): 370–93, esp. 373–77.

31. It is true, writes Karl Popper, that our cultural world is created by men, but emphasizing the man-made character of our cultural world is a mistake. Instead,

INTELLECTUAL HISTORY AND THE SOCIAL SCIENCES

"it is to be stressed that this world exists to a large extent autonomously; that it generates its own problems . . . and that its impact on any one of us, even on the most original of creative thinkers, vastly exceeds the impact which any of us can make upon it." Popper, "Epistemology without a Knowing Subject," in *Philosophy Today No. 2*, ed. Jerry H. Gill (New York: Macmillan, 1969), p. 272.

HISTORIANS AND
THE DISCOURSE OF INTELLECTUALS

DAVID A. HOLLINGER

Much of the scholarly work that goes by the name of "intellectual history" consists of efforts to study the discourse of communities of intellectuals. The obviousness of this fact is sometimes concealed by the easy way we have of speaking of our subject as "ideas" or "attitudes," and by our habit of describing these ideas and attitudes with such sweeping adjectives as "Western," "modern," "American," "European," "white," and "nineteenth-century." To be sure, there are works of history comprehensive enough to justify the use of these adjectives, and there are works whose subjects are indeed ideas and attitudes in their autonomy. By "autonomy" here I mean the absence, on the part of the historian, of conscious attention to any discourse in which an idea or an attitude might have functioned. Yet a great many of the books and articles produced by scholars known conventionally as intellectual historians are implicitly or explicitly addressed to the performance of minds in discourse. Moreover, many of these books and articles address the discourse of certain kinds of people whom, for want of a better term, we often call "intellectuals."

Why should these points deserve the explicit formulation and elaboration that this paper seeks to provide? That ideas are articulated in a communicative context of some kind is scarcely news to historians or to anyone else. How this basic insight is commonly possessed and employed by intellectual historians, however, is not quite so clearly and widely understood. The existing literature on aims and methods in the field, compatible as much of it is with what I want to say, focuses on other aspects of the endeavor. A critical explication of the role played by the notion of discourse in the work of intellectual historians may serve to increase the control practitioners have over their metier and thereby to improve its practice. This explication may also serve to help explain to historians in other fields, and to nonhistorians, just what it is that intellectual historians do.

By identifying "discourse" as a basic subject matter of inquiry I intend several implications. Discourse is a social as well as an intellectual activity; it entails interaction between minds, and it revolves around some-

42

HISTORIANS AND THE DISCOURSE OF INTELLECTUALS

thing possessed in common. Participants in any given discourse are bound to share certain values, beliefs, perceptions, and concepts— "ideas," as these potentially distinctive mental phenomena are called for short—but the most concrete and functional elements shared, surely, are *questions*. Even when one grants that the choice of questions on the part of contributors to a discourse is in itself an act of evaluation, and when one grants further that conflicting "answers" offered to these questions will be structured partly by the ethical, aesthetic, and cognitive agreements among the participants, it remains true that questions are at the active heart of the discourse. Questions are the points of contact between minds, where agreements are consolidated and where differences are acknowledged and dealt with; questions are the dynamisms whereby membership in a community of discourse is established, renewed, and sometimes terminated. To focus instead on a belief or value attributable to an individual or to a collectivity of individuals is at once to move back from those authentic, contingent relationships; when historical subjects are said to hold a belief or value, those subjects are endowed with merely abstract, static characteristics (for example, a belief in "progress" or in "republicanism") that may or may not be shared by a virtual infinity of other subjects who may or may not interact with each other. Yet when these same ideas are viewed in their capacity as answers to questions shared with other persons (for example, "What is the national destiny of America?" or "What kinds of political conduct are virtuous?"), they become contributions to discourse.

They become so in different senses, depending upon the degree of explicitness with which a given question is being addressed. An idea about national destiny, for example, is easily understood to be a contribution to discourse if the context of its assertion is decidedly a discussion about national destiny. Yet a society that so takes for granted its national destiny as to obviate any discussion of it may also possess, in the unarticulated presuppositions of its members, an "answer" to what the historian may treat as a "question" about national destiny. Clear as the distinction may be between questions actually asked and those not asked —between what is talked about and what is not—the infinity of the unsaid includes within it a class of ideas that stand as answers to certain basic questions for particular groups of people and that silently serve, thereby, to limit, direct, and sustain what members of those groups actually say to each other. Presuppositions, then, lie in socially undifferentiated space no more than do explicit questions and answers; presuppositions have a distinctive role within specific systems of communication.

That the history of thought consists of a series of answers to questions was, of course, pointed out eloquently by R. G. Collingwood,[1] and it has

DAVID A. HOLLINGER

been a prominent observation in recent theoretical literature. Yet the point of entry for this literature, as for Collingwood, is the particular historical artifact, usually the *text*: it is in order to discover the intentions behind particular texts, such as Hobbes's *Leviathan*, that historians are understood to scrutinize the realm of discourse in which such texts were designed to speak. The discovery of the meaning of texts is obviously essential, but a distinction exists between, first, the study of discourse as a means of interpreting particular texts and, second, that study as a project of its own. It is one thing to explicate Huxley's response to Bishop Wilberforce and it is quite another to write a history of the Darwinian controversy. My point is not that either of these two enterprises can go forward without the insights derived from the other; rather, we must simply acknowledge that the most rigorous of our recent theoretical literature describes and advocates the first of these and says little about the second.[2]

This fact about our own methodological conversations derives, I think, from the distinctive needs of the branch of intellectual history whose practitioners have written the most compelling and widely quoted methodological treatises in recent years: the history of political philosophy. By "distinctive needs" I refer first to the emphasis historians of political philosophy place on particular artifacts of intellect; indeed, if the history of political philosophy did not focus on texts like Hobbes's we would certainly need to create a discipline that did. A second distinctive need has been the imperative to overcome the residual Whiggery and moralism that there remain a more formidable obstacle to historical scholarship than they do in other fields. This second need has quite clearly been a motive force behind the theoretical literature to which I refer, just as—to cite a more well-known and momentous example of this syndrome—social scientists of the late-nineteenth century produced a substantial body of writing on the nature of "science" while trying to transform the various branches of moral philosophy into sciences. And, just as natural scientists were then—to carry the analogy a step farther—inclined to describe the nature of their own enterprise a bit more precisely and explicitly, so, too, is it now appropriate that intellectual historians articulate more clearly the general outlook that has been taken up and put to such creative and effective use by historians of political philosophy.[3] This articulation must include, above all, the reminder that discourse and the communities formed around it are "central subjects"[4] as authentic as are ideas and the texts in which ideas are embedded.

In the context of this conviction, a number of issues demand attention. Does the notion of discourse restrict itself to minds that were active at the same historical moment, and even to those aware of each other? Do communities of discourse necessarily correspond to national, linguistic, and occupational units? Must such communities consist of social equals? Can discourse be fairly construed to include paintings, statues, rituals, and other nonverbal modes of communication? Are discourse-defining questions presumed to be perennial? To what extent does the designation of communities of discourse as the primary unit of study restrict the attention of historians to ideas that appear to directly "answer" the discourse-defining question, and thereby exclude from inquiry aspects of the designated discourse generated by the engagement of its participants with other questions and other communities of discourse? Does the notion of discourse imply any general theory about the impetus for, and sustaining conditions of, intellectual change, including changes in questions as well as answers? To what extent would the more conscious reliance upon the notion of discourse entail acceptance of the "archaeological" outlook on discourse advanced recently by Michel Foucault?

Let me try to speak to several of these issues by translating into their terms the prominent features of several well-known works of intellectual history, none of which, I trust, is so idiosyncratic as to render it an inappropriate example of what many intellectual historians do. I have in mind three works written about different centuries by students of different national cultures: William J. Bouwsma's *Venice and the Defense of Republican Liberty*, Charles Coulston Gillispie's *Genesis and Geology*, and Perry Miller's *The New England Mind*.[5] None of the authors of these books has made a pointed methodological assertion about "communities of discourse," but I believe this notion fits their work comfortably.

Bouwsma's title refers to the Venetian writers who sought to defend the interests of their republic through the theoretical refinement and articulation of Venice's political tradition in the immediate context of the imperatives of the Counter-Reformation. These writers participated, with spokesmen for Rome and for Florence, in a Catholic discourse about the proper structure of authority in a Christian society. Specifically, the questions at issue were the extent of papal powers vis-à-vis those of secular states, and the foundations of those powers in the nature of things and in the history of the Mediterranean world. If these questions were created for the disputants by their common membership in the geographic, political, economic, and religious continuities of northern Italian life, the grounds for differing answers were laid by the contrasting circumstances of the commercial city, Venice, and the capital, Rome, responsible for the maintenance of the universal Catholic order. The "republican liberty" that had flourished in the trader's world was placed in a new light by the appearance, in the Reformation, of a particularism more radical than that of the Italian republics; hence the questions were sharpened, and the contrasting interests of the opposing Italian parties became more threatening to each of those parties. Bouwsma concludes with Paolo Sarpi, the last—before his republic's decline—Venetian polemicist to create out of the terms of the argument with Rome a compelling theoretical statement of Renaissance republicanism. Sarpi's writings eventually became vehicles for the recollection, on the part of Europe as a whole, of the example of freedom set by the Venetian republic. Since the memory of Venice was indissolubly bound up with a more "modern," particularistic, secular world view, that memory, in turn, was an agent in the political imagination of Europe for several centuries.

The discourse of these northern Italian Catholics of the late-sixteenth century thus emerges from Bouwsma's account as a distinctive historical moment, significant for the functions the discourse itself performed in the larger history of Europe. Bouwsma's ultimate interest throughout is actually in attitudes and values of a general order, not in the exact questions around which the discourse revolved. The methodological point I want to make at the risk of belaboring it, however, is that Bouwsma's means of getting at the salient values and attitudes (for example, "particularism," "historicism,") is to study exactly those now-arcane questions and answers that were on the surface, that carried debate forward, and that drew out of one group of participants a distinctive exemplar of Republicanism.

Gillispie's book is about British geologists from the turn of the nineteenth century to the eve of the Darwinian controversy. These geologists argued over the merits of various theories designed to account for the origins of the earth (for example, catastrophism and uniformitarianism), but their arguments turn out to be demonstrably conditioned by commitments each had developed in his capacity as a Protestant, and, less demonstrably, by commitments developed as a citizen of Britain. There were three discourses, then, that overlapped: while the primary one had to do with technical questions in geology, the contributors to this discourse simultaneously sought—with varying degrees of conscious intentions—to answer questions in natural theology and social philosophy that were being addressed at the same moment by natural theologians and social philosophers. Gillispie is aware that geology was not confined to Britain (although British naturalists were then preponderant in geological research and writing), but he chooses to single out for study the British participants in geological discourse precisely because this enables him to more vividly show the presence of Protestant natural theology and British social philosophy within geology.[6]

Students of American intellectual history need no guide to the most commanding and justly famous work in our own scholarly tradition,

HISTORIANS AND THE DISCOURSE OF INTELLECTUALS

Perry Miller's *The New England Mind*. I can allude briefly to its relevance to the concerns of this paper. The first volume of *The New England Mind* gives some attention to the intellectual and religious origins of Puritan ideas, but treats these ideas, for the most part, as a structure, and attributes the structure to a community of interacting minds. Miller's aim was to describe the contents of the minds of the first generation of New England's intellectual leaders; at one point he explicitly characterized these contents as "the premises of all Puritan discourse."[7] And what is the second volume if not the narrative of that discourse during the following two generations? The questions addressed by Miller's subjects run a gamut from explicit theological issues, such as the extent to which one can be "prepared" for salvation, to such implicit issues as the relative goodness of human nature. Throughout, Miller is concerned with how the formulation and attempted resolutions of these questions is conditioned by not only the "premises" outlined in volume one, but also by a variety of contingent experiences, including, among others, the growth of commerce, the transformation by events in England of issues in church polity and in the relations between church and state, the general emergence in Europe of the "new learning," and the development over time of attachments to America as a place. Specialists may complain that Miller's judgments require correction—as they may complain that Bouwsma subsumes the Venetians and their foes too strictly under "medieval" and "modern" world views, or that Gillispie distinguishes too sharply between "scientists" and other educated Englishmen —but complaints of this order need not distract us from recognizing the kind of history Miller has executed. Volume two of *The New England Mind* is held together less by "ideas" than by the seventy-year conversation to which those ideas were contributed; to read this book chapter by chapter is to immerse oneself in a succession of disputes, of discussions, of arguments—here, if anywhere in our professional literature, is the life of the mind depicted as a *life* rather than as a set of discrete units of thought or artifacts of intellect possessed of either common or unique attributes.

It will scarcely have gone unnoticed that the examples I am using address, in each case, a discourse carried on predominantly in verbal form among disputants who were essentially peers, who were cognizant of each other's views, and who shared both a language and what we could loosely call, even in the instance of Bouwsma's northern Italians, a national culture. Moreover, the temporal scope of these works covers two or three generations. The notion of a community of discourse need not be given so restricted a denotation, but I begin with works of this sort because so many studies of intellectual history do, in fact, operate within these parameters. This pattern in the selection of topics is a result

DAVID A. HOLLINGER

not only of sloth, but of the historian's proverbially tenacious loyalty to the particularity and density of experience more easily grasped within these parameters than beyond them.

This loyalty to what Gilbert Ryle and Clifford Geertz have now led historians to think of as "thickness"[8] has made the work of Arthur O. Lovejoy anomalous, and therefore instructive here as a contrast to the books I have cited. Lovejoy's brilliant *Great Chain of Being* exemplifies "thin" description. Here is a study of a single "idea"—or, more precisely, a mutually reinforcing cluster of three beliefs about the nature of things —over many centuries and within many languages and national cultures. What makes the book "thin" is Lovejoy's purposive disregard of the distinctive contexts in which the idea of the great chain ostensibly appeared and was put to service. Lovejoy does observe that the great chain was an answer to a question that kept getting asked throughout Western history,[9] so one could insist that Lovejoy performs for a single "premise" of all Western discussion of "being" the same sort of analysis Miller's volume one achieves for many premises of Puritanism. This insistence might save—formally—the notion of a community of discourse, but in fact Lovejoy does not study the evolving constitution of the question supposedly involved, only the continuity of the answer. Now, the very idea that a single question can exist in so many times and places I do not find so thoroughly outrageous as do some of Lovejoy's critics, but most of us can surely agree that no question, however general, can escape being constituted by some particulars of the language, the national culture, and the genre of expression in which a given formulation of the question may have existed. Lovejoy would not dissent from this, but the insight has little impact on his work because he frankly eschews the desire to understand ideas as they variously function, a desire that of course lies behind most discourse-conscious scholarship. Lovejoy explicitly directs his ideal historian to "cut into" philosophical argument, for example, in order to isolate the "unit ideas" the historian will then similarly isolate by cutting into art, science, literature, etc.[10]

Reference to Lovejoy's aloofness from the discursive thickness of the ideas he studies need not imply that such aloofness is endemic to histories with multigenerational and multilinguistic subjects. In epistemology, for example, or in physics, it is not invariably a mistake to regard members of different societies living in different centuries as participants in a single discussion. To so regard certain aspects of the history of epistemology and physics does not necessarily imply a timeless status for the questions to which these disciplines are addressed, nor even that epistemologists and physicists lack salient involvement in other, more temporally and geographically bound, contexts of discourse. What is implied, rather, is only that questions in epistemology and physics can

HISTORIANS AND THE DISCOURSE OF INTELLECTUALS

sometimes be *demonstrated* to be so constant, even as such questions are addressed by persons greatly separated in time and place, that there exists as an appropriate subject a community of discourse having boundaries very different from those within which Bouwsma's Italians or Miller's Massachusetts clergy conversed. For example, one could say that there has been, among a substantial number of British, American, German, and French philosophers since the time of Kant, a considerable agreement on what the problems of epistemology are; it is not necessarily wrong to regard Kant, Josiah Royce, and some of today's philosophers as participants in a continuous discussion.

A number of issues remain; in order to eliminate any inference that the scholarly tradition I am seeking to explicate is moribund or esoteric, I will explore these issues through texts "closer to home": American history imprints of 1975, 1976, and 1977. A convenient example is a book of 1977, Theodore Dwight Bozeman's *Protestants in an Age of Science*.[11] This book, which is much narrower in scope than any to which I have alluded until now, is about Baconian ideas as held by the conservative faction of antebellum American Presbyterian theologians. Now, one can call it a history of "ideas" if one wishes, but in so doing one might not convey the fact that Bozeman's Princetonians are discussed in explicit relation not only to other Presbyterians, but also to their Unitarian and Evangelical enemies. The discourse in which Bozeman's crowd participated also embraced most of the intellectually ambitious Protestant clergy in America and Scotland, but Bozeman's "narrow" book is no less grounded in that discourse than would be a volume that sought to interpret all of it. Strictly speaking, Bozeman's book is not a description of Baconian ideas as they can be found in the writings of these professors; it is rather an explanation of the appeal of these ideas and an analysis of their function in the apologetic endeavor thrust upon Old School Presbyterians by the religious behavior and thought of those of their contemporaries and immediate predecessors about whom these Princetonians greatly cared, and of whom they took careful notice. The book is also an attempt to discover the role that Princeton Baconianism, in turn, played in the larger discourse to which it was a contribution: how, for example, it affected the context in which the Darwinian controversy could take shape among American Protestants during the next generation. Hence *Protestants in an Age of Science* is built on a grid strikingly similar to that on which Bouwsma's undeniably more imposing and important work was constructed.

Bozeman's book, like the others I have cited thus far, focuses on arguments made by people whose chief business it was to argue, and to do so as rationally as they could. It is in relation to studies of this kind that the word "discourse" makes the clearest intuitive sense.[12] Yet the

DAVID A. HOLLINGER

notion can also be an anchor for studies of a very different kind, as is shown by the example of Ronald G. Walters's *The Antislavery Appeal.* The immediate abolitionists who are Walters's subjects bear to the world of antebellum American reform a relation not unlike that borne by Old School Presbyterians to American Protestant theology; both have a position on a set of related questions that are being argued over with other parties. Debates among antebellum American reformers, however, entailed more direct and extensive efforts to change the social behavior of masses of people than did debates among theologians, and the community of reformers did not put nearly so high a value on logical consistency as did the community of theologians. Now, one could still write a book on the arguments of the immediatists, and of the ideas embedded in those arguments, but Walters has instead addressed the immediatist movement on the level of the "structure of perception"[13] that integrated its world and informed the full range of its activities, from the most earnest efforts at rational argument, through the most frank of emotional appeals, to the most direct of political action. Walters explores this structure of perception by documenting certain patterns in the way slaves, slaveholders, and related social conditions were depicted by immediatists in a variety of modes of expression, including diaries, fiction, letters, drawings, speeches, and treatises. Hence *The Antislavery Appeal*, while a study of neither the arguments contributed by the immediatists nor even of the style of thought embodied in those arguments, defines its topic according to a specific referent point in reformist discourse—the immediatist position—and illuminates that topic by showing how a distinctive set of perceptions conduced more directly than others to the assertion, in discourse, of a particular position. One could insist that a book more about "seeing" than about "thinking" is marginal to intellectual history as a discipline, but that would not render the volume's foundation in the notion of discourse any less striking.

By now I trust it is clear that the notion of discourse can apply to communities with varying degrees of commitment to the ideal of rationality, can sustain studies of parts as well as of wholes, and, further, that the notion entails neither an obliviousness toward the ways in which distinctive communities of discourse overlap nor an insensitivity to the fact that a single artifact of intellect may serve as an answer to more than one question. It ought to be clear, moreover, that the notion does not imply any attribution of sufficient causal efficacy to any generically defined component or sustaining condition of a discourse, including values, beliefs, perceptions, social structure, economic function, political position, and psychological state. All of these things may or may not be agents in a given discourse, and it is the responsibility of a given historian to persuade us of the validity of whatever causal claims or implications he or she introduces with regard to a given aspect of a given discourse. The point about "discourse" is not a point about causal explanation at all, but about the nature of the reality to which causal claims and implications often apply. In any event, a truism that seems always in need of repetition is that providing causal explanations is only one of the things historians do; it would be impossible to translate without remainder any of the books I have mentioned into the strict terms of a causal explanation.

I trust it is also clear by now that the notion of discourse applies the least ambiguously to studies of men and women of words. The histories I cite are, for the most part, devoted to preachers, scientists, philosophers, theologians, political polemicists, and to a lesser extent, writers of fiction, rather than to painters, sculptors, architects, and performers of religious rituals. The extent to which an etching and an essay can be said to "share a question" is an interesting issue, and one that can no more be resolved by complacent affirmations of the integrity and autonomy of contrasting modes of expression than by the prior conviction that each age has a spirit that manifests itself in all cultural activities.[14] It is rather a matter for empirical study on a case-by-case basis; we have a number of books that convincingly treat certain nonverbal artifacts as contributions to the same discourse to which certain verbal artifacts have been contributed. A number of classics could illustrate this point, but I will instead mention a recent book by John F. Kasson simply because the volume's treatment of the arts is so representative of American scholarship during the past generation, and because the book also exemplifies the study of discourse across the lines of class and power.

Kasson's *Civilizing the Machine*[15] is about those literate Americans between the Revolution and the end of the nineteenth century who remained loyal to "republicanism" as a political culture and who sought to assess the implications of the growth of technology. These Americans participated in a discourse in which questions were less sharply formulated than in that of Bouwsma's Catholics or Bozeman's Princeton theologians, but it was one in which the assertion of technology's benign and "republican" character was undoubtedly a position held in opposition, for example, to such other positions on technology's moral and political meaning as the more skeptical ones taken by working-class leaders, some of whom saw in technology the potential replacement of republicanism with slavery. Kasson does not insist that technology's claims to benignity and republican virtue were *argued*, strictly speaking, by paintings like John Ferguson Weir's *Gun Foundry*, etchings like J. O. Davidson's *Southern Cotton Press by Night*, or the railroad scenes by Currier and Ives; but only the most querulous of Kasson's readers will doubt that the positions he attributes to these artists were indeed ad-

DAVID A. HOLLINGER

vanced and publicly reinforced by them, regardless of what other functions, discursive or otherwise, their art may have performed. To be sure, some of Kasson's subjects did not hear each other's answers to their shared questions as clearly as do the subjects of most studies of political or philosophical discourse. Distinctions between degrees of directness in communication must be maintained, but our access to these distinctions need not be lost when we simply recognize how thoroughly Kasson's book is grounded in the awareness that the attitudes he studies were not invented independently by a succession of mysteriously similar individuals; rather, Kasson's book is informed by the insight that these attitudes were generated, learned, possessed, asserted, criticized, and defended in a historically and socially specific context of public discussion. In that context, certain questions endured and certain answers seem more compelling than others to people who had particular economic relationships with machines. Currier and Ives helped to extend the domain of "Republican technology" within the public culture of the United States, and Mark Twain's *Connecticut Yankee* extended the domain of certain doubts about technology's consistency with republicanism; to regard the industrial landscapes of Currier and Ives and this novel of Twain's as contributions to a discourse does not, I believe, strain the notion of discourse altogether beyond its descriptive utility.

The extent to which the writer of an essay and the maker of an etching "share a question" is of course only a sharper form of an issue that can legitimately be raised about contrasting verbal modes, or even about particular works within one of these modes, such as the essay. The issue, as it is most often put, is one of *intentions*: did a given person, through whatever he or she wrote or otherwise created, intend to speak to a given question, and thereby intend to express the particular ideas that we as historians are inclined to attribute to him or her? Near the beginning of this paper I referred to the distinction between the instrumental use of a discourse in order to better understand a given text and the study of discourse itself. The latter enterprise might be said to use texts as instruments in order to better understand discourse. Since the two types of study reinforce each other so vitally, it would be a mistake to get scholastic about their distinctness; yet their differences on "intention" need to be clarified because it is on this single but important matter that methodological essays for one cannot speak effectively on behalf of the other.[16] The difference can be put both negatively and positively.

To state the difference in the negative, when a text (or other artifact of intellect) is used as a means of understanding a discourse, the historian need be concerned neither with the *complete* recovery of all the intentions behind a work, including intentions to speak to a variety of

HISTORIANS AND THE DISCOURSE OF INTELLECTUALS

questions which themselves are the foundation for discourses other than the one the historian is addressing, nor with the rigorous determination of the author's hierarchy of priorities; when, by contrast, the point of the inquiry is to establish the intentions behind a text, all of the discursive contexts in which the text appears to participate become tools for the interpreting of the text. Joseph Wood Krutch's *The Modern Temper*,[17] for example, is a text that speaks to a number of questions of interest to students of twentieth-century intellectual history. Now, the text may have a particular, definite structure of intentions the recovery of which is a legitimate enterprise, but the explication of this entire structure is not incumbent on a student of the efforts of Krutch and his contemporaries to define the meaning of love, say, or upon historians differentially addressing discourse about the social role of art, about the moral implications of laboratory science, or about the extent to which civilization was making "progress."

What *would* be incumbent on the historian of any one of these discourses—to turn now to the positive way of stating the difference—is above all reference to how Krutch's text functioned in the designated community of discourse, and to whatever freight from Krutch's various "other" involvements was brought into the life of the designated conversation. The same obligations, of course, attend upon the contributions of other participants than Krutch in the designated discourse. Thus the meaning of a text for the historian of discourse consists not exclusively in the intentions of its author, but also in the text's functions, including the answering for readers of questions that the author had not been especially concerned to answer.[18] Just as one enterprise employs the apparent functions of a text as a clue to its intentions, so does the other employ its apparent intentions as a clue to the text's function in discourse.

So conceived, the study of discourse can include inquiries of a number of kinds, as the examples of Bozeman, Walters, and Kasson indicate.[19] Although this breadth in the tradition is exactly what I want to emphasize, it would be a mistake to lose sight of the contrast between this tradition and other sorts of intellectual history. Obviously Lovejoy and his immediate followers have pursued a calling very different from the one I am describing. So, too, have the many historians of philosophy, of the social and natural sciences, and of political thought who have sought to show how thinkers in the past responded, in effect, to questions cast in the terms peculiar to *today's* discourse. These "Whiggish" historians, after all, were the object during the 1960s of much-discussed critiques by Thomas S. Kuhn, George W. Stocking, Jr., and Quentin Skinner, all of whom asked, for one or more of these branches of the history of thought, the development of a historiography congruent with the broad but reso-

DAVID A. HOLLINGER

lutely "historical" scholarly tradition I have been describing.[20] Less obvious is what to make of the most methodologically articulate and distinctive cluster of scholars within the ranks of American intellectual historians, the "myth and symbol school."

It is possible to project onto some of the better works of this school—especially Henry Nash Smith's *Virgin Land*[21] and John William Ward's *Andrew Jackson: Symbol for an Age*[22]—a vast community of Americans of various stations addressing in several contexts a set of related questions about the meaning of their society. But even these two carefully designed books are more vague about the social constituency of the images they attribute to the collective mind of the United States and are less tightly focused on the particular uses to which such images were put than is Kasson's book, which otherwise resembles the books by Smith and Ward. Perhaps the works of the "myth and symbol school" could be more successfully defended against critics had the notion of community of discourse been more operative in the execution of these works and more explicit in the methodological pronouncements of its authors.[23]

Christopher Lasch's *The New Radicalism in America, 1889–1963*[24] is far indeed from the "myth and symbol school" and from "the American mind," but this provocative, extensively discussed volume can also serve as a counterpoint to the tradition of scholarship I am concerned to explicate. Lasch's successive chapter-biographies of selected twentieth-century intellectuals aim to chart the growth of a collectivity of *individuals* who manifest the general social characteristics (for example, detachment, reliance upon the mind in work and play) that Lasch believes can distinguish "an intellectual" from other individuals. As with the works of Ward and Smith, it is not impossible to project onto Lasch's book a community of discourse. Yet what the reader then might take as Lasch's account of a given thinker's contribution to the ongoing life of that community Lasch himself has consciously and consistently depicted as just one more occasion for the emergence of a single and generic "social type."[25]

This recognition about the nature of Lasch's book can bring us now back to my opening observation that most intellectual historians study the discourse of certain kinds of people whom, for lack of a better term, we call "intellectuals." The introduction of this notorious term into methodological discussions is usually an invitation to swap red herrings with all interested parties, but before trying to eliminate those red herrings let me underline two related disclaimers that until now have remained only implicit: (1) there is no reason in principle the notion of a community of discourse could not inform the study of *any* population that has left a record of having addressed "shared questions," regardless of the nature of the questions and of the educational level and mental capabilities of those who shared the questions; and (2) there is no reason in principle the term "intellectual history" has to be confined to the study of the discourse of "intellectuals."

What then, are we to do with the appellation "intellectual"? Or, to put the issue more sharply, what is it that gives the "discourse *of intellectuals*" a measure of identity sufficient to mark it off as a major variety of intellectual history? Certainly, the standard distinction between "elites" and "ordinary people" has much to do with it. Even if members of the powerless and uneducated classes of Renaissance Venice or Cambridge of the 1890s expressed opinions on the nature of liberty or on the structure of the universe, they shared questions only superficially with Paolo Sarpi and Josiah Royce. The same must be said of a large percentage of the "elite" population. Much of the intellectual activity that goes on within social and political elites belongs to what we now call popular culture or popular ideology. Moreover, someone who belongs to an "elite" for the purposes of some discussions may be "ordinary" for others. In our historiographical tradition, then, the "discourse of intellectuals" is identified chiefly by the extent to which participants draw upon and bring into precise focus the theoretical knowledge, literary and religious traditions, and other cultural resources that historians know to have been accessible to the most well-informed members of a given society at a given historical moment.

The demarcation to which I allude is not to be translated into the terms of the distinction between "articulate" and "inarticulate," for this distinction is often taken to imply either that persons who speak effectively and extensively do so not only on their own behalf, but also on behalf of silent neighbors with varying social characteristics, or that persons who do little to perpetuate or advance the scientific, literary, political, and theological debates of their time are "inarticulate" about all other matters, too. The distinction I wish to make is a more strictly behavioral one, which I hope can be clarified by reference to how differently a group of children may relate to "lego," the popular toy.

When children are given several boxes of lego, some will single out one or two structures to build and play with, while other children, given the same amount of time, will manage to use most of the lego in all of the boxes, and in so doing create definite and well-connected structures. The children who only use a few pieces are not necessarily "inarticulate." They may have simply chosen, for whatever reason, to exploit in an articulate fashion fewer of the resources at hand than have the children who end up using most of the pieces. To make the example stronger, one can confine the contrast to children with essentially the same apparent

DAVID A. HOLLINGER

purpose, to create, say, a vehicle for the transportation of a single imaginary person; this purpose for one child can be achieved by a half-dozen pieces, or even a single piece, while another may require 100.

Why does one child use only a few pieces? Has this child not seen all the pieces in one box, or not noticed the other boxes? Does he or she simply put little value on the building of things, including imaginary vehicles? Does he or she simply not like lego, and prefer other modes of expression? Has another child hidden the other boxes of lego while we adults were not looking? Why do some people apparently interested in supporting a given claim about the authorship of the Bible settle for using one or two of many ideas at hand without taking seriously the potential utility of the other ideas? Do they not understand the relevance of these other ideas? Is their experience too limited to enable them to employ these other ideas? Do they simply not care very much about the issue, and devote their intellectual energies to other interests of which the historian may or may not be aware? Do they think the issue is important but so easily answered as to require no fuss? What role in these differences is played by education, intelligence, class position, cultural thievery, economic function, personal temperament, etc.? Pursuing these issues is an interesting and valuable activity, but the resolution of these issues is not a precondition for making the basic distinction to which I refer. It ought to be sufficient to observe that interaction among people who are using most of the pieces in all of the boxes, and who are able to order them in a variety of ways, is different from interaction among people who use no more than a handful of pieces and who arrange them in few ways.

This observation recognizes that questions of a general kind can indeed be shared by persons with varying resources for the formulation and pursuit of such questions, that communications across educational levels can be authentic, and that "ordinary people" as well as intellectuals think, even formally and systematically, with or without the same analytic tools used by contemporary intellectuals. Yet the observation *also* recognizes that relatively distinctive discourses can develop among people who precisely formulate questions that may be shared with people who remain oblivious to these more specific and often more precise formulations. Participants in these distinctive communities of discourse may come to see as constitutive of these very questions a range of highly particular elements—elements that must be ignored if the historian looks only upon the denominators common to both this specific discourse and the larger, more general one. Certainly, histories can be, have been, and should be written about intellectual experiences common to intellectuals and other sentient beings, but these histories, as well as those confined either to those experiences in which a given class of

HISTORIANS AND THE DISCOURSE OF INTELLECTUALS

intellectuals apparently did not share or to those that seem to have been peculiar to intellectuals, can best locate their own subjects and define the relations between those subjects and the subjects of other histories by more deliberate attention to the discursive setting of thought.

This is to suggest that many of the traditional missions of historians, including the asking of exactly what ideas were formulated and possessed by whom, and put to what use, can be reinforced and equipped with more rigor if the notion of discourse is made somewhat more prominent in the methodological consciousness of scholars, and if it is cojoined with the operational definition of intellectuals outlined above. The discourse of intellectuals, then, has in any given case boundaries that are ostensibly empirical, that mark shifting differences in intellectual behavior, and that, by virtue of their very distinctness, encourage historians to inquire more diligently into the relations between these bounded entities and other communities of discourse than, perhaps, historians inquire if they fail to view as distinctive the thought of a society's apparent intellectual leaders. Inquiries into how and why a set of preoccupations moves from one interacting group to another, for example, are more likely to be stimulated when distinctive discourses are recognized.[26]

This sensitivity to the distinctness of communities of discourse may promise an enriched scholarship, but nothing could more resoundingly betray that promise than a literal-minded determination to fix boundaries more exactly and firmly than good sense will allow. Devoutly as one may wish for general rules of method with which rigor may be consummated and the "precise" boundaries of communities discovered, such rules (for example, the imperative to identify shared questions) are more effectively grasped and applied when learned from concrete examples of historical scholarship than when stated in the abstract. Examples such as those that form the elements out of which this paper is built can convey both rules and the sorts of limits imposed on their application by the concrete sources with which a historian works. The boundaries of many communities of discourse are no more or less definite than the boundaries of the historiographical tradition this paper seeks to explicate; just as one could go on, at yet greater length than I have above, trying to clarify the parameters of this tradition, so could a historian of a given community of discourse risk losing sight of that community's essence by relentlessly seeking to verify in each of its apparent members the existence of a fully uniform pattern of intellectual behavior.

If the promise of a more rigorous exploration of relations between ideas and their various social constituencies is one benefit of a heightened recognition of the discursive context of thought, another benefit is

DAVID A. HOLLINGER

the placing in perspective of an "idealist" vocabulary that, when used uncritically, misrepresents the tradition as actually practiced. The notion of discourse avoids the deleterious effects of the idea-event dichotomy while preserving the recognition of the intellectuality of the subject matter of intellectual history: an idea contributed to a discourse is no less an "event" (and no less trivial or momentous, in itself) than a bullet fired in a war or the invention of a machine. The notion of discourse sidesteps the Cartesianism that afflicts the language of many prefaces, if not of the texts that follow; it recasts the "internal-external" problem in terms that transcend the conceptual prison of "intellectual" versus "social" phenomena; and it recognizes in our subject matter an authenticity that the rhetoric of a dessicated rationalism has too often concealed from both practitioners and critics of intellectual history.

The notion of discourse, as I have tried to indicate throughout, implies the historicity, temporality, dynamism, and contingency in human thinking that have long been seen as the special province of historians and that are helpfully brought into bold relief by this notion at the present moment, when historians are so admirably eager to absorb as much insight as possible from such ahistorical disciplines as anthropology, linguistics, philosophy, and sociology. A hint of how endemically "historical" is this notion can be gleaned from the *Oxford English Dictionary's* entry for discourse, in which static meanings are well submerged beneath those entailing development.[27] A more dramatic and instructive index is the work of Michel Foucault. There, an effort to retain the notion of discourse within a program designed to obliterate the historical way of looking at human knowledge has located Foucault's argument in an undercurrent that constantly threatens to pull him down into historical depths the very reality of which it is his great mission to deny.[28] Nothing nettles him so much as to be mistaken for a writer of intellectual histories, and nothing in his theoretical writing is more obscure and unpersuasive than his efforts to explain why this characterization of his *Order of Things*, for example, is a mistake.[29] Although this is not the place to attempt an adequate exposition of Foucault's prescriptions,[30] attention to some of their features can serve to distinguish this paper's implications from Foucault's and to underline more of the methodological attractions of the notion of discourse.

Foucault charges "archaeology" with the tasks of discovering the "rules" that govern particular "discursive practices," and transcribing the changes from one set of rules to another. What goes on in discourse at any given time, then, is analyzed by Foucault in pointedly synchronic rather than diachronic terms, and what transitions there are—the substitution of one synchronic, rule-bound discourse for another—archaeology does not seek to explain, only to record. Foucault professes no interest

HISTORIANS AND THE DISCOURSE OF INTELLECTUALS

in the political and social matrix of discourse, and is so determined to focus on what he regards as the unmediated, empirical surface of discourse—the dispersion of enunciative events—that he altogether eschews reference to "questions." These imply a measure of agency and coherence on the part of participants in discourse that is not implied by the mere existence of objective rules according to which utterances, including those a speaker may subjectively regard as questions, are constructed. Foucault's vision of discourse is in effect dehumanized, in comparison, at least, with the outlook basic to the historiographical tradition I have reviewed. How, then, can anyone seeking to critically extend that tradition learn anything from Foucault, and experience while reading his work an increase in enthusiasm for the notion of discourse?

In his effort to drain effective volition from artifacts of intellect, particularly texts and oeuvre, Foucault attributes to discourse itself a vivid positivity, a truly primal existence in contrast to the almost phantasmic being allowed to books, careers, genres, traditions, and other presences commonly felt to be concretely visible in discourse. To profit from this suspension of such conventional "unities" as books—to treat them, that is, as a mere space in which a population of events are dispersed—one need not accept Foucault's demand that only on the basis of discovered rules for discursive practice can the reality of these unities be reestablished, nor need one accept Foucault's radically antihermeneutic claim that the "population of dispersed events" that makes up discourse is available in its primal state if we but exercise the appropriate effort to apprehend it. This suspension has its attractions: it can subject to more rigorous interrogation the texts, oeuvres, genres, and traditions that appear to be *given*; of them one can ask, with conscious naiveté, "What are they?" what are the networks of which a book is a "node"? Out of what "complex field of discourse" is it constructed? "What specific phenomena" does it "reveal in the field of discourse?"[31] By refusing, for a moment, to answer these questions only in terms of the obvious antecedents of texts (for example, the intention of an author or the influence of an exemplar), the historian can gain critical distance from the presuppositions he or she brings to the study of discourse, and may be more likely to discover connections and gaps between artifacts of intellect that have been overlooked. It is Foucault's rasping, audacious, almost exasperated testimony to the substantiality of the particulars of discourse that most commends his work, and is also the most easily detached from his Olympian faith that these particulars are controlled by discoverable rules immune to human agency.

The heuristic suspension of conventional categories, like other benefits of heightened awareness of discourse, can apply in a general way to

DAVID A. HOLLINGER

almost everything intellectual historians write about. In practice, however, the notion of discourse has a more constant and intimate utility for studies of historical figures who share well-defined questions and who are conscious of their common engagement with such questions—studies of the sort represented by Bouwsma, Gillispie, Miller, and some of the recent American history imprints discussed or cited early in this essay.

Even for such studies, the benefits of the notion of discourse are not to be misconstrued as ready solutions to the methodological dilemmas that practitioners regard as standard. How does one decide, for example, exactly where and how the perspectives of the major theoretical traditions in the human sciences ought to inform the selection, design, and execution of a project in the historical analysis of thought? The role of the notion of discourse is not to answer such questions, but clarify the setting in which they need to be asked.[32]

Notes

This paper owes much to the lively discussion given an earlier version of it at the Wingspread Conference. To give fair acknowledgment would be to list here the names of most of the participants. Instead, let me say simply that criticisms I have worked especially hard to meet were raised at Racine by Michael Fellman, Thomas L. Haskell, John Higham, Bruce Kuklick, and Warren Susman. The same applies to points made by several readers not present at the conference: Felix Gilbert, John F. Kasson, Lewis C. Perry, Daniel Scott Smith, and Ronald G. Walters. For stimulating talks about the issues addressed by this paper I am grateful to Quentin Skinner.

1. R. G. Collingwood, *An Autobiography* (Oxford, England: Oxford University Press, 1939), p. 31.
2. I have in mind particularly John Dunn, "The Identity of the History of Ideas," *Philosophy* 43 (April 1968): 85–104; Quentin Skinner, "Meaning and Understanding in the History of Ideas," *History and Theory* 8 (1969): 3–53; J. G. A. Pocock, *Politics, Language, and Time: Essays on Political Thought and History* (New York: Atheneum, 1971), esp. pp. 3–41. Pocock is closest to the second enterprise on pp. 24 and 25 and 28 and 29, but he manifests throughout this important essay a tendency to return always to the particular "speech act" as the unit of study. An intelligent discussion of these three methodologists from the perspective, again, of strictly "political thought," is Charles D. Tarlton's "Historicity, Meaning, and Revisionism in the Study of Political Thought," *History and Theory* 12 (1973): 307–28. Skinner's most recent writings are refreshingly more explicit in promoting the investigation of entire political languages, including the asking of how they interact with and gain predominance over one another; see especially his "Political Language and the Explanation of Political Action" (Paper presented to the Annual Meeting of the American Political Science Association, Washington, D.C., September 1977).
3. A number of methodological treatises on intellectual history were written between twenty and thirty years ago, when the field was becoming established in the curricula of American universities. A number of contributions to this earlier literature made sound observations, especially John C. Greene's "Objectives and Methods in Intellectual History," *Mississippi Valley Historical Review* 44 (June

HISTORIANS AND THE DISCOURSE OF INTELLECTUALS

1957): 58–74, which, if read without a mean-spirited eagerness to find Hegel between the lines, remains one of the most sensible articles in the field.

4. On this concept, see the helpful remarks of David L. Hull, "Central Subjects and Historical Narratives," *History and Theory* 14 (1975): 253–74.

5. William J. Bouwsma, *Venice and the Defense of Republican Liberty: Renaissance Values in the Age of the Counter Reformation* (Berkeley: University of California Press, 1968); Charles Coulston Gillispie, *Genesis and Geology: A Study in the Relations of Scientific Thought, Natural Theology, and Social Opinion in Great Britain, 1790–1850* (Cambridge: Harvard University Press, 1951); Perry Miller, *The New England Mind: The Seventeenth Century* (New York: Macmillan, 1939); Perry Miller, *The New England Mind: From Colony to Province* (Cambridge: Harvard University Press, 1953).

6. See also Robert Young, "Malthus and the Evolutionists: The Common Context of Biological and Social Theory," *Past and Present*, no. 43 (May 1969), pp. 109–45.

7. Miller, *Seventeenth Century*, p. x. Compare with Miller the references to "discourse," "dialogue," and "cultural conversation" in the introduction to another classic work in American intellectual history, R. W. B. Lewis, *The American Adam: Innocence, Tragedy and Tradition in the Nineteenth Century* (Chicago: University of Chicago Press, 1955), pp. 1–3.

8. Clifford Geertz, *The Interpretation of Cultures* (New York: Basic Books, 1973), esp. pp. 3–30.

9. Arthur O. Lovejoy, *The Great Chain of Being: A Study of the History of an Idea* (Cambridge: Harvard University Press, 1936), p. 14. Although an extensive literature exists on Lovejoy, one recent contribution is especially helpful: Thomas Bredsdorff, "Lovejoy's Idea of Idea," *New Literary History* 8 (1977): 195–211. See also Daniel J. Wilson, "Arthur O. Lovejoy: An Intellectual Biography" (Ph.D. diss., The Johns Hopkins University, 1975).

10. Lovejoy, *Chain*, p. 3.

11. Theodore Dwight Bozeman, *Protestants in an Age of Science: The Baconian Ideal and Antebellum American Religious Thought* (Chapel Hill: University of North Carolina Press, 1977).

12. Representative examples from 1975, 1976, and 1977 imprints in American history include the following: Mary O. Furner, *Advocacy and Objectivity: A Crisis in the Professionalization of American Social Science, 1865–1905* (Lexington: The University Press of Kentucky, 1975); William R. Hutchison, *The Modernist Impulse in American Protestantism* (Cambridge: Harvard University Press, 1976); Thomas L. Haskell, *The Emergence of Professional Social Science: The American Social Science Association and the Nineteenth-Century Crisis of Authority* (Urbana: University of Illinois Press, 1977); Bruce Kuklick, *The Rise of American Philosophy: Cambridge, Massachusetts, 1860–1930* (New Haven, Conn.: Yale University Press, 1977). One intellectual biography designed explicitly as a study of the functions performed by a single career in the overlapping communities of discourse of an American academic generation is David A. Hollinger, *Morris R. Cohen and the Scientific Ideal* (Cambridge: M.I.T. Press, 1975).

13. Ronald G. Walters, *The Antislavery Appeal: American Abolitionism After 1830* (Baltimore, Md.: The Johns Hopkins University Press, 1976), p. xiii.

14. On this problem, see E. H. Gombrich, *In Search of Cultural History* (Oxford: England, Oxford University Press, 1969).

15. John F. Kasson, *Civilizing the Machine: Technology and Republican Values in America, 1776–1900* (New York: Grossman, 1976).

16. I am thinking here even of the important essays of Quentin Skinner, above all "Meaning and Understanding," by far his most widely quoted and influential article. Skinner's focus on texts is somewhat less pronounced in a more carefully wrought article that is, unfortunately, read by all too few historians, "Some Problems in the Analysis of Political Thought and Action," *Political Theory* 2 (August 1974): 277–303, but even here "the recovery of the historical meaning

DAVID A. HOLLINGER

of a text" is for Skinner "obviously the main question" (p. 283). Closer to my concerns are his unpublished paper, "Political Language and the Explanation of Political Action," and his *The Foundation of Modern Political Thought*, 2 vols. (Cambridge: At the University Press, 1978).

17. Joseph Wood Krutch, *The Modern Temper* (New York: Harcourt, 1929).
18. This extremely common phenomenon might be called, with apologies to Robert K. Merton, the "unanticipated consequences of purposive intellectual acts." A recent and well-known case involves Thomas S. Kuhn, *The Structure of Scientific Revolutions*, rev. ed. (1962; Chicago: University of Chicago Press, 1970). An inquiry into this book's intentions and an inquiry into the questions it was used to answer by many of its readers, especially in the social sciences and the humanities, would produce very different results. Less common, perhaps, but equally interesting is the opposite phenomenon, the obliviousness of the discourse of an author's generation to work that a later generation makes integral to its own discourse, and in relation exactly to the questions the author aimed to answer; classic examples of this involve Spinoza and Mendel.
19. An example of a yet different kind is Daniel Walker Howe, "American Victorianism as a Culture," *American Quarterly* 27 (1975): 507–32, which takes one of the more notorious and amorphous "isms" of nineteenth-century intellectual history and gives it definition as both a "communication system" and a "value system."
20. Kuhn, *Structure*; George W. Stocking, Jr., "On the Limits of 'Presentism' and 'Historicism' in the Historiography of the Behavioral Sciences," *Journal of the History of the Behavioral Sciences* 1 (1965): 211–18; idem, *Race, Culture, and Evolution: Essays in the History of Anthropology* (New York: Free Press, 1968); Skinner, "Meaning and Understanding." The extent to which Kuhn's theory of scientific change is rooted in traditional historiography is emphasized in David A. Hollinger, "T. S. Kuhn's Theory of Science and Its Implications for History," *American Historical Review* 78 (April 1973): 370–93.
21. Henry Nash Smith, *Virgin Land: The American West as Symbol and Myth* (Cambridge: Harvard University Press, 1950). Frustrating as is its lack of exactness, *Virgin Land* remains one of the most informative contributions ever made to the study of American intellectual history.
22. John William Ward, *Andrew Jackson: Symbol for an Age* (New York: Oxford University Press, 1955).
23. One sharply drawn critique of this school is effective chiefly as a demonstration of the inadequacy of the theoretical efforts its members have offered as commentaries on their own enterprise: Bruce Kuklick, "Myth and Symbol in American Studies," *American Quarterly* 24 (1972): 435–50.
24. Christopher Lasch, *The New Radicalism in America, 1889–1963: The Emergence of the Intellectual as a Social Type* (New York: Alfred A. Knopf, 1965).
25. For a more explicitly discourse-based view of the development of an intellectual "class" in America, see David A. Hollinger, "Ethnic Diversity, Cosmopolitanism, and the Emergence of the American Liberal Intelligentsia," *American Quarterly* 28 (1975): 133–51.
26. See the suggestions made in papers at the Wingspread Conference and published herein by Thomas Bender (ch. 11) and Murray Murphey (ch. 9). Another pertinent paper was presented at Wingspread by Michael Fellman, "Approaching Popular Ideology in Nineteenth-Century America." See also Howe, "Victorianism."
27. The *OED* entry begins with "Onward course; process or succession of time, events, actions, etc." and with the ancient association between the word "discourse" and "running to and fro."
28. For a hint of Foucault's awareness of this problem, see his *The Archaeology of Knowledge* (New York: Harper & Row, 1976), p. 200.
29. For example, "Forward to the English edition," Michel Foucault, *The Order of Things: An Archaeology of the Human Sciences* (New York: Pantheon Books, 1971), and Foucault, *Archaeology of Knowledge*, passim. I find it a general rule

HISTORIANS AND THE DISCOURSE OF INTELLECTUALS

in Foucault that whenever the name of "the history of ideas" is invoked, something particularly wrongheaded and unhelpful is about to follow.

30. A cogent discussion can be found in Hayden V. White, "Foucault Decoded: Notes from the Underground," *History and Theory* 12 (1973): 23–54. White is more sympathetic than I am to Foucault's entire program. Practitioners of American history have written remarkably little about Foucault, whose *The Archaeology of Knowledge* is surely one of the most ambitious and intelligent theoretical essays on intellectual history. A partial exception to this silence—partial since the piece remains unpublished—is Robert F. Berkhofer, Jr., "Does History Have a Future? The Challenge of New Ways of Understanding Past Human Behavior for Traditional Historical Analysis" (Paper delivered at the Annual Meeting of the Organization of American Historians, Denver, Colorado, April 1974). This paper is the liveliest of recent discussions, by Americanists, of methodological issues in intellectual history. A helpful piece more directly on Foucault is Alexander N. Block, "Archaeological Analysis and Historiography" (Seminar paper, Department of History, State University of New York at Buffalo, 1974).

31. Foucault, *Archaeology of Knowledge*, esp. pp. 22–26.

32. Since this paper has an essentially affirmative tone regarding American intellectual history, I want to acknowledge that I share the widespread conviction that the subdiscipline has not been living up to its potential in recent years. My complaints, however, are not at all the ones that have been the most loudly proclaimed (for example, the field is elitist, excessively fascinated by ambiguity and complexity, idealist, oblivious to the social origins of ideas, and too literary). Four of the most keenly felt of my own disappointments are these: (1) our books and articles often are not sufficiently rigorous in clarifying the questions they ask about the American past; (2) our field has been slow to come to grips with natural knowledge as produced by scientists and as differentially assimilated and employed by various individuals and groups in the twentieth century; (3) we remain too concerned—despite some exemplary repudiations of this limitation—with the uniqueness of American history and not enough with the place of American intellectual history in the history of the West, side-by-side with the national cultures of England, Germany, France, etc.; (4) we have failed to make as clear as we might have that our subject is often the history of the discourse of intellectuals. This fourth complaint alone is a basis for the present paper.

ON STUDYING THE NATIONAL MIND

RUSH WELTER

So far as it is possible to generalize successfully about the findings of a
meeting that arrived at no formal conclusions, it may be said that participants in the Wingspread Conference on Intellectual History largely
agreed that inclusive historical studies of the sort attempted by either
Perry Miller or Vernon Louis Parrington are at best a risky undertaking,
if indeed they have any utility at all. On their view, scholars know too
much about the complexity of the nation's high intellectual traditions,
and too little about the intellectual orientations of lesser men and
women, to attempt to identify and analyze national beliefs or attitudes.
Rather, their remarks typically suggested, a national or even a regional
"mind" never existed; or if it did, it is not accessible to the methods by
which intellectual historians have normally approached their materials,
and they would best be advised either to pursue more limited inquiries
or to embrace the materials and methods of the new social history (especially those of the *mentalités* school) if they hope to arrive at something worth saying.

It seems to me that the participants' concerns were more significant
than their recommendations were persuasive. Granted that much of
what has passed for the intellectual history of the United States has been
tainted by methodological inadequacies, it does not follow that it can be
so comfortably dispensed with. Indeed, the converse is probably true:
intellectual history will probably lose much of its significance if its practitioners do not continue to attempt broad-gauged analyses of American
thought. I propose in this essay to discuss why I think attempts to reach
an American "mind" are necessary, what form they may most profitably
take, what objections they may risk, and wherein their promise lies. In
the final analysis I judge, not only that the effort is both plausible and
necessary, but that, properly conceived, it is one of the historian's most
promising tools for analyzing and even explaining the events he purports
to understand.

It is necessary for several reasons. For one thing, as Quentin Skinner
has suggested, we literally cannot understand historic statements or arguments unless we have a most perspicuous grasp of the intellectual
context in which they were made. If we treat words out of context we

ON STUDYING THE NATIONAL MIND

will not know what they were intended to convey or how they were perceived, and—as Peter Laslett has demonstrated with respect to John Locke's treatises of civil government—we are also likely to miss the point and emphasis of the larger discourse in which they appeared.[1] Aileen Kraditor has made the same point, albeit for different purposes, in criticizing radical historians who take seemingly revolutionary exhortations out of context and impose their own vision of class struggle on a society in which such struggles notably did not materialize.[2] Considered in this light, good intellectual history requires an extraordinarily broad awareness of the intellectual orientation of the whole society or region in which any given statements were made; generalization of this sort is an indispensable preamble to understanding intellectual events.

Such a preamble is necessary even if it is the purpose of the historian to trace the attitudes or careers of a clearly defined group of individuals, for the treatment of any such group will suffer if it cannot be anchored in a close understanding of the larger intellectual context in which it had its being. The historian who does not know what that larger context was has no way of measuring the peculiarity or idiosyncrasy of his chosen subjects, or of truly understanding the perspectives that made them distinctive. The more sharply defined their identity, the greater may be his need to understand the intellectual premises against which they asserted it; for unless he has a firm grasp of those premises he cannot assess either the intellectual import or the practical significance of their statements.

The obverse is also true: particular studies of discrete groups can have little meaning unless they serve to illuminate a more general perception of historic phenomena. Here we must distinguish between the internal and the external significance of works of historical scholarship. No matter how persuasive they may be when measured by internal standards like factual accuracy and logical coherence, there is relatively little they can persuade us of unless they make some sort of contribution toward extending, modifying, or even denying a more general interpretation of events in which the particular events were immersed. The proposition is, indeed, self-evident, in that a reader necessarily assimilates the results of any new study to an existing frame of reference, but it is more pertinent than this psychological truism suggests. Only competent understanding of the larger context of events will lend appropriate meaning and significance to any particular study, no matter how carefully conducted.

The character of the nation's history has created additional reasons for the American intellectual historian to seek out general patterns of thought alongside the narrower patterns in which he may take a particular interest. To the extent that the United States has been egalitarian in its social aspirations, to the extent that its educational institutions and media of information or persuasion have been popular rather than elite in their bias, to the extent that popular opinion (however misinformed) has been a given within which its political leaders were forced to work, the ideas current in the society at large have had more to do with how it conducted its affairs than have comparable ideas in other societies. One need not celebrate this proposition in order to find it compelling. For example, it does not matter whether the historian believes that the whole American "ideology" was an invention of the common man or a contrivance of the possessing classes to maintain their economic hegemony; the fact is that the ideology seems to have existed, and that it apparently had large consequences. So, too, with any version of the contention that ideas always trickle down from the upper classes to the lower; their presence among the lower classes is the key historic fact. Hence it is arguable that American historians cannot make significant statements about the actions national leaders took without understanding the larger intellectual context in which they acted. Even diplomatic history, once the most narrowly defined of the traditional forms of historical inquiry, has been much deepened and enlarged by assumptions of this sort, whether those of William Appleman Williams or Ernest May.[3]

Nevertheless, the effort to write about an American mind has proceeded by interpretive devices that seem inadequate to the purpose. One of them has been what we may well describe as agglomeration, the assembling into a larger intellectual structure of bits and pieces of historical analysis developed by many historians. This has its roots in the view of historical study that flourished at the turn of the century, according to which historical research is a form of scientific inquiry that will, when properly conducted, arrive at uniformly plausible and methodologically compatible statements about historic phenomena. Unfortunately the same philosophical perspectives that have undermined the ideal of scientific history have also undermined agglomeration: if objectivity is impossible, then the bits and pieces of interpretation that various historians have developed do not occupy the same universe of discourse and cannot safely be assembled into synthetic statements about historic phenomena. It is true that, reading between the lines and seeking data relevant to their own concerns, scholars may well be able to turn earlier studies to account in spite of the different perspectives of their authors, but even this prospect offers no great hope to intellectual historians. However much it may be possible (for example) to assemble data about a wide variety of economic activities into a convincing portrait of the national economy, there is no good reason to believe that a collection of studies of what various men and women thought will sufficiently identify the intellectual commitments and transactions central to a given epoch

ON STUDYING THE NATIONAL MIND

or region. In short, successful generalization by agglomeration seems to be all but impossible in intellectual history.[4]

In any case, intellectual historians have commonly employed other means to serve the intended purpose. Among them has been extrapolation, the conscious extension of discoveries made on a lesser scale to the explication of events on another and larger scale. One can understand the attractions that extrapolation holds even for the conscientious scholar: it enables him both to grapple closely with a manageable phenomenon and to place his results in a context that lends a broader significance to what he has discovered. Indeed, it is psychologically impossible for any of us as human beings to avoid some kinds of extrapolation; we cannot help but comprehend the phenomena we encounter in our historical inquiries in terms of phenomena that are already familiar to us. Nevertheless we also have good reason to doubt the history that is written by these means, and nowhere more than in its intellectual branches. At one time it seemed possible to write American intellectual history as if it were identical with the intellectual biographies of a handful of literary figures. Now it clearly is not, and the work of Perry Miller comes under attack because it describes a New England mind (sometimes an American mind) haunted by problems peculiar to a learned seventeenth-century ministry—this quite apart from questions that have been raised about Miller's interpretation of the ministers' theology.[5] The same kinds of criticism have called into question other, less significant, studies. It is now widely recognized, for example, that the Social Darwinism Richard Hofstadter described in his first book simply did not hold the kinds of influence or authority that he and his continuators initially attributed to it.[6] Under these circumstances it is no wonder that highly competent scholars have more or less abandoned conscious generalization by extrapolation even while they continue to practice it out of necessity.

Prompted in part by the defects of extrapolation, American historians have pursued another approach to the national mind, which may best be described as generalization by imputation. Like extrapolation from the lesser to the larger scale, imputation rests upon the psychologically inevitable practice of reading the unknown in terms of the known, but it also involves a conscious effort to solve the problems of interpreting historic events by employing principles of explanation derived from other disciplines. The practice has acquired special luster in intellectual history because many disciplines peculiar to the twentieth century—the psychology of the subconscious, the sociology of knowledge, and cultural anthropology among them—have increasingly impressed historians as ways of conceiving mental processes beyond the reach of their tradi-

RUSH WELTER

tional analytical operations. These circumstances have apparently encouraged them to embrace novel and essentially paradigmatic models of analysis and explanation, which they have applied not only to conventional literary documents but also to a far wider range of literary and nonliterary remains than their predecessors typically examined. Hence they have arrived at challenging new perspectives on the general patterns of American thought; but it is in the nature of their methods that the thought patterns they have discovered exemplify the conceptual schemes the historians bring to them. They have overcome the difficulties of finding out how a generation thought by interpreting the sources they work with in the light of assumed models of human behavior.

Much of the best work in American Studies exemplifies both this broadening of inquiry and the problems of interpretation it creates. For example, the scholars who are most commonly identified as proponents of the American Studies approach—Henry Nash Smith, R. W. B. Lewis, Leo Marx, John William Ward—have made a positive virtue of applying essentially literary constructs to the documentary materials they deal with, at the expense of attempting a broader understanding of American thought.[7] But the practice extends well beyond American Studies; many modern works, often of the most venturesome character, suffer because of the extent to which they substitute elaboration of the historian's scheme of analysis for open-ended consideration of what he reads. This is apparent in Louis Hartz's study of the liberal tradition in America, which literally depends upon the imputation to American political life of a dialectic of perception and analysis borrowed from the history of European political thought, and which is as a result simply insensitive to many of the considerations that seem to have shaped the American political tradition.[8] So, too, with studies in psychohistory. These are at their most programmatic when they seek to explain the behavior of groups of men, let alone whole nations, but even individual biographies demonstrate the peculiar thrust of their inquiries: witness Robert D. Thomas's recent study of John Humphrey Noyes, in which the footnotes consist of references to psychoanalytic studies of personality disorders rather than data from Noyes's own life.[9] But the difficulty is not peculiar to psychohistory, it is only highlighted by it; historians of many different kinds cast about for models of explanation that will illuminate events they cannot reach by agglomeration or extrapolation. Doing so, they employ the paradigm as a substitute for more traditional modes of historical inquiry.

In part this is an inevitable development, a consequence of the proliferation of knowledge, the accumulation of data, the ramifications of modern philosophy, the psychology of inquiry, and the creative bent of the human mind. But it also imposes burdens on intellectual history that it cannot and should not be asked to accommodate. For one thing, it tends to reinforce the practice of asking self-fulfilling questions, which Aileen Kraditor has so sharply criticized; if one asks only questions that are to be answered by a priori criteria, one tends both to obtain the answers one was looking for and to arrive at answers that do not significantly deepen the investigation. More important, any inquiry based upon sociological or psychological generalizations is by definition an attempt to gather knowledge by reconceiving the explicit content and logic of the materials the historian is dealing with. If a concern for content and logic has often led intellectual historians to develop assertions that proved in retrospect to have been absurd, the concern for other kinds of significance ultimately denies their discipline its reason for being.

The proposition invites us to approach our inquiries with a different perspective, not forgetting the lessons we may have learned from the failures of past efforts or the discoveries of the social sciences, but working our way through to a mode of analysis that is appropriate to the special circumstances of our discipline. When we have done so we may also find that we have defined a method of inquiry that offers singular opportunities for effective interpretation of the nation's thought.

We may best begin by recognizing that intellectual historians should presumably seek to deal with ideas: with conceptual and essentially cognitive statements that can be understood in discursive terms and subjected to discursive analysis. We do not need to claim that men are always rational or that their perceptions are always intellectual to declare our interest in studying them when they were. At the same time, we need not limit the definition of rationality to patterns of thought that meet scholarly criteria for philosophical or scientific inquiry. It is true that if we measure commonplace mental dispositions by the standards of academic discourse, we cannot help but conclude that most of them are subrational (if not irrational) and infer that they cannot be approached by attempts to analyze their intellectual content and logic, but must be understood as the instinctive articulation of deeper motives that are revealed rather than expressed. Yet even if ordinary men and women do not apprehend events with the same intellectual system and the same analytical rigor as their erudite betters, it seems evident that they conceptualize them in terms of categories of belief or expectation they have already acquired; they undertake to deal with the disparities they recognize between those expectations and their experience by some form of thought; and they seek means (however ineffectual) to "solve" the problems their experience thus presents. Given this condition of affairs, we have reason to examine even popular thought directly as thought rather than indirectly through paradigmatic analysis.[10] In particular, using

RUSH WELTER

documentary residues of human thinking to guide our analysis, we can address as explicit objects of historical inquiry the connections that speakers or writers seem to have made between idea and idea (the inferences they drew) as well as between idea and phenomenon (the recognition, conceptualization, or comprehension of facts).

It seems almost equally apparent that we should deal with ideas in their practical significance. The proposition helps to distinguish between the primary objectives of intellectual history and some of the concerns its practitioners have embraced. On occasion they have written as if either the internal consistency or the putative origins of ideas were their most significant characteristic; far from treating ideas as if they had made a difference in the world, these enthusiasts have dealt with them as if they were interesting in their own right. Nevertheless, even historians who have devoted themselves to tracing changes in major ideas have usually implied that they illuminated other aspects of human behavior by identifying the ways in which successive generations of thinkers defined their worlds, while their counterparts in the sociology of knowledge have written as if the commitments they wished to account for were none the less influential for the fact of being explicable. Hence the central problem for intellectual historians today would seem to be not *whether* but *how* ideas may be construed as consequential phenomena, to develop ways of perceiving them that will maximize their potential for explaining the actions that men historically took.

In 1979 it is inconceivable that we should do so without drawing upon aspects of psychology, nor do we lack psychological models that can help us to define our purposes more clearly. Two relatively recent studies have reviewed much of the literature and extracted the relevant inferences. The first, by Robert F. Berkhofer, Jr., attempts to work out what the author calls *A Behavioral Approach to Historical Analysis*. It is especially compelling, therefore, both when it argues for the need to establish the "internal" components of historic behaviors and when it employs current psychological doctrine to help define the effort. In particular, Berkhofer argues that mental dispositions that affect behavior but are normally thought to be beyond the reach of empirical inquiry are potentially accessible when they are reconceived as collective cultural orientations. By this means, he argues, we may overcome what psychologists refer to as the "black box" phenomenon—the inaccessibility of mental operations to direct empirical analysis. At the same time, he warns against the dangers of imposing modern ideational constructs on the cultural expressions of an earlier generation, an admonition that reinforces our suspicion of paradigmatic analysis and has the important ancillary effect of suggesting that there may be ways in which we can reach these mental dispositions without distorting them unduly by imputation. In short, his book suggests that intellectual historians may well be able to identify the role that thought played in historic events if only they can find means to deepen their analysis of ideas.[11]

While Berkhofer testifies only indirectly to the psychological legitimacy and explanatory significance of intellectual history, Gene Wise elaborates specific psychological perspectives that should govern the historical treatment of ideas. His study, *American Historical Explanations*, comes to a focus in formal analysis of types of intellectual history, but his argument rests upon an extended consideration of patterns of behavior common to all mankind. He holds on the basis of cognitive psychology and philosophical anthropology that men cannot help but engage in selective perceptions of the world, which order their experiences according to established symbolic categories even while they are also shaping those categories to fit the events the men seek to deal with. Wise applies the proposition to professional historians, whom he depicts in the act of noticing, conceptualizing, and diagnosing historic phenomena according to one or another of the paradigms of historical explanation available to them from their previous training and experience, but there is nothing in his analysis that restricts its application to scholars. What he calls "minding" is a characteristic human act, and (although he does not say so) the techniques of analysis by which he establishes the distinctive biases and dispositions of different historians are also available for the analysis of documentary evidence of the ways that other kinds of men sought both to understand and to prescribe for their experience.[12]

In other words, these volumes point to a kinetic rather than a descriptive consideration of ideas in history: to an effort wherever and however possible to enter into the intellectual operations by which historic men and women conducted their lives, rather than simply analyze their expressions and take their significance for granted. In practice, however, most intellectual historians have been concerned with identifying the positions men took—with noting the sides they arrived at rather than contemplating the means by which they apparently got there—and the effect has been to dismiss from consideration the cognitive processes that would seem to have led them to embrace one rather than another response to the stimuli they experienced. The achievements and the limitations of this approach are well exemplified by Ronald Walters' recent study, *The Antislavery Appeal*, an outstanding work in the genre. Attempting to identify the perceptions that entered into American abolitionism, Walters ends by denying that historians can do more than locate the abolitionists in their times and their culture, when it would seem evident that the key question to have asked is what intellectual processes may be thought to have brought these particular Americans to the point of being abolitionists. It is not their Americanness that needs explaining, but the idiosyncratic conclusions they derived from premises they apparently shared with the rest of the nation.[13]

Even so, we still confront the "black box" phenomenon Berkhofer refers to. In keeping with his behavioral orientation, he is inclined to look to cultural anthropology to identify the mental preoccupations of a given generation. Nevertheless, the anthropological concept of culture would seem to cut off the analysis of human thought just at the point at which it becomes most useful to the intellectual historian. For one thing, it seems to harbor at least the residue of ethnographic studies of "primitive religion," in which purportedly rational explanations of events appear rather as rationalizations of ancient ritual or as presenting a view of the world that "explains" but does not comprehend the phenomena it addresses. Furthermore, despite their criticisms of both functional and structural analysis, anthropologists tend to visualize culture in holistic terms and to treat its separate manifestations as elements in a larger scheme of behavior.[14] Neither tendency is especially helpful to us as intellectual historians: ideas can be shared without being systemic and can be significant without fulfilling needs external to them.

Much the same judgment applies to the claims some scholars have made for cultural history, which is thought to improve upon the intellectual version by eliciting the unstated mental dispositions of the nation as a whole. For one thing, much of it seems to verge on an attempt to define the national character rather than a national intelligence; it often concentrates on dispositions that were not discursive on the grounds that these were more significant than those which may be analyzed as logical statements.[15] In addition, it is apparently premised on an assumption that almost any given datum can exemplify patterns of mental orientation characteristic of a nation or an epoch.[16] Hence it more or less invites the historian to use his ingenuity in examining cultural artifacts as evidence of a pattern of interpretation he favors rather than encourages him to elucidate the pattern of analysis historic figures seem to have applied to events. Whatever its merits, cultural history so understood is no more able than cultural anthropology to take the place of intellectual history.

More generally, we have a choice between imputing specific contents to the "black box" of the mind on the strength of essentially anthropological assumptions and seeking to understand the contents of that mind by analyzing documents that seem to reflect the train of thought individuals followed in dealing with the phenomena they encountered. Obviously any such effort must confront the problem of distinguishing between the intellectual operations of an author and the form in which he chose to articulate his conclusions. Few men record their thoughts in process of formation, and fewer still publish the record. In any case, surviving documents are bound to have been influenced by the circumstances in

ON STUDYING THE NATIONAL MIND

which they were produced and the audience to which they were addressed; for example, they may have the character of rhetorical celebration, of polemical misrepresentation, or of personal justification or rationalization. Hence we cannot treat them as exact representations of the motives of the author; yet this fact does not preclude us from seeking to establish the intellectual framework within which he stated his case or the mental processes by which he purported to address the phenomena he was dealing with. Even if his motives are not available to us, some parts of his thought are; in the language I have already used, we can identify his categories of belief or expectation, perceive his attempted explanations of the disparities between expectations and experience, and recognize the thrust of a deliberative process in the solutions he espouses. To this extent, having abandoned the search for motives understood as "real" reasons for verbal behavior, we may also begin to perceive ideas themselves as motives to actions.

None of this is intended to deny the difficulties that must confront us if we try to reconstruct the thought patterns of men and women who must forever remain strangers to us. It is a truism of modern historiography that we cannot hope to understand them as they understood themselves; but it is also true that our capabilities as historians give us kinds of access to them that are not readily open to literary scholars or philosophers. (This is the logical although not the intended implication of Quentin Skinner's criticisms of classic studies in the history of political ideas. Only if we know a good deal about the circumstances in which statements were made and the audience to whom they were addressed, Skinner's arguments suggest, can we even hope to understand their meaning.[17]) Political philosophers and literary critics tended to interest themselves in formal verbal analysis; we are far more accustomed to dealing with the context of ideas as well as with the ideas themselves, and this gives us an immense practical advantage. Too often, indeed, we have slipped into examining the context of ideas rather than their content, but if we can perform both tasks simultaneously we should come as close as it is possible to come to understanding how given figures coped with their experience. In short, our training as historians is an asset we should treasure rather than a limitation we should seek to overcome in our attempts to understand intellectual history as intellection.

The problem of achieving a kinetic grasp of intellectual commitments deepens when we attempt to treat them as general phenomena. One solution may be to conceive of the undertaking as an exercise in orchestration, the placing of ideas held by different classes, groups, or sections in an essentially dialectical relationship with each other, in which no idea is assumed to be dominant yet in which there is ample room to examine what ideas actually flourished and how men seem to have employed them. This is an approach that characterizes Gordon Wood's masterful *The Creation of the American Republic*, which is successful in part because it portrays the revolutionary generation as competing groups seeking to establish their own distinctive versions of republican self-government. The men Wood describes use their minds in a dynamic rather than a static fashion, adjusting their ideas to their circumstances and their arguments to the arguments of their opponents. Hence his account represents much more than an agglomeration of the results of previous studies—valuable as they are to his analysis—yet it avoids the danger of limiting the scope of the generation's discourse to a single mode of thinking about public issues. It is, in short, pluralistic rather than holistic, as well as insistently pragmatic in its analysis, and on both these counts it serves to indicate how intellectual historians may profitably deal with a national mind without sacrificing either intellection or diversity to the needs of systematic analysis.[18]

At the same time, Wood's account presents certain problems that seem to be inherent in the orchestral mode he develops. For one thing, although he clearly makes an effort to deal with the content of ideas, he also treats them in context as expressions of practical interests. This is particularly true of his treatment of the disagreements the people of the time expressed as distinguished from the ideas they generally adhered to, as if to suggest that when "real" issues surfaced they automatically subordinated general conceptions and thought processes to these more cogent imperatives. On the other hand, in pursuing the common principles men put forward to justify acts of rebellion, he tends to trace continuities in rhetoric rather than ask whether the themes these men invoked occupied a central place in their ways of comprehending their situation. Although these two criticisms may seem at first glance to cancel each other out, I think they point to a disposition that unites them: to some extent, at least, Wood has conceived an analysis that is focused on a history of the ideas men appealed to rather than a history of the ways they came to terms with their experience. The effect is to limit the utility of his account in explaining how the thinking of the generation led to the consequences he describes.[19]

As I have already argued, however, we probably need somehow to address this larger question before we can really understand the lesser ones. To do so, we need to visualize the revolutionary generation as a whole engaged in dialogue with events before we try to visualize it as parts engaged in dialogue with each other. The work Karl W. Deutsch has undertaken in the study of nationalism gives us additional reason to look for national patterns of thought. Although Deutsch points out that no single circumstance guarantees the rise of nationalism, and although other scholars have argued that even the concept of nationalism is fuzzy,

ON STUDYING THE NATIONAL MIND

there is no doubting that a cluster of intellectual constructs we give that name has played a major role in shaping the political and economic behaviors of modern nation-states. Hence Deutsch's attempt to analyze the phenomenon is suggestive even if it is not conclusive. In particular he notes that practical circumstances like geographical mobility, economic interchange, a common language, and a shared history make for a "community" of "minds and memories" that is different from the community of habits, preferences, and institutions that he labels "culture." In effect he invites us, not to assume that these circumstances always lead to community, but that an intellectual community can exist or come into being even where some of the "objective" bases for it are not present.[20]

More briefly, Deutsch testifies to the proposition that nationalism both depends upon a commonalty of discourse and contributes to it. Even without his saying so, the proposition would suggest the probable existence of an American national discourse that resembled patterns of behavior common to most of the modern world yet assumed forms that were peculiar to the United States. For that matter, Deutsch argues that even "objective" considerations like class and vocation do not distinguish the inhabitants of a modern nation from each other as sharply as their common national orientation distinguishes them from the inhabitants of a neighboring country who play comparably divergent roles in its society. Nor is he an advocate of nationalism, or of a national consensus; rather, the best thought he has been able to give to the subject points to the existence of a national phenomenon best described as a community of mind.[21]

His conclusion is even more persuasive if we consider some of the suggestions latent in social psychology about the nature of the socialization process. In general, following the work of George Herbert Mead, they imply that an individual finds himself in the world neither by fulfilling wholly private imperatives nor by deferring to wholly external controls, but by defining his personal imperatives in terms of the responses his behaviors elicit from "significant others." Various ideas now current in social psychology, for example that of role playing, stem from this basic characterization of the human experience, and it seems plausible to believe that this kind of transactional analysis goes far toward explaining how individuals come to share in national as well as less extended intellectual orientations.[22]

Significantly, however, while such a formulation goes far toward accounting for shared perceptions and modes of cognition, it also leaves room for individual idiosyncrasy; the individual may be "socialized" and yet retain distinctive characteristics. Hence any effort to identify general patterns of thought requires that we look for them as widely as possible in the documents available to us. The wider the range of our inquiry the

RUSH WELTER

more persuasive our interpretation will be; it is not small groups of self-conscious intellectuals but a host of different kinds of speakers and writers that will reveal to us the intellectual transactions characteristic of a nation. Only if we can familiarize ourselves with a sufficient number of statements by a sufficient variety of men and women will we have reason to think that we have established the intellectual categories with which its members approached their experience and reconstructed the intellectual processes by which they arrived at the formulas that shaped their actions.

At this point we confront the chief stumbling block in the way of general intellectual history. It is easy to see that only a small handful of literate men and women leave documentary residues of their thought, and plausible to infer that discursive analysis of such residues can tell us nothing about the thought patterns of the majority of the population. In addition, many historians apparently believe that the existence of what they perceive as objective class differences obviates the possibility of shared intellectual dispositions. On this view, general intellectual history is impossible no matter what the documents say, unless perhaps it is assimilated to a dialectical model of history in which the alleged discrepancies are made parts of the larger synthesis.

There are two kinds of question buried in such objections. One is whether the absence of direct evidence cuts us off from any prospect of recapturing popular thought; the other is whether that thought must have been different from its more elevated counterpart. But if it is true that most men do not think like intellectuals, it does not follow that intellectuals never think like ordinary men; the problem for the historian is to find means to get at patterns of thought that extended across class or educational lines, not to find versions of elevated thought in the ruminations of lesser men. Much the same proposition applies to the presumption that objective class differences create disparate intellectual orientations. For one thing, the question may properly be resolved only by inquiry, so far as inquiry is possible at all. For another, the argument that class differences necessitate intellectual differences is suspect because it suggests that ideas are purely derivative formulas and somehow only represent or reflect an external reality—as if thinking were not part of reality, and human belief about that reality not a mental construct. To the extent that ideas give men ways of conceptualizing their experience, it is at least possible that some of their constructs will deny class differences—as radical critics of an American ideology have long complained.

It is less easy to dispose of the contention that the absence of documents cuts us off from the popular mind, but even this proposition is far from conclusive. To some extent it seems to rest upon a descriptive rather

ON STUDYING THE NATIONAL MIND

than an analytical conception of intellectual history, a belief (akin to that of agglomeration) that distinctively American thought is no more than a composite of all the thoughts that the inhabitants of the society engaged in. Of course no competent historian makes this argument in so many words, but it remains with us at least as a principle by which to cast doubt on the findings of the discipline. (For example, it seems to be part of the appeal of Daniel Boorstin's famous gibe to the effect that intellectual history is the history of intellectuals.[23]) It also largely influences the current attempt to incorporate the disadvantaged and the dispossessed into the study of intellectual history. Acting with the best of motives, proponents of Black Studies and Women's Studies, not to mention what no one calls "Lower-Class Studies," have sought to define the black experience and its social equivalents quite apart from the attitudes and values of dominant white males. Too often, however, they have succeeded only in demonstrating that there *was* a black experience or its equivalent; they have dealt with sources usually neglected by traditional historians as if retrieving them from obscurity were sufficient to identify their meaning and demonstrate their importance.

Nevertheless, there is nothing in the mere broadening of the subject matter of intellectual history that will deepen our operations as historians; if anything, the kinds of materials that socially subordinate groups have left us lend themselves only sparingly to the kinetic analysis I have proposed. Not only are many of the most interesting remains subliterary and very simple in their apparent arguments—one thinks of work songs and broadsides—but many of the more literary sources that come to our attention seem to have been couched as arguments intended to reach the dominant culture, hence have little value for identifying the commitments that distinguished subordinate groups' thought from that of their superiors. In short, we should not be misled by our approval for a more democratic definition of the American experience into thinking that additional studies of this sort will enable us to generalize in intellectual history. Our chief question should not be whether everybody is heard from, but how well we can grasp ideas and intellectual processes that are in some real sense within our reach.

This proposition hardly exempts us from the need to inspect the full range of literary evidence available to us. Here, however, our primary objective should not be to attempt a hypothetical "coverage" that we know to be impossible; if the documents do not exist, any attempt at coverage will be illusory. (Even the study of *mentalités* rests upon sources that are at best selective representations of popular thought.) Rather, we should seek to examine the materials we possess as evidence of the range of intellectual resources (both concepts and inferences) open to the generation. We may hypothesize that in a society like that of

RUSH WELTER

the United States, in which literary vehicles have been widely available and major libraries most assiduous in collecting ephemeral publications, we have access to a significant variety of documents even if we also know that most of them reflect the views of only a small number of the total population. But even if this is not so—even if we cannot hope to retrieve more than a fraction of the ideas men thought—we may well surmise that the statements we possess represent the *range* of ideas they employed to understand their lives. We will still have a problem in deciding what proportion of any given group or groups adhered to given ideas, and there will be times when doubts on this point may call our conclusions into question, but we will also have made major strides toward recognizing which ideas men employed and how they entered into the actions men took. Our first problem is not to dissect the "mass mind" but to establish the alternatives open to it, the better to understand the directions it actually took.

To this extent we must embrace the very task that Quentin Skinner has ridiculed: to develop a history of thoughts no one actually thought at a level of coherence no one actually attained. Applied to the study of major texts in political theory on an essentially ahistorical basis, his protest was well warranted; it *is* foolish to treat Niccolò Machiavelli and John Locke as if they were engaged in some kind of conversation with us about the meaning of liberty.[24] But the criticism is largely irrelevant to the broader reaches of intellectual history. In order to escape from the limiting effects of literary evidence without simply using it to exemplify our own paradigms we must look at available documents as particular expressions of a more general intellectual discourse that we cannot retrieve directly. Carefully examined, a wide range of literary remains should indicate (although not conclusively demonstrate) patterns of analysis and belief that transcended the particular statements of individual men; they should give access to patterns of thought that were presumably shared by men who did not engage in recorded exchanges as well as those who did.

To put matters another way, it is the fetish of writing only about recorded exchanges of thought, not the difficulty of finding relevant documents, that presents the greatest obstacle to general studies in intellectual history. If we visualize intellectual events in essentially academic terms as a series of reasoned exchanges on problematical topics, we have no choice but to treat intellectual biographies (including collective intellectual biographies) as the core of our discipline. Doing so, however, we cannot help but be dissatisfied with our grasp of popular thought and be forced to spend our time in cultural or social history when we attempt to deal with it. But if we can visualize thinking as a social activity in which all men participated although few recorded the products of their effort,

ON STUDYING THE NATIONAL MIND

we should be able to treat surviving statements as clues to broader transactions. Under these circumstances the similarities of stance or analysis we find among writers who had no apparent contact with each other will be more significant than the similarities we find among men whom we know to have corresponded or otherwise communicated; they will suggest that we have indeed discovered intellectual processes that were not peculiar to any single group in the society. (The fact that the speakers apparently did not communicate will help to demonstrate the existence of thinking that was shared rather than idiosyncratic.) So, too, with the occasional document that says exactly what we want it to say. If it expresses the analytical scheme we think we have discovered, it will suggest, not that here is a solitary document to prove what we want to prove, but that here is the explicit affirmation of a mode of thinking we have been able to infer from the analysis of a host of other documents. In short, we may be confident that we have discovered rather than presupposed the representative figures of a generation, and that we have identified its intellectual commitments less by agglomeration, extrapolation, or imputation than by inference from the available evidence.

It also follows that if we proceed so far as possible by inference we will have means to accommodate the interpretations we develop to the data we examine: our statements can be comprehensive without being monolithic. Analysis of a variety of documents may in some cases demonstrate the presence and operative force of two or more basic orientations, which may either compete with or complement each other. Moreover, in tracing the ideas we discover to their probable or presumed consequences we should also be able to determine when shared premises led to different practical conclusions as well as when divergent premises led to shared conclusions, which will help us still further in assessing the precise roles given ideas may have played in shaping given actions. So, too, if we judge that the relationship among different groups of men was dialectical rather than fixed, we can essay to establish the terms in which they grappled with each other and the manner in which their ideas and perceptions contributed to the transactions in which they engaged; we may orchestrate their relationship according to their logic rather than ours.

Finally, intellectual history pursued along the lines I have sketched should also locate it more securely vis-à-vis history in general. Despite the greater sympathy institutional historians have displayed toward the discipline, they have often accommodated to it rather than embraced it. Hence the tendency to redefine it as cultural history or the new social history or the history of *mentalités*; hence also the tendency of standard surveys in American history to intersperse chapters on institutional developments with less frequent chapters on cultural and intellectual de-

RUSH WELTER

velopments, as if how men perceived themselves and their problems were ancillary to how they got their living and how they voted. Nevertheless, it seems plausible that the intellectual developments sensitive historians should be able to chart are likely to go at least as far toward explaining what happened in history as any of the external considerations to which modern historians characteristically turn. Even if they cannot hope to accomplish this much, moreover, intellectual historians should be able to establish well-considered portraits of mental dispositions and mental activity that will deepen institutional historians' understandings of the behavior they now purport to explain by other means. On any terms, the search for an American "mind" is not only inviting, necessary, and plausible, but also a most promising avenue for historical inquiry.[25]

Notes

1. Quentin Skinner, "Meaning and Understanding in the History of Ideas," *History and Theory* 8 (1969): 3–39; Peter Laslett, Introduction to John Locke, *Two Treatises of Government*, ed. Peter Laslett, rev. ed. (New York: New American Library, 1965), esp. pp. 58–92.
2. Aileen Kraditor, "American Radical Historians on Their Heritage," *Past & Present*, no. 56 (August 1972), 136–153.
3. Williams demonstrated the potential value of such analysis in an early essay, "The Frontier Thesis and American Foreign Policy," *Pacific Historical Review* 24 (November 1955): 379–95. For Ernest May, see "American Imperialism: A Reinterpretation," *Perspectives in American History* 1 (1967): 123–283.
4. I think this is the practical import of the reception now granted Merle Curti's *The Growth of American Thought* (New York: Harper & Row, 1943; 3rd ed., 1964), which is an outstanding work of its kind but which is seldom used as the basis for specialized inquiries into American thought. Curti's accomplishment is, finally, additive rather than analytical, and does not often serve as a foil for lesser studies.
5. See particularly Darrett B. Rutman, "The Mirror of Puritan Authority," in *Law and Authority in Colonial America*, ed. George A. Billias (New York: Dover Publications, 1970), esp. pp. 42–47 and 58–61.
6. See, for example, Edward C. Kirkland, *Dream and Thought in the Business Community, 1860–1900* (Ithaca, N.Y.: Cornell University Press, 1956), passim, and Irvin G. Wyllie, "Social Darwinism and the Businessman," *Proceedings of the American Philosophical Society* 103 (1959): 629–35.
7. Henry Nash Smith, *Virgin Land: The American West as Symbol and Myth* (Cambridge: Harvard University Press, 1950); R. W. B. Lewis, *The American Adam: Innocence, Tragedy, and Tradition in the Nineteenth Century* (Chicago: University of Chicago Press, 1955); Leo Marx, *The Machine in the Garden: Technology and the Pastoral Ideal in America* (New York: Oxford University Press, 1964); John William Ward, *Andrew Jackson: Symbol for an Age* (New York: Oxford University Press, 1955). I describe these approaches as literary because even when the authors have drawn upon cultural anthropology to vindicate their concerns their actual analytical operations have closely resembled traditional literary analysis. For an indirect and unintended confirmation of this view, see Cecil F. Tate, *The Search for a Method in American Studies* (Minneapolis: University of Minnesota Press, 1973).

ON STUDYING THE NATIONAL MIND

8. Louis Hartz, *The Liberal Tradition in America: An Interpretation of American Political Thought since the Revolution* (New York: Harcourt, Brace, 1955).

9. Robert D. Thomas, *The Man Who Would Be Perfect: John Humphrey Noyes and the Utopian Impulse* (Philadelphia: University of Pennsylvania Press, 1977).

10. This is true even of formulations with which we may totally disagree. For example, although it is undoubtedly true that the American people have often behaved irrationally, attempts to characterize their behavior as paranoid have succeeded only in deprecating rather than comprehending the train of thought that led them to embrace nativism and similar prejudices. Given prevailing American commitments, nativism and its neighbors were understandable if reprehensible public attitudes.

11. Robert F. Berkhofer, Jr., *A Behavioral Approach to Historical Analysis* (New York: Free Press, 1969).

12. Gene Wise, *American Historical Explanations: A Strategy for Grounded Inquiry* (Homewood, Ill.: Dorsey Press, 1973).

13. Ronald G. Walters, *The Antislavery Appeal: American Abolitionism After 1830* (Baltimore, Md.: The Johns Hopkins University Press, 1976), pp. 146–49. Walters's conclusion is the more interesting in light of the debt he expresses to David Donald, who initiated much of the debate about the antislavery crusade by his effort to account for its leaders sociologically and psychologically. (See Donald, "Toward a Reconsideration of Abolitionists," in *Lincoln Reconsidered: Essays on the Civil War Era* [New York: Alfred A. Knopf, 1956], pp. 19–36.)

14. See, for example, the essays of Clifford Geertz, whose work has been hailed by many historians. See especially "Thick Description: Toward an Interpretive Theory of Culture," in Geertz, *The Interpretation of Cultures: Selected Essays* (New York: Basic Books, 1973), pp. 3–30.

15. See, for example, Daniel Walker Howe, "Victorian Culture in America," in *Victorian America*, ed. Daniel Walker Howe (Philadelphia: University of Pennsylvania Press, 1976), pp. 3–28.

16. David Grimsted justifies this approach in his Introduction to his *Notions of the Americans, 1820–1860* (New York: Braziller, 1970), pp. 3–7.

17. Quentin Skinner, "Meaning and Understanding"; also "Conventions and the Understanding of Speech Acts," *Philosophical Quarterly* 48 (May 1970): 118–38, and "Some Problems in the Analysis of Political Thought and Action," *Political Theory* 2 (August 1974): 277–303. Skinner discusses alternative modes of explanation in " 'Social Meaning' and the Explanation of Social Action," in *Philosophy, Politics and Society*, ed. Peter Laslett, W. G. Runciman, and Quentin Skinner, 4th ser. (Oxford, England: Blackwell, 1972), pp. 136–57; and see John Dunn, "The Identity of the History of Ideas," *Philosophy* 43 (April 1968): 85–104.

18. Gordon Wood, *The Creation of the American Republic, 1776–1787* (Chapel Hill: University of North Carolina Press, 1969).

19. This interpretation of Wood's analysis is reinforced by his essay on "Rhetoric and Reality in the American Revolution," in which he seems to deny the legitimacy of much of what his book attempts. It receives additional if indirect confirmation from the recent work of Joyce Appleby, which demonstrates the existence and the practical significance of a broadly liberal or laissez-faire strain in American revolutionary thought that competed with and ultimately supplanted the commonwealthsman tradition emphasized by Bernard Bailyn and discussed by Wood. See Wood, "Rhetoric and Reality in the American Revolution," *William and Mary Quarterly* 23 (January 1966): 3–32, and Appleby, "The Social Origins of American Revolutionary Ideology," *Journal of American History* 64 (March 1978): 935–58.

20. Karl W. Deutsch, *Nationalism and Social Communication: An Inquiry into the Foundations of Nationality*, 2d ed. (Cambridge: M.I.T. Press, 1966).

21. Ibid., pp. 95–96.

22. George Herbert Mead, *Mind, Self & Society from the Standpoint of a Social*

RUSH WELTER

Behaviorist, ed. Charles W. Morris (Chicago: University of Chicago Press, 1934), esp. part 3; and see Peter L. Berger and Thomas Luckmann, *The Social Construction of Reality: A Treatise in the Sociology of Knowledge* (Garden City, N.Y.: Doubleday, 1966), esp. part 3.

23. Daniel Boorstin, "The Place of Thought in American Life," in Boorstin, *America and the Image of Europe: Reflections on American Thought* (New York: Meridian, 1960), p. 44.

24. Skinner, "Meaning and Understanding."

25. Needless to say, the promise of generalization conducted on these premises depends upon the resourcefulness with which it is carried out, and the argument I have developed here only points to a possibility; it does not establish a model of analysis that will work well no matter how it is implemented. Methodological exhortations cannot take the place of intellectual breadth and imagination, a penchant for close and conscientious analysis of documentary materials, an awareness of the complexity of human behavior, and an ability to use language to elucidate it rather than obscure it.

II

HISTORY OF IDEAS

NEW ENGLAND'S ERRAND REAPPRAISED

⊂⊃ ⊘ ⊙ ⊂⊃

SACVAN BERCOVITCH

Perry Miller's "Errand into the Wilderness" may be the single most influential essay in early American studies. Written just after the completion of the second volume of *The New England Mind*, it offers an eloquent and impassioned summing-up of what remains the most impressive achievement in American intellectual history. To say that the essay is also deeply problematic in no way detracts from that achievement. What I would suggest is that Miller's "Errand" has become influential in the wrong way—that it has shaped our view of Puritanism rather than engaging us in the Puritan writings themselves. My purpose is to reopen our inquiry into the meaning of the errand by comparing Miller's essay with its equally eloquent and impassioned precursor, Samuel Danforth's election-day address of 1670, *A Brief Recognition of New England's Errand into the Wilderness*.

Let me begin with the better known of the two addresses. Perry Miller centers his argument on what he terms a "figure of speech," the ambiguity inherent in the Puritan concept of errand. An errand, Miller observes, may be either a venture on another's behalf or a venture of one's own, and the tragedy of the New England Puritans was that their errand shifted from one meaning to another in the course of the seventeenth century. The first settlers saw themselves on an errand for the Protestant Reformation. Their New England Way was to be a detour (and, they hoped, a shortcut) on the road leading from the Anglican establishment to a renovated England. After 1660, however, with the collapse of Cromwell's revolution, the colonists found themselves isolated, abandoned. "Their errand having failed in the first sense of the term, they were left with the second." They turned inward, accordingly, to fill their venture "with meaning by themselves and out of themselves" —and discovered there, in what was meant to be utopia, "nothing but a sink of iniquity." Hence the vehemence of their self-condemnation: they had been twice betrayed. Not only had the world passed them by, but the colony itself, their city set on a hill, had degenerated into another Sodom. They vented their outrage in an "unending monotonous wail," a long threnody over a lost cause, in which they came increasingly to acknowledge that New England was sick unto death. But the very

SACVAN BERCOVITCH

vehemence of the lament, Miller tells us, implied something quite different. The latter-day New England jeremiad registers

> bewilderment, confusion, chagrin but there is no surrender. A task has been assigned upon which the populace are in fact intensely engaged . . . [Thus] while the social or economic historian may read this literature for its contents—and so construct from the expanding catalogue of denunciations a record of social progress—the cultural anthropologist will look slightly askance at these jeremiads. If you read them all through, the total effect, curiously enough, is not at all depressing: you come to the paradoxical realization that they do not bespeak a despairing frame of mind . . . whatever they may signify in the realm of theology, in that of psychology they are purgations of the soul; they do not discourage but actually encourage the community to persist in its heinous conduct. The exhortation to a reformation which never materializes serves as a token payment upon the obligation, and so liberates the debtors. Changes there had to be: adaptations to environment, expansion of the frontier, mansions constructed, commercial ventures undertaken. These activities were not specifically nominated in the bond Winthrop had framed. They were thrust upon the society by American experience. . . . Land speculation meant not only wealth but dispersion of the people, and what was to stop the march of settlements? . . . [The first emigrants] had been utterly oblivious of what the fact of the frontier would do. . . . Hence I suggest that under the guise of this mounting wail of sinfulness, this incessant and never successful cry for repentance, the Puritans launched themselves upon the process of Americanization.[1]

I have quoted the passage at length because it so clearly shows the grounds of Miller's analysis. What he meant by ambiguity was opposition: the errand is either for oneself or for someone else; the jeremiads either discourage or encourage. Clearly, this stems from a "paradoxical realization" that somehow the errand functioned both ways, and that the jeremiads included both threat and hope. But the realization is an ironic one, a paradox. It lies in the reader's capacity to see conflicting elements at work in the same act. For Miller, the Puritans' sense of a failed errand ironically led them to make the errand their own. Paradoxically, their "cry for repentance" furthered the community's "heinous conduct." And the reader's ironic awareness, in turn, builds upon what amounts to a series of static oppositions: content versus intent, social progress versus catalogues of denunciations, psychology versus theology, the march of settlements versus a reactionary church-state, and summarily "the American experience" (manifest in land speculations, growing wealth, population dispersion) versus the Puritan lament, a "mounting wail of sinfulness" that issues in a self-defeating ritual of purgation. Methodologically, this implies the dichotomy of fact and rhetoric. Historically, it posits an end to Puritanism with the collapse of the church-state. From either perspective, in what is surely a nice irony in its own right, Miller's analysis lends support to the dominant anti-Puritan view of national development—that the "American character" was shaped (in Miller's phrase) by "the fact of the frontier."

We need not discount the validity of this frontier thesis to see what it does *not* explain: the persistence of the rhetoric of "errand" throughout the eighteenth and nineteenth centuries, in all forms of the literature, including the literature of westward expansion. Indeed, what first attracted me to the study of Puritanism was my astonishment, as a Canadian immigrant, at learning about the prophetic errand of America. Not of North America, for the prophecies stopped short at the Canadian and Mexican borders, but of a country that, despite its arbitrary territorial boundaries—despite its bewildering mixture of race and genealogy —could believe in something called America's mission, and could invest that patent fiction with all the emotional, spiritual, and intellectual appeal of a religious quest. I felt then like Sancho Panza in a land of Don Quixotes. Here was the anarchist Thoreau describing his "westward walk" as an emblem of "America's errand into the future"; here, the solitary singer Walt Whitman, claiming to *be* the "American Way"; here, the civil-rights leader Martin Luther King, descendant of slaves, denouncing segregation as a violation of "America's errand to freedom"; here, an endless debate about national directions, full of rage and faith, Jeffersonians claiming that they, and not the priggish heirs of Calvin, really represented the errand, conservative politicians defending the errand against its "un-American" critics, left-wing polemics recalling the nation to its true origins and mission. The problem in these latter-day jeremiads was never "Who are we?" but, as though deliberately evading that common-sense question, "When is our errand to be fulfilled?"— "How long, O Lord, how long?" And the answers, again as in the seventeenth-century sermons, invariably joined lament and celebration in reaffirming American exceptionalism.

This litany of hope, which seems to me a direct challenge to Miller's concept of ambiguity, leads back to Danforth's *A Brief Recognition of New England's Errand into the Wilderness.* Danforth delivered the address forty years after the *Arbella* fleet landed, and no one at that emotional gathering felt more keenly than he that the new promised land was far from won. Yet what he said then remains a great testament to the persistence of the founders' dream. Taking his text (Matt. 11:7–9) from Christ's "encomium of John the Baptist," Danforth praises the errand as a migration from a "soft" civilization to the purity of the "wilderness-condition." To forsake worldly vanities for Christ, he points out, is the mark of every believer, in any time or place; and accordingly he invests the errand with the general import of *pilgrimage.* "What went

SACVAN BERCOVITCH

ye out into the wilderness to see?" becomes the Christian's ultimate challenge: "What must I do to be saved in the wilderness of this world?" "How shall I seek the spirit through the wilderness of my own hard heart and recalcitrant will?" The subject was wholly fitting to the occasion. Election days in the Puritan church-state were a civic affair, but an affair nonetheless reserved for the regenerate and their children. Drawn by their spiritual calling, they had gathered together and shipped for America. They had built their theocracy to serve God. Like all saints, Danforth reminded them, they needed constantly to rededicate themselves to the *itinerarum mentis*, the errand within from self to Christ.[2]

The rhetorical effect here may be termed ambiguous, but emphatically not in the sense of contradiction. Danforth is not posing an alternative between pilgrimage and migration, but offering a resolution. His terms are not *either/or* but *both/and*. They imply the union of saint and society, the spiritual and the historical errand; and in this context they lead him to still another ambiguity. The parallels that Danforth urges upon his listeners, between John the Baptist and Danforth the preacher, between the Arabian and the New England deserts, develop into a sweeping prophetic comparison of the errand then, at the birth of Christianity, with the errand now, to bring history itself to an end. In this sense, *errand* means *progress*. It denotes the Church's gradual conquest of Satan's wilderness world for Christ. Significantly, Danforth's exegesis devolves neither on "errand" nor on "wilderness," but as it were beyond these, on the relative stature of John the Baptist. the question "What went ye out for to see?" is "determined and concluded," Danforth points out, when Christ describes John as "A prophet . . . and more than a prophet." The Baptist, that is, both resembles and supersedes his predecessors; his role as exemplum is at once recapitulative and prospective.

> John was the Christ's herald sent immediately before his face to proclaim his coming and kingdom and prepare the people for the reception of him. . . . John was greater than any of the prophets that were before him, not in respect of his personal graces and virtues (for who shall persuade us that he excelled Abraham in the grace of faith . . . or Moses in meekness . . . or David in faithfulness . . . or Solomon in wisdom? . . .), but in respect of the manner of his dispensation. All the prophets foretold Christ's coming, his sufferings and glory, but the Baptist was the harbinger and forerunner. . . . All the prophets saw Christ afar off, but the Baptist saw him present, baptized him, and applied the types to him personally. . . . "But he that is least in the kingdom of heaven is greater than John" (Mat. 11.11; Luke 7.28). The least prophet in the kingdom of heaven, i.e., the least minister of the Gospel since Christ's ascension, is greater than John; not in respect of the measure of his personal gifts nor in respect of the manner of his calling, but in respect of the . . . degree of the revelation of Christ, which is far more clear and full . . . than in the day when John the Baptist arose

like a bright and burning light . . . proclaiming the coming and kingdom of
the Messiah (which had oft been promised and long expected).[3]

All the prophets saw Christ. Who could excel Abraham or Moses?—
this is history seen in the eye of eternity. All the faithful, Danforth is
saying, are one in Christ; our errand here in New England is that of any
other saint, or group of saints; our wilderness no different essentially
from that of Moses or John the Baptist. And yet the passage makes the
difference abundantly clear. Sacred history unfolds in a series of stages
or *dispensations*, each with its own (increasingly greater) *degree of
revelation*. Hence the insistent temporality of the rhetoric: *prepare, fore-
told, herald, harbinger, forerunner*, and, summarily, *types*. Finally, Danforth insists, there are crucial discriminations to be made. All of the Old
Testament is an errand to the New; and all of history after the Incarnation, an errand to Christ's Second Coming. It leads from promise to
fulfillment: from Moses to John the Baptist to Samuel Danforth; from
the Old World to the New; from Israel in Canaan to New Israel in
America; from Adam to Christ to the Second Adam of the Apocalypse.
The wilderness that Danforth invokes is "typical" of New England's
situation above all in that it reveals the dual nature of the errand as
prophecy. In fulfilling the type, New England becomes itself a harbinger
of things to come. Like John the Baptist, though with a brighter and
fuller degree of revelation, the Puritan colony is itself a herald, sent to
prepare the world for Christ's often-promised, long-expected kingdom.

For Danforth, in short, *errand* has the ambiguity of the *figura*. It
unites allegory and chronicle in the framework of the work of redemption. And in doing so, it redefines the meaning not only of *errand* but of
every term in *New England's Errand into the Wilderness*. The *new*ness
of New England becomes both literal and eschatological, and (in what
was surely the most far-reaching of these rhetorical effects) the American wilderness takes on the double significance of secular and sacred
place. If for the individual believer it remained part of the wilderness of
the world, for "God's peculiar people" it was a territory endowed with
special meaning, like the wilderness through which the Israelites passed
to the promised land. In one sense it was historical, in another sense
prophetic; and as Nicholas Noyes explained in a sermon on the errand
more than three decades after Danforth's, "*Prophesie* is *Historie an-
tedated*; and *Historie* is *Postdated Prophesie*: the same thing is told in
both."[4] For these New England Jeremiahs, and all their second- and
third-generation colleagues, the ambiguity confirmed the founders' design. They dwelt on it, dissected it, elaborated upon it, because they
believed it opened into a triumphant assertion of corporate destiny,
migration and pilgrimage entwined in the progress of New England's
holy commonwealth.

SACVAN BERCOVITCH

From that figural vantage point Danforth condemns the colonists' failings and justifies their afflictions. "We have . . . in a great measure forgotten our errand into the wilderness," he charges, invoking the familiar precedent of exodus:

> The Lord foreseeing the defection of Israel after Moses his death, commands him to write that prophetical song recorded in Deuteronomy 32 as a testimony against them, wherein the chief remedy which he prescribes for the prevention and healing of their apostasy is their calling to remembrance God's great and signal love in manifesting himself to them in the wilderness, in conducting them safely and mercifully, and giving them possession of their promised inheritance (ver. 7–14). And when Israel was apostatized and fallen, the Lord, to convince them of their ingratitude and folly, brings to their remembrance his deliverance of them out of Egypt, his leading them through the wilderness for the space of forty years, and not only giving them possession of their enemies' land but also raising up even of their own sons, prophets . . . all which were great and obliging mercies.[5]

The ambiguities of the biblical parallel not only obviate the threat but transform self-doubt into consolation. "Apostasy" itself serves as prelude to deliverance. For as every member of Danforth's audience knew, Moses' "prophetical song" was traditionally interpreted as an address to the inhabitants of spiritual Israel, the true believers who were to have the "promised inheritance" of Christ, when He would literally transform the world's wilderness into the millennial kingdom. It is in this framework, both atemporal and temporal, that Danforth compares New England's "howling wilderness" with that of Moses and John the Baptist. The story of all three errands is one of ingratitude, folly, and backsliding, but the progression itself, from one errand to the next, attests to a process of fulfillment. Moses' rebuke is really a "remedy" for "healing"; Christ's "admonition," above all a "direction how to recover"; and Danforth's lament, an affirmation of God's "great and obliging mercies." And the affirmation, in Danforth's case as in those of the others, is absolute, unequivocal. He assures the colonists of success not because of their efforts, but God's: "the great Physician of Israel hath undertaken the cure . . . he will provide . . . we have the promise."[6]

In all this Danforth's strategy is characteristic of the American jeremiad throughout the seventeenth century: first, a precedent from scripture that sets out the communal norms; then, a series of condemnations that detail the actual state of the community; and finally, a prophetic vision that unveils the good things to come, and so explains away the gap between fact and ideal. Perry Miller seems to have understood this form as a triptych, a static three-part configuration in which the centerpiece (the condemnation) conveys the meaning of the whole. So interpreted, the New England sermons embody a cyclical view of history: the

NEW ENGLAND'S ERRAND REAPPRAISED

futile, recurrent rise and fall of nations that sustained the traditional European jeremiad. But the rhetoric itself suggests something different. It posits a movement from promise to experience—from the ideal of community to the facts of community life—and thence forward, with prophetic assurance, toward a resolution that incorporates both fact and ideal. The dynamic of the errand, that is, involves a use of ambiguity that is not divisive but progressive, and that is impervious to the reversals of history, because the very meaning of progress is inherent in the rhetoric itself.

This errand into ambiguity, if I may call it so, speaks directly to the contrast Miller posited between rhetoric and history. What Miller meant by history was the course of events, the "process of Americanization," that led to the theocracy's decline; by rhetoric, he meant the lament, "unremitting and never successful," over a failed enterprise. Thus while he stressed the affirmative "psychology" of the Puritan sermons, he interpreted the sermons themselves as certain psychologists interpret wish-fulfillment dreams. What counts is not the happy ending but the conflicts that prompted the need for fantasy in the first place. The conflicts are "real," the happy ending transparently a means to something else—avoidance, compensation, substitute gratification, or simply self-delusion. Now, the fact of the theocracy's decline is incontrovertible. But we need not interpret it as Miller does. His "Errand into the Wilderness" is a hail and farewell to the Puritan vision. Danforth's *Errand into the Wilderness* attests to the orthodoxy's refusal to abandon the vision, and the fact is that the vision survived, from colony to province, and from province to nation. The fact is, furthermore, that it survived through a mode of ambiguity that denied the contradiction between history and rhetoric— or rather translated this into a discrepancy between appearance and promise, which nourished the imagination and inspired ever grander flights of self-justification, and so continued to provide a source of social cohesion. In fact, that is, the New England orthodoxy succeeded, precisely through their commitment to the Puritan ideal, in transmitting a myth that has remained central to the culture.

So perceived, the evidence suggests a different relation between rhetoric and history. Even if we grant that the jeremiads were a form of wish-fulfillment—even if we agree with Miller that their rhetoric served as a "guise" for "real" conflicts—we need not see them in opposition to the course of events. Suppose, for example, that the wish-fulfillment is profoundly relevant to those conflicts. What if it actually offers a resolution of sorts, a realistic way to deal with crisis and change? Miller likened the second-generation Puritans to a husband who, while on an errand for his wife, discovers that his wife has forgotten all about her request—or worse still, denies she ever made a request at all. The

SACVAN BERCOVITCH

analogy is accurate so far as it goes. But suppose the husband simply refuses to acknowledge that as fact. What if he persuades himself, in compensation for what everyone else sees as a mistake, that in fact his errand has nothing to do with his wife, and that in fact *he is correct?* What if, moreover, he does not harbor that "fantasy" in secret, like Walter Mitty, but proudly declares it to others, and for sound, pragmatic reasons, reasons that conform to the "real" course of events, *persuades them, too?*

I am suggesting that "the process of Americanization" began in Massachusetts not with the decline of Puritanism but with the Great Migration, and that the concept of errand, accordingly, as a prime expression of the Puritan venture, played a significant role in the development of what was to become modern middle-class American culture. I hope that in suggesting this I do not seem to be overstraining the worn links between Puritanism and the rise of capitalism. My point is simply that certain elements in Puritanism lent themselves powerfully to that conjunction, and precisely those elements came to the fore when the Bay emigrants severed their ties with the feudal forms of Old England and set up a relatively fluid society on the American strand—a society that devalued aristocracy, denounced beggary, and opened up political, educational, and commercial opportunities to a relatively broad spectrum of the population.

The argument has been demonstrated elsewhere so persuasively, and from so many perspectives, as hardly to need comment here. Tocqueville's well-known views on this matter are representative of a host of others, from Adam Smith through Frederick Engels, down to a variety of social and economic historians in our own time:

> It was in the states of New England, that the two or three main principles now forming the basic social theory of the United States were combined. . . . [These] colonies as they came to birth seemed destined to let freedom grow, not the aristocratic freedom of their motherland, but a middle-class and democratic freedom of which the world's history had not previously provided a complete example. . . . In England the nucleus of the Puritan movement continued to be in the middle classes, and it was from those classes that most of the emigrants sprang. The population of New England grew fast, and while in their homeland men were despotically divided by class hierarchies, the colony came more and more to present the novel phenomenon of a society homogeneous in all its parts. . . . [Thus] the whole destiny of America [is] contained in the first Puritan who landed on these shores, as that of the whole human race in the first man.[7]

Tocqueville was making the point by hyperbole, but the point itself is valid enough to suggest a fundamental truth about our culture. The economists Douglass North and Robert Thomas have shown that "the

NEW ENGLAND'S ERRAND REAPPRAISED

colonization of [Anglo-] America was a direct outgrowth of . . . the decline of feudalism." The philosopher Ralph Barton Perry has argued the "affinity" of "Puritan individualism . . . with laissez-faire capitalism." The historian Robert Brown has pointed out that property was so easily acquired in New England that "the great majority of men" could meet the requirements for political franchise.[8] These and many similar quantitative differences between old and New England are symptomatic, I believe, of a sweeping qualitative distinction between America and all other modern countries. In England (and the Old World in general), capitalism was an economic system that evolved dialectically, through conflict with earlier but persisting ways of life and belief. Basically New England bypassed the conflict. This is by no means to say that conflict was avoided. On the contrary, the first century of New England history is a remarkable instance of rapid social change, involving widespread moral, psychic, and political tensions. The emergent structures of a free-enterprise economy did not all at once transform the guild and craft mentality; for a time mercantile capitalism actually helped maintain aristocratic privilege; for an even longer time premodern modes of social and familial relationship resisted the commercial revolution underway in the Northern Anglo-American colonies. But *ideologically* the resistance was as ineffectual as it was anachronistic. It signified not a contest between an established and an evolving system, but a troubled period of maturation. The emigrant leaders did not give up their class prerogatives when they landed at Massachusetts Bay, and yet the forms they instituted tended to erode traditional forms of deference. They restricted opportunity in commerce and property-ownership, yet social power in the colony increasingly shifted to the commercial and property-owning classes. In all fundamental ideological aspects, New England was from the start an outpost of the modern world. It evolved from its own origins, as it were, into a middle-class culture—a commercially oriented economy buttressed by the decline of European feudalism, unhampered by lingering traditions of aristocracy and crown, and sustained by the prospect (if not always the fact) of personal advancement—an ideologically homogeneous society whose enterprise was consecrated, according to its civic and clerical leadership, by a divine plan of progress.

I think it can be said without hyperbole that the process of consecration began with the Great Migration of 1630. In his *Model of Christian Charity*, John Winthrop advocated a doctrine of vocational calling that (as Michael Walzer and others have shown) effectually undermined feudal hierarchy by its appeal to self-discipline and self-sufficiency. And several weeks before, as the *Arbella* passengers were about to embark from Southampton pier, John Cotton defended *God's Promise to His Plantations* through analogies to commerce for "gainesake":

SACVAN BERCOVITCH

Daily bread may be sought from farre. Yea our Saviour approveth travaile
for Merchants, when hee compareth a Christian to a Merchantman seeking
pearles: For he never fetcheth a comparison with any unlawfull thing to
illustrate a thing lawfull. . . . Nature teacheth Bees . . . when as the hive is
too full . . . [to] seeke abroad for new dwellings: So when the hive of the
Common wealth is so full, that Tradesmen cannot live one by another, but
eate up one another, in this case it is lawfull to remove. . . . God alloweth a
man to remove, when he may employ his Talents and gifts better elsewhere,
especially when where he is, he is not bound by any speciall engagement.
Thus God sent *Ioseph* before to preserve the Church: *Iosephs* wisdome and
spirit was not fit for a shepheard, but for a Counsellour of State.[9]

Cotton's analogies, like Winthrop's concept of vocation, bespeak a moment of cultural transition: they reflect earlier ideals as well as fore-
shadow later developments. But in both cases the direction is unmistakable. All of Cotton's examples, from nature and the Bible, are geared
toward sanctifying an errand of entrepreneurs whose aim is religion, or
mutatis mutandis legalizing an errand of saints whose aim is entrepreneurial.

In this respect, as in others, a direct line may be traced from the first
emigrants to the latter-day Jeremiahs. It runs from the *Arbella* sermons
by Cotton and Winthrop to Cotton Mather's *Magnalia Christi Americana*, where Joseph appears as a model for the rags-to-riches errand of
several famous New Englanders, and it includes *A Brief Recognition of
New England's Errand into the Wilderness*. "John preached in the wilderness, which was no fit place for silken and soft raiment," Danforth
observes, because the Baptist's "work was to prepare a people for the
Lord." How could he do so amidst the "superfluous ornaments," the
"delicate and costly apparel [of] . . . princes' courts"? This is neither a
plea for the sanctity of poverty nor a summons to some ascetic retreat
from the world. Nor is it merely a denunciation of the rich, in the
manner of the Old Testament prophets. In effect, Danforth is urging
upon New Israel the middle way of the Protestant ethic, reinforcing
Cotton's analogies and Winthrop's model of vocation by reminding his
audience that the prophecies they inherited, their promised future, entailed "the values of piety, frugality, and diligence in one's worldly calling." Economically as well as figurally, it was their mission to leave a
"soft" Old World order, with its "courtly pomp and decay," for a "purer"
kind of society, one that would provide them with the proper means for
both "respectable competence in this world and eternal salvation in the
world to come."[10]

Thanks largely to Perry Miller, Danforth's sermon has become a *locus
classicus* for defining the American jeremiad. So it should be, but not in
the terms Miller suggests. The American Puritan jeremiad, let me repeat,

NEW ENGLAND'S ERRAND REAPPRAISED

was a mode of celebration rather than of lament. In deliberate opposition to the traditional mode, it set out to transform threat into promise,
and the nature of the Puritan errand helps explain the transformation.
The European jeremiad developed within a static hierarchical order; the
lessons it taught, about historical recurrence and the vanity of human
wishes, amounted to a massive ritual reinforcement of tradition. Its function was to make social practice conform to a completed and perfected
social ideal. The American Puritan jeremiad was the ritual of a culture
on an errand, which is to say, a culture based on a faith in process.
Substituting teleology for hierarchy, it discarded the Old World ideal of
stasis for a New World vision of the future. Its function was to create a
climate of anxiety that helped release the restless "progressivist" energies
required for the success of the venture. The European jeremiad also
thrived on anxiety, of course. Like all "traditionalist" forms of ritual, it
used fear and trembling to teach acceptance of fixed social norms. But
the American Puritan jeremiad went much further. It made anxiety its
end as well as its means. Crisis was the social norm it sought to inculcate.
The very concept of errand, after all, implied a state of unfulfillment.
The future, though divinely assured, was never quite there, and New
England's Jeremiahs helped provide the sense of insecurity that would
ensure the outcome. Denouncing or affirming, their vision fed on the
distance between promise and fact.

I need hardly say that they were not revelling in crisis for its own sake.
Anxiety was one result of the ritual, its day-by-day aspect. The other
aspect, equally crucial to the concept of errand, was direction and purpose. Together, these two elements define the ritual import of the early
New England jeremiad: to sustain process by imposing control, and to
justify control by presenting a certain form of process as the only road to
the future kingdom. The emphasis on control is not difficult to explain.
As Christopher Hill points out in arguing the connection between
Cromwell's revolution and the growth of the English middle class, Puritanism served in important ways to harness "the turbulent force of
individualism." That force was nowhere more turbulently manifest than
in Puritan New England, a colony of radical dissenters—militant,
apocalyptic, "irrepressibly particularistic and anti-authoritarian." In
1630, Edmund Morgan notes, "emigration offered a substitute for revolution."[11] But the hazards of settlement required the colonial leaders to
seek a more permanent substitute. They found it, after a precarious
beginning, in the New England Way of church-state, a sort of institu-
tionalized migration, consciously modeled on the pattern of exodus. And
they sought to enforce their Way through what proved to be perhaps
their most durable creation, the ritual of the errand.

Danforth's sermon testifies eloquently to its distinctive qualities. In

SACVAN BERCOVITCH

contrast to traditionalist rituals, the American Puritan jeremiad evokes the mythic past not merely to elicit imitation but above all to demand progress. The fathers, says Danforth, were mighty men, as were Moses, Elijah, and John the Baptist—unexcelled in their piety, wisdom, and fervor—but the errand they began leads us toward a higher, brighter dispensation. Precisely because of their greatness, we have a sacred duty to go beyond them. To venerate and emulate is to supersede; in God's New Canaan all of life is a passage to something better. This outlook obviously derives from Protestant ritual. One need only think of Bunyan's Pilgrim, Christian, whose lifelong progress is shaped by a series of crises that point him forever forward toward a single preordained goal. But Christian's crises, like those of every Reformed Christian, are personal and eschatological; they involve the conflict between flesh and spirit, worldly commitments and "last things." More often than not, therefore, Christian finds himself defying social authority. The society to which he conforms instead is the community of the elect, wherever they happen to be, journeying from a wicked world to their heavenly home. And the journey, moreover, is essentially retrospective, an imitation of Christ. Christian advances with his eyes fixed on the past. The New England Puritans fixed their gaze on the future. Christ's victory over Satan, they stressed, was itself a shadow or type of His greater victory to come, when He would usher in the millennium. Accordingly, they grounded their covenant in prophecies still to be fulfilled. Even as they strove individually to imitate Christ, they invested their hopes in the success of their venture. In effect, they identified eschatology with regional teleology, the individual's way to salvation with the progress of their church-state. What for European Protestants was an ideational structure—the "New World" of regeneration, the "promised land" of heaven, the "wilderness" of temptation, the "garden" of the spirit—was for Danforth and his colleagues also a political reality, the civic, religious, and economic structures of a covenanted New World society.

The contrast has far-reaching implications. Both Bunyan's Christian and the New England saint are on an errand, constantly "betwixt and between," forever at the brink of some momentous decision, but as rituals their errands tend in opposite directions. The ritual Bunyan adopts leads Christian into what anthropologists call a "liminal state," a sort of cultural no man's land, where all social norms may be challenged.[12] And given the Calvinist tenet that salvation is a lifelong enterprise, it is an errand fraught with all the religious and economic dangers of unfettered individualism: the excesses of both antinomianism and self-interest. The American Puritan jeremiads seek (in effect) to prevent these excesses by turning liminality itself into a mode of socialization. Their errand entails a ritual that obviates the traditional distinctions

NEW ENGLAND'S ERRAND REAPPRAISED

between preparation for salvation and social conformity, a carefully reg-
ulated process where the fear for one's soul is a function of social
progress, personal discipline a means to public success, and success a
matter of constant anxiety about the future. More than that, the ritual
of errand offers a new mode of social identity: it defines the members
of the community not by their English background but by their exodus from Europe to America,[13] it establishes a mode of consensus by
ideology rather than by popular tradition; and it implies a form of na-
tionhood without geographical boundaries, since the wilderness is by definition unbounded, the *terra profana* "out there" yet to be conquered,
precisely as the wilderness of the world is being conquered, step by
inevitable step, by the advancing armies of Christ.

In all this, as it turned out, the Puritan concept of errand was well
suited to the process of Americanization. Let me briefly outline a few
implications of the concept—or as Danforth might have put it, some of
its uses and applications. Perhaps the most striking of these, in view of
Miller's analysis, is the relation between the errand and the frontier
movement. Traditionally, *frontier* meant a border dividing one people
from another. It implied an acceptance of differences between nations.
In a sense, the Puritans recognized such differences—their "frontier"
separated them from the Indian "outer darkness"—but they could hardly
accept the restriction as permanent. America was God's country, after
all. By promise, as John Cotton argued in 1630, the land belonged to
them before they belonged to the land, and they took possession, accordingly, first by imposing their own image upon it and then by seeing
themselves reflected back in the image they had imposed. The wilderness became their mirror of prophecy. They saw themselves revealed in
it as the New Israel that would make the wilderness blossom as the rose.
They also discerned in it those who did *not* belong to the land, because
they were excluded from the errand: Indians, heretics, opponents of the
New England Way, adherents to the ways of the Old World.[14]

In sum, the concept of errand issued in a decisive shift in the meaning
of frontier, from a secular barrier to a mythical threshold. Even as they
spoke of their frontier as a meeting-ground between two civilizations,
Christian and heathen, the Puritans redefined it, in a rhetorical inversion
characteristic of the myth-making imagination, to mean a *figural* outpost,
the outskirts of the advancing kingdom of God. It became, that is, not a
dividing line but a summons to territorial expansion. And as in time the
holy commonwealth spread westward across the continent, bringing
light into darkness—or in a recurrent Puritan phrase, "irradiating an
Indian wilderness"—the frontier movement came to provide a sort of
serial enactment of the Great Migration. It was the moving stage for the
quintessentially "American" drama of destined progress. By the early

SACVAN BERCOVITCH

nineteenth century the Puritan inversion was standardized. What in Europe signified historical restriction, came in America to signify limitlessness, open opportunity, the revelation of things to come.

It also came to signify a special notion of consensus. I use the term *consensus* in its Puritan and ideological sense. When the emigrants constituted themselves New Israel on an errand, they set out what I just referred to as a radically new mode of cohesion, a form of hegemony based on cultural, as distinct from tribal or national, norms and ideals. The biblical Hebrews were nationalists. Although they too claimed their land by promise, Canaan itself was a country (like any other) with fixed boundaries; and though they too defined themselves as a "peculiar" people, the definition itself was based (like that of any other people of their time) upon genealogy, popular tradition, and a certain form of religion. The Puritans' belief in a spiritual New Israel denied the importance of genealogy; their concept of wilderness allowed their "walled garden" to expand into what later Americans would call the Western "garden of the world"; and their ritual of errand issued in a religious identity that was as ambiguous, potentially (and purposefully) as vague in scope and in theological content, as their geographical identity. For by the terms of their errand, the Puritans were not just a particular sect, but the vanguard of Protestantism; and Protestantism, by the same logic, was not just a religious movement, but the last stage of the worldwide work of redemption. For Danforth, those general claims were restricted to a scrupulously self-contained community. But once the community had established itself, it could discard its scruples as it moved outward to fulfill its mission. Eventually, the errand led from tribal covenant to mass revivals, and thence forward, through the Revolution, into a flowering of America's multidenominational "civil religion."

The ambiguous role of "American nationality" in this development deserves special emphasis. Elsewhere in the modern world, nationalism has remained local, historical, and complex, even when it makes universalist claims. European national heroes, for all their "representative" qualities, are circumscribed by paternity and class; the messianic dreams of German and Russian nationalism are rooted in atavistic distinctions of race, religion, and geography. The "American" community, on the contrary, defines itself by its relation to a promised future. Especially when its adherents invoke the legend of the fathers, as Danforth did, "American" identity obviates the usual distinctions of national history, the conflicts, say, of ideological and economic interest, because the very word *American* implies a *cultural* identity, a commitment to a certain way of life and to the quasi-religious myths and symbols through which that way of life has perpetuated itself. The Puritans used the myth to restrict their consensus to visible saints. Later, the consensus was restricted (by the same means) to visible WASPs. But in both cases, restriction was effectually a strategic device, a means of control that facilitated process while making process a means of sustaining the culture. The American consensus could include blacks and Indians, too, when in the fullness of time they would come to adopt the tenets of black and red capitalism. Women could also learn to be "True" Americans, so long as feminism would lead into the middle-class American Way. On that provision, Jews and even Catholics could eventually join the errand into the Theopolis Americana. On those grounds, even such unlikely candidates for perfection as Puerto Rico, Hawaii, and Alaska could become America.

The success of the ritual is reflected in the enormous power of "America" as symbol; and both the ritual and the symbol reflect the growth of the major capitalist power of our times. They also express an ideological consensus unmatched in any other modern country. Consider the ambiguities spawned by the errand: a social enterprise that carries with it the Christian meaning of the sacred; a prophetic vision that combines eschatology and chauvinism; a mode of identity, American, that fuses civic and spiritual selfhood, nationality and universality, secular and redemptive history, the country's past and paradise-to-be, in a single synthetic ideal. These ambiguities are intrinsic to our culture, on all levels; and I would like to urge, as a last application of the doctrine, that we would do well to recognize their impact upon our literary tradition.

To see how deeply our classic writers were involved with the concept of errand, and how much that involvement contributed toward shaping their imaginations, is not to reduce their works to ideology. Indeed, it may be no more than to speak of Chaucer's debt to medieval thought, or Shakespeare's to the Renaissance world picture, except in one important detail. Chaucer and Shakespeare wrote more or less openly from within their culture. Our classical writers tended to see themselves as outcasts and isolatoes, prophets crying in the wilderness. So they have been, as a rule, *American* prophets, simultaneously lamenting a declension and celebrating a national dream; hypersensitive to social failings, and yet offering in their most communitarian, idealistic works a mimesis of cultural beliefs; profoundly suspicious of the uses of the errand, but describing the errand itself, as did the early Puritans, in the ambiguous terms of millennium or doomsday.

We have not been alert enough to the nature of such ambiguities. No doubt the self-proclaimed alienation of our writers helped them perceive and struggle against cultural limitations. But Danforth's sermon shows how this kind of opposition may serve to revitalize society, since the very standards by which society is found wanting are the standards by which the culture continues to justify itself. Insofar as we teach works like *Walden* as a source of transcendent truth, we transform moral complaint

SACVAN BERCOVITCH

into a summons to get on with the errand. Insofar as we render *The American Scholar* or *Democratic Vistas* the basis of native radical dissent, we make literary criticism a version of the American jeremiad—which is to say, part of a continuing ritual of socialization.[15]

⊂⟳⟲⊃

I do not mean to say, of course, that Thoreau, Emerson, and Whitman were Puritan Jeremiahs. Indeed, I invoke their works partly to emphasize the distance between early New England and what we have come to call American culture—to qualify the assertions of historians like Carl Degler that "capitalism came to America in the first ships."[16] Danforth's sermon, after all, despite its affirmative power, reminds us that in many of its specific attributes the Puritan state was transitional, the substance of a new social order encased in squirearchical and quasi-biblical forms. It reminds us, too, that by 1670 the New England theocrats were already on the defensive. One of Danforth's purposes was to reproach aspiring merchants and landholding "lay brethren of the congregation" for challenging clerical control—or better, for trying to assume control in face of the inadequacy of theocratic forms.[17] For whether or not this indicated a decline in piety, as he and his colleagues wailed, clearly the second-generation colonists were increasingly forcing the institutions they lived under to comply with the political and economic realities of their New World society.

In this sense, there is some justice in Perry Miller's ironic image of the Old Guard "backing into modernity" at the end of the seventeenth century, in "crablike progress" from an "aristocratic" order to "a middle-class empirical enterprising society."[18] But his irony neglects the import of the Puritan rhetoric of ambiguity, and hence obscures the most vital aspect of the transition from Puritan to Yankee New England. For the emigrant leaders, the concept of errand was a means of social control, but the society they established proved inadequate to their "wilderness condition." Primarily, to be sure, they based their authority on an agency superior to human failings, the prophecies of scripture. But they were too sanguine about their experiment to rely on prophecy altogether, and accordingly their sermons constantly reveal the friction between promise and reality—between their vision of a holy commonwealth and the fact that the New England Way was above all the product of a modern new world. In the last decades of the century, when it became clear that practical measures would no longer suffice, the Old Guard ministers withdrew into the ambiguities of the rhetoric itself. They understood this shift in strategy as an effort to make the errand impervious to the ravages of time. In fact, they were being forced by history to enlarge their concept of the errand into a vision that was so broad in its implications, and so specifically American in its application, that it could survive the failure of theocracy.

In that fact, I would suggest, lies the major irony of colonial history. Insisting that the errand was the one sure way to success, the ministers drained it of its discrete theological and institutional content. Intent on preserving the past, they transformed it, as legend, into a malleable guide to the future. Seeking to defend the theocracy, they abstracted from its antiquated social forms the larger, vaguer, and more flexible forms of metaphor and myth (New Israel, wilderness, promised land, destined progress), and so facilitated the movement from the New England to the American Way, and from errand to manifest destiny, American mission and the dream. Determined, in sum, to sustain the rhetoric and vision of the fathers, the latter-day Jeremiahs forged what was in effect a powerful vehicle of middle-class ideology: a ritual of progress through consensus, a system of sacred-secular symbols for a laissez-faire creed, a "civil" or "political" religion for a people chosen to spring fully formed into the modern world—"America," the first-begotten daughter of democratic capitalism, the only country that developed, from the seventeenth through the nineteenth centuries, into a wholly middle-class culture.

Notes

1. Perry Miller, "Errand into the Wilderness" (1952), in *Errand into the Wilderness* (Cambridge: Harvard University Press, 1956), pp. 2, 8–9, 15. Materials for this essay were taken from Sacvan Bercovitch, *The American Jeremiad* (Madison: University of Wisconsin Press, 1978).
2. Samuel Danforth, *A Brief Recognition of New England's Errand into the Wilderness*, in *The Wall and the Garden: Selected Massachusetts Election Sermons*, ed. A. William Plumstead (Minneapolis: University of Minnesota Press, 1968), p. 59.
3. Danforth, *Brief Recognition*, pp. 60, 62.
4. Nicholas Noyes, *New England's Duty* (Boston: Bartholomew Green and John Allen, 1698), p. 43.
5. Danforth, *Brief Recognition*, pp. 64–65.
6. Danforth, *Brief Recognition*, pp. 75–76.
7. Alexis de Tocqueville, *Democracy in America*, tr. George Lawrence, ed. J. P. Mayer (Garden City, N.Y.: Doubleday, 1969), pp. 34–39, 56, 279.
8. Douglass C. North and Robert Paul Thomas, eds., *The Growth of the American Economy to 1860* (New York: Harper & Row, 1968), p. 5; Ralph Barton Perry, *Puritanism and Democracy* (New York: Vanguard, 1944), p. 297; Robert E. Brown, *Middle-Class Democracy and the Revolution in Massachusetts, 1691–1780* (Ithaca, N.Y.: Cornell University Press, 1955), p. 82. I do not, of course

SACVAN BERCOVITCH

mean to blur the stages of economic growth from agrarian economy through urbanization, including the "transportation revolution," credit economy, industrialization, corporate enterprise, and expansionist finance. My assumption is that every one of those stages (including the War of Independence) was more or less organic, that in effect the culture was committed from the start to what social scientists have termed the process of modernization. The assumption itself, I might add, is neither "monolithic" nor "teleological," nor does it imply a belief in providence. The development I speak of was historically organic—rooted in the conditions of American society and in the symbols through which that society defined itself. Various recent historians have shown that the rise of European capitalism was attended by a clash of cultures, a lingering struggle of emergent middle-class values against traditions inherited from some ancien régime. (See for example Keith Thomas, *Religion and the Decline of Magic* [New York: Charles Scribner's Sons, 1971], and Robert Mandrou, *Introduction to Modern France, 1500–1640* [Paris: Halmer and Meier, 1976].) The growth of what we now call America shows no significant ideological warfare of that kind. Those Southern leaders, for example, who advocated anti- or precapitalist forms of life explicitly dissociated their region from the American Way. As Louis Hartz put it, they were alien children "in a liberal family, tortured and confused driven to a fantasy life" (quoted in C. Vann Woodward, *The Burden of Southern History* [Baton Rouge: Louisiana State University Press, 1960], pp. 21–22; see also Woodward's contrast here between the "native tradition" of Lockean liberalism and the South's "uniquely un-American experience"). But the family itself grew rapidly in strength and numbers, and in accordance with its specific historical situation. The fantasies *it* spawned took the form of a comprehensive, officially endorsed cultural myth that became entrenched in New England and that subsequently, through a series of highly effective rituals of socialization, spread across the Western territories and the South.

9. John Cotton, *God's Promise to His Plantations* (1630), in *Old South Leaflets 3*, no. 53 (Boston, 1874–76): 5 (see also p. 14). John Winthrop's "Christian Charitie. A Modell Hereof" is reprinted in *Puritan Political Ideas, 1558–1794*, ed. Edmund S. Morgan (Indianapolis: Bobbs-Merrill, 1966), pp. 75–94; Michael Walzer's fullest statement of the ideological implications of Puritanism is *The Revolution of the Saints: A Study in the Origins of Radical Politics* (Cambridge: Harvard University Press, 1965). I mention this sermon and Winthrop's partly because they define the prophetic as well as the theocratic aims of the *Arbella* migrations; in an important sense, they may be said to be the first examples of a state-of-the-errand genre that extends past the seventeenth century through the Revolution and the Civil War.

10. Danforth, *Brief Recognition*, pp. 59, 72; John G. Cawelti, *Apostles of the Self-Made Man* (Chicago: University of Chicago Press, 1965), p. 4.

11. Christopher Hill, *The Century of Revolution, 1603–1714* (Edinburgh: T. Nelson, 1961), p. 97; Emery Battis, *Saints and Sectaries: Ann Hutchinson and the Antinomian Controversy in the Massachusetts Bay Colony* (Chapel Hill: University of North Carolina Press, 1962), p. 255; Edmund S. Morgan, "The Revolutionary Era as an Age of Politics," in *The Role of Ideology in the American Revolution*, ed. John R. Howe, Jr. (New York: Holt, Rinehart and Winston, 1970), p. 11.

12. I am indebted here to the works of Victor Turner.

13. As it turned out, this implication of the concept of errand had far-reaching effects, and so warrants a word of explanation. The Puritans, as we have seen, saw progress in terms of a series of "dispensations," each of which was (like the biblical Jesus) simultaneously a fulfillment of things past and a promise of things to come—simultaneously, that is, an antitype and a foreshadowing. Hence Danforth's appeal to the fathers: in his Janus-faced vision, the Great Migration was a *figura* that confirmed New England's destiny. In effect, his concept of errand involved a typology of the New England Way. And in time this was to become, in a flagrantly secular sense, the typology of the American Way. The

NEW ENGLAND'S ERRAND REAPPRAISED

process of this development may be traced by comparing Danforth's sermon with (for example) Samuel Sherwood's *The Church's Flight into the Wilderness* (New York, 1776), the most popular and most inflammatory sermon of 1776. Danforth bases his figuralism on the Bible, and on a scriptural mode of identity. Assuming the authority of tradition, he uses the tradition to justify the venture. Sherwood takes that justification, rather than the tradition behind it, as his authority. Ultimately, he appeals not to Church tradition, and not even to the Bible, but to the American experience. Pushing Danforth's tenuous figuralism to its extreme, Sherwood virtually reverses the hermeneutical process—turns figuralism inside out. His authority is the country's progress, his text the Puritan past, his exegetical framework the typology of America's "errand of liberty." He and his Whig compatriots used that typology to good effect in answering the Tory charges of filial rebellion. The real fathers of the country, the Whigs argued, were the emigrants who began the errand toward a libertarian republic; and of course their argument involved the old figural imperative: what the fathers began, the sons were destined to complete. The War of Independence, in short, was at once an act of filiopietism and America's long-prepared-for errand into national maturity.

14. Eventually these images would come to include English royalists, "Jacobin conspirators," the Western Indian nations, etc. See John Juricek, "American Usage of the Word 'Frontier' from Colonial Times to Frederick Jackson Turner," *Proceedings of the American Philosophical Society* 110 (1966): 15, 32–33.

15. This statement is extravagant, perhaps, but my purpose is simply (as Thoreau put it) to make the point emphatic. I discuss the subject in some detail in chapter 6 of *The American Jeremiad*.

16. Quoted in Stuart Bruchey, *The Roots of American Economic Growth, 1607–1861* (New York: Harper & Row, 1968), p. 44. See also, for example, Johan Huizinga, *America*, trans. Herbert H. Rowen (New York: Harper & Row, 1972), esp. pp. 8–9, and of course Max Weber, *The Protestant Ethic and the Spirit of Capitalism*, trans. Talcott Parsons (New York, Charles Scribner's Sons, 1948). In a recent essay, Michael Zuckerman has argued that in the early colonies "both the self-assertion that inform the modern psyche and the coercive mutuality that marks the modern community achieved something of their subsequent scope. . . . Communities made excessive claims of concord for themselves and then fell into a dismayed sense of declension whenever they failed to sustain such ideological aspirations" ("The Fabrication of Identity in Early America," *William and Mary Quarterly* 34 [1977]: 184–85). I would add that this dual tendency is particularly a Puritan characteristic, and that the New England Puritans contributed in particular to modernization through a rhetorical mode specifically devised to transform a "dismayed sense of declension" into a ritual of cultural aspiration.

17. The immediate political background of Danforth's election-day address indicates the transitional nature of the theocracy. In 1669, a Third Church of Boston was formed by a group of tradesmen who dissented from the orthodox First Church. Shortly after this Richard Bellingham, the sternest of the Old Guard magistrates who followed John Winthrop to the post of governor, expressed his fear of "sudden tumult," and his council warned against "an invasion of the rights, liberties, and privileges of churches" (Larzer Ziff, *Puritanism in America: New Culture in a New World* [New York: Viking, 1973], pp. 188–89). Only twenty of the fifty deputies in the General Court of 1669 were reelected in 1670. And yet the freemen of 1670 who elected a new government in defiance of Governor Bellingham were covenanted members of the visible churches of Massachusetts. The Third Church was built on land donated for that purpose by the widow of John Norton, a pillar of the first-generation orthodoxy; among its first members was Sarah Cotton Mather, the widow of John Cotton and Richard Mather. And these widows were not betraying the "grand design" their husbands had sought to realize. Despite their allegiance to theocracy, the emigrant Puritans were part of the movement toward the future.

SACVAN BERCOVITCH

18. Perry Miller, *The New England Mind: From Colony to Province*, reprint ed. (1953; Boston: Beacon Press, 1961), p. 442. Miller's argument, it is worth noting, essentially follows from the lament of the Old Guard Puritans, who, like Danforth, bewailed their alienation from their times. No doubt they felt alienated, but we need not simply accept their view of the situation, as Miller does.

INTELLECTUAL HISTORY
AND RELIGIOUS HISTORY

HENRY F. MAY

What I am going to say about this subject is personal, because I think history-writing is a rather personal business. Perhaps this is especially true of intellectual history, but I suspect that it is true to some degree of all kinds of history. However many teams assemble the information, and however many computers they run it through, in the long run the decisions about what it is worth and how to present it need to be made by an individual. There are really very few successful examples to the contrary.

This is, I think, because the data do not tell us what they are for; the answers do not generate the questions. Each historian has to decide what he is trying to do, and why, and how to go about it according to everything he has learned, not just in graduate school, but in his life. Thus we will have as many visions of the past as we have historians. Gradually most historians may come to agree on some things, but whatever consensus is reached will continue to be fleeting and unstable. In every generation, at least since the Enlightenment, there have been some people who were made profoundly uncomfortable by this state of affairs, who demanded that we adopt a new method that will arrive at objective, scientific truth. But most practicing historians give up this ambition rather early and hope no more than to get a usable insight or two.

Perhaps this is tolerable because history is not a policy science; its goals are not, or not obviously, utilitarian. In some fields people have to struggle hard for consensus. Some consensus is necessary, for instance, in engineering, or in medicine. It would be nice if a little more could be achieved in economics. In some cultures, consensus has been and is imposed, and there the writing of history does not thrive. Chairman Mao found that he could not afford to let a hundred flowers bloom; we can and must. It may be that the irreducible independence of the historian explains in part what I find a poignant phenomenon: that able people still throng to graduate study in history even though they know that there are few jobs.

All this is by way of apology for offering some remarks based on my own work. My main hope is that what I have to say will prove interesting to others who have struggled with the problems of intellectual history. I can say for myself that I would rather hear another historian—even one I disagreed with—talking about what he has learned through his work than hear the same person say what he thinks everyone ought to do.

My own work, not through design but through a series of circumstantial and apparently random choices, has proved always to involve an effort to bring together religious and intellectual history, and to a lesser extent to place both against a social history background. I started with a religious history topic treated as social and intellectual history. My next major effort was an intellectual history topic that proved at all points to have a quasi-religious dimension. Most recently I have tried to treat a familiar major topic in intellectual history, the Enlightenment, arguing that it makes most sense when treated as religious history. My teaching has moved from a concentration on intellectual history to a concentration on religious history. But I have not ever been able to escape either field, and now realize that for me the two have always proved to illuminate each other.

At one point I was attracted by the suggestion that the two fields might turn out to be the same thing. That is if, with Tillich, one defines religion as ultimate concern, most intellectual history turns out to deal with religion whether it is called that or not—it deals with whatever people have found inescapably important. At the moment, however, I am not satisfied with this unification of the two fields. Both intellectual history and religious history do indeed deal with the ideals and values held to be most important by people in past time. But religious history deals with certain *kinds* of ideas and values, expressed in certain ways.

Some say that religion is concerned with the transcendent, a special kind of ultimate concern that nonreligious people do not share. But to define *transcendence* clearly seems to be difficult even for theologians, and is still harder for historians. For some people who have considered themselves religious—deists and some kinds of liberal Christians—God himself has not been clearly transcendent. For some patriots and romantic democrats, the nation or the people have had transcendent meaning. For Transcendentalists, all nature was an incarnation of spirit and thus transcended itself.

I find somewhat more helpful an insight I find in the essays of Clifford Geertz, which suggests that religion deals with symbols in a different way from other divisions of human culture. To Geertz and to some other anthropologists, all culture consists of systems of symbols. Religion involves a set of symbols endowed with ultimate authority and tremendous motivating power, whose function is to bring together a conception of the universe and a code of conduct.[1]

INTELLECTUAL HISTORY AND RELIGIOUS HISTORY

Sometimes this special kind of extremely powerful symbol system cannot be reduced to systematic verbal formulation. Here, perhaps, in the vast and rapidly changing field of language and symbol—a perilous jungle unfamiliar to most historians and certainly to me—one must begin one's search for a clue to the difference between religious and intellectual history. Both these deal with human culture and therefore with sets of symbols. Intellectual history in theory draws its subject matter from a great many aspects of culture. In practice, its writers tend to concentrate on those kinds of thought that have been systematically expressed in words, and in words used discursively. Religious history, on the other hand, deals with supremely powerful ideas and emotions that often cannot be expressed in this manner. Religious ideas and feelings have been expressed in many different ways, partly in words, and in words used in various ways, and partly otherwise, for instance in liturgical acts, demonstrations of devotion, or works of art.

Let us then rely for the moment on this difference in means of expression for our distinction between the two fields, bearing in mind also the somewhat tenuous matter of transcendence. Obviously this will leave a considerable overlap. Jonathan Edwards, for instance, clearly is part of the subject matter of both fields. His *Nature of True Virtue* uses words in the same way they are used by other eighteenth-century moral philosophers, seldom invoking any kinds of symbols not acceptable to nonbelieving opponents. On the other hand many of his sermons and meditations are in a completely different mode of discourse, much less approachable from outside religion. Perry Miller and his critics do not agree on what Edwards really meant by "eternal fires," and no scholar is likely to explain to us just how Edwards, walking in the fields, suddenly discovered the gentleness of God.

If we say that religion deals with many kinds of symbols and not only with words, it may be objected that precise verbal formulas like the Westminister Confession play a large part in the history of some kinds of American religion. Yet the first article of that confession declares that the light of nature is not sufficient to give the knowledge of God, and the second describes him not only as invisible but also as incomprehensible. Verbal formulas, from the Westminster Confession to the various platforms of late–nineteenth-century Fundamentalists, have usually played the role of unsuccessful efforts to dam and channel the flood of religious intuitions and emotions. The history of religion, in America as elsewhere, has to be much more than the history of creedal statements.

At the opposite end from Edwards in the religious spectrum, both Thomas Jefferson and John Dewey sometimes approach the border between religious and intellectual history. Both spent a lot of time worrying about ultimate matters and proposing new religious formulas. But

HENRY F. MAY

neither was able to develop sufficiently powerful symbols to make his religious insight authoritative for many people. Nature's God and the *Common Faith* remain elusive in a way that the Crucifixion or the Exodus are not elusive, although the meaning of these last may in turn be difficult even for a believer to state in clear grammatical sentences. On the other hand, some people who we think of as living on the far borders of religious history have developed a pretty powerful set of symbols, which is authoritative and perhaps transcendent for them. Here one thinks especially of the proponents of Manifest Destiny, the religion of the Great Republic, whose symbols include both objects—the flag—and events—the landing of the Pilgrims. For some adherents of the quasi-religion of American nationalism, the assassination of Lincoln in the moment of victory and forgiveness has tremendous symbolic authority, clearly dependent in large part on its Christian parallel.

There is indeed a blurred border area, and yet the distinction is not entirely without its uses. For instance, the endlessly repeated emotional formulas of the revival sermon, or the ritual of the camp meeting with its mourner's bench and anxious seat belong with religious and not with intellectual history. The exercises in deductive or inductive reasoning of modern academic philosophers or sociologists belong with intellectual and not with religious history. And as these examples suggest, a major difference between the two fields, at least when one sees them in the American context, is that intellectual historians are likely to deal mainly with an educated elite, religious historians with many kinds of people on many levels of articulateness and education.

This has, I think, been a division that scholars and teachers of American intellectual history, including me, have been reluctant to admit. Part of the difficulty has arisen from the emotionally complicated relation between American intellectuals and the masses. Most academic Americans in recent times have considered themselves liberal democrats. They —or rather we—have wanted to be on the side of the people, even perhaps to love the people. But most of us have been made aware at some time in our lives, perhaps painfully, that large sections of the people do not share our tastes and opinions and do not feel that they need or want our work. Thus sometimes we have stopped looking at the people as they are and have been, and have instead constructed an ideal version of the history of American culture as it ought to have been from a liberal intellectual point of view.

I will call this version, loosely, the Parringtonian synthesis. It goes something like this: Americans of the seventeenth century were obsessed with religion, especially Calvinism. From this they were liberated in the eighteenth century by the combined influence of the Enlightenment and the Revolution. In the nineteenth century, as Americans became less

INTELLECTUAL HISTORY AND RELIGIOUS HISTORY

European and therefore more egalitarian, they progressively turned away from supernaturalism to various kinds of religious liberalism, and eventually some of them moved beyond this to scientific naturalism. In the twentieth century, this process has gone far enough so that one need take little account of religion at all; where it survives it is mere social convention. Contemporary cultural history is expressed mainly through science, social science, and literature.

This is no doubt a caricature, and it may seem that I am setting up a straw man. Yet I would ask you to think about this mode in relation to our actual presentation to students. A good deal of it, I find, was implied in the organization and selection of topics in the course in intellectual history I taught for more than twenty years and have now happily turned over to a very able colleague. Something that always made me uncomfortable in this course, and that was sometimes noticed by bright students, was that it skipped back and forth between an attempt to deal with the community or with large groups and a concentration on elites, sometimes tiny elite groups like the Transcendentalists, or even on isolated individuals. Was a lecture on the Great Awakening or the Social Gospel really part of the same sequence as one on Thorstein Veblen or the expatriates of the 1920s? Part of the difficulty I think was that I was moving back and forth, without realizing it, between intellectual history —the history of ideas systematically expressed in words—and religious history, the history of ideas and feelings expressed in other kinds of symbols as well as in words, and in words used in various ways. More recently I have begun teaching instead a short survey of American religion, broadly defined. This too of course has its epistemological and organizational problems, and always will. But I feel a little more as though I am talking about the same thing all through the course, even though I am dealing with extremely different kinds and numbers of people. And to me, at least, the version of American culture I now present seems richer and more various.

I should like briefly to run through some of our standard topics, and to try to suggest how they look different if one moves from intellectual history to religious history, and how making this change helps to lay to rest the ghost of the Parringtonian synthesis.

In dealing with seventeenth-century intellectual history, most of us used to draw heavily on the work of one great, dramatically compelling scholar. Our lectures were likely to deal with the Puritan errand, with the covenant, and with declension. Like all great scholars, Perry Miller has attracted swarms of critics, and in his case some of them have made telling points. We have learned to question the theory of the covenant theology as a strategy shaped to deal with declension. We have learned

HENRY F. MAY

to ask whether one has finished with the cultural history of the New England colonies when one has dealt with the ideas of the leading clergy. And we have been reminded that New England was not America. All this makes Miller's subjects, the Puritan clergy, more real and interesting. Their task becomes more significant when we realize that not everyone in seventeenth-century Massachusetts Bay was obsessed full time with religious ideas, any more than was everyone in thirteenth-century France. (Perry Miller knew this, of course, and sometimes made it clear that he knew it.) It is valuable to see the tasks of the Puritan clergy in terms of their daily round of religious duties, carried on in an environment that was precarious from the beginning.[2] The theory of decline set forth in jeremiad sermons is more interesting when it is seen not as a report on the actual situation but rather as a hortatory device. Without going back to the rather silly cynicism of some of Miller's predecessors, fully recognizing the importance of all he has taught us, we can perhaps see religion in early New England in somewhat the same way as we see religion in other periods of American history—as part of an adaptation of traditional beliefs and symbols to a new situation, a situation involving some degree of voluntarism and pluralism from the start. We may be able to argue that religion was important in the seventeenth century in New England without implying that it was unimportant in other times and places.

When we come to the eighteenth century we have the task of fitting together, in America as in the world, the Age of Enthusiasm and the Age of Reason. We have learned from many excellent scholars that the relation between evangelical Protestantism, the Enlightenment, and the Revolution is extremely complicated, and different in different American places and subcultures. We know that if many of the leading Revolutionaries were inclined towards deism, many of their most ardently committed and even violently revolutionary troops were evangelical, that many people saw the revolutionary struggle not as liberation from Calvinism but as a means of arresting moral and sometimes doctrinal decay. I have argued that parts of the Enlightenment—especially in its most antireligious aspects—were tied closely to the culture of the European upper classes and thus to those Americans who clung most firmly to that culture. Some of the Enlightenment was at once religiously radical, socially aristocratic, and politically conservative—some but by no means all. If this is so it was clearly not possible that the Enlightenment in anything like its European shape could carry with it the independent American people. As American culture became more democratic and less European, the Enlightenment could survive only in drastically adapted form. Another way of putting this might be to say

INTELLECTUAL HISTORY AND RELIGIOUS HISTORY

that it remained an intellectual movement and failed to become a religion.

The themes of our cultural history in the early nineteenth century—perhaps the most formative period—are four: the growth of evangelical religion, social and political egalitarianism, nationalism, and reform. All these grew together and cannot be separated, and their relation with each other was complex and shifting. It has not worked, for instance, to range evangelical religion *against* either democracy or reform—it was too much the heart and soul of both. Yet it is also true that the leaders of certain important kinds of evangelical religion distrusted democracy and engaged in a no-holds-barred battle against certain kinds of reform.

To make sense of this complicated story (and I believe no one has quite done this) one has to make some use of religious distinctions and even terminology. For political and social as well as religious history one has to speak of theocrats and antinomians, millenarians and comeouters. Among the fascinating problems is the relation of that important but tiny group of self-appointed spokesmen, the Transcendentalists, to the whole national scene. It was clearly an ambivalent relation: like so many American intellectuals, Emerson and his friends were deeply on the side of the people but differed with most of them on almost every religious or political question. And yet for some odd reason Concord intellectuals were saying some of the same things as revivalist preachers and Jacksonian editors[3] about certain matters crucially important to all: the sources of knowledge and the tests of truth. Really to understand Emerson and Thoreau, or for that matter Whitman and Hawthorne, one has to bear in mind, among others, Charles Grandison Finney, Phoebe Palmer, and Joseph Smith. Of course no one can do that adequately; that is what makes our enterprise so inexhaustibly absorbing.

For the late nineteenth century almost everyone starts with the immense facts of industrialization and urbanization. Here and at many other points we must go well outside the bounds of religious or intellectual history if we are to understand either. And yet it must be borne in mind that people of this generation were reacting to these physical stimuli in terms of the complex intellectual and religious tradition carried on from earlier periods. Industrializing America is not even the same as industrial England, and utterly different from industrializing France or Germany or Russia. Part of the difference must be sought in religious history.

The country was still officially Protestant in its odd unofficial way, and leading political spokesmen saw American Protestantism as part of the coming worldwide social and political millennium. And yet this dominantly Protestant country was developing a working class a large part of which was Catholic—a situation quite special in the world. Within

HENRY F. MAY

Protestantism a rather bland variety of theological liberalism was powerfully entrenched in the socially dominant churches.[4] From the same liberal theological principles different kinds of sincere Protestants drew political and social conclusions ranging from the most rigid laissez-faire conservatism to reformist semisocialism. This socially dominant Protestant liberalism was so powerful that it exerted a strong and disruptive pull on both Catholics and Jews. Yet in the Protestant camp itself, liberalism was increasingly challenged by orthodox revivalism and militant religious conservatism. It would be hard to say whether more people were influenced by Henry Ward Beecher or Dwight L. Moody.

More than we used to realize, in this period of social upheaval social critics made natural and fervent use of religious terminology. This was true not only of millennial socialists like Edward Bellamy but also of Populists, raised on camp meetings and revival hymns and by no means abandoning either their forms or their message.[5] It is true, and important, that on the top intellectual level various people challenged, qualified, abandoned, or fought against all the dominant religious assumptions. But one cannot understand William James, Thorstein Veblen, or John Dewey without remembering the agonies and struggles of doubters in an age when religious commitment was taken for granted.

Finally, let us consider the last article of the Parringtonian synthesis. Is religion a nearly negligible topic in American culture of the twentieth century, as many intellectuals living in that time have assumed?[6] Here I want to be careful not to overstate my case for polemical purposes. It is clear enough that religion does not occupy the same place in American culture that it did in the days of Henry Ward Beecher, let alone in those of his father, Lyman. It is indeed still part of the official rhetoric. It would probably be harder for a critic of majority religion to be elected president now than in the days of Jefferson. It is tempting to dismiss political religiosity as meaningless verbiage, but this is clearly inadequate in the days of Jimmy Carter. Even if one finds official religion meaningless, the reasons politicians find it necessary are important to think about.

On the other hand, since the First World War or a little earlier, religion has ceased to have a place in the established culture of the intellectuals. In some intellectual centers it probably takes more courage for a writer or painter or professor to go to church or synagogue than not to—though neither choice involves any serious disabilities. About middle-class religion, the problem raised by Will Herberg is a real one: Is it possible in a country with several equal religions to talk about "religion in general" in a way that has any meaning? Robert Bellah has suggested that one of the powerful surviving religions is the civil religion, a suggestion that some people find depressing if true.[7] For a number of reasons then, it is

INTELLECTUAL HISTORY AND RELIGIOUS HISTORY

plausibly and widely suggested that religion is now merely a meaning-less camouflage for conservative patriotism, the pseudoreligion of Americanism.

I would call this a corollary of neo-Parringtonianism and suggest that it is at most only partly true. To begin to move toward a full understanding of the present complicated religious situation one would have to take into consideration a whole series of phenomena that challenge this thesis.

First, one must bear in mind the familiar statistics that show an almost steady growth in church membership, which reached its peak in 1965, and has declined only slightly since. To say that something which attracts some concrete allegiance from 60 percent of the population is insignificant one must be extraordinarily certain about what is important and what is not. Second, one must look hard at the great and rising popularity of many kinds of evangelical Christianity and pentecostalism, kinds of religion that are not anything like civil religion, and that have all sorts of different relations, antagonistic as well as friendly, to the religion of Americanism.[8] Third, one cannot omit the flourishing of the mystical cults, old and new, Eastern and indigenous, many of them centrally related to complaints against the materialism of American culture. Finally, right in the intellectual center, or at least in the intellectual centers, one has to confront the youth movement of the 1960s, which seemed to many observers to be full of echoes of the period of transcendentalism. Much of the New Left and its residues can, I believe, be seen as centrally a repudiation of all varieties of scientific naturalism and a search for transcendent values and symbols in which to express these. Naturally enough, this tendency has deeply distressed many partisans of the Old Left. To summarize: in recent times the position of religion in American culture is different and difficult, but we get nowhere in understanding it by dismissing the problem.

Now I come to the difficult question. Is it possible to draw any helpful conclusions from this sketch, which by no means pretends to offer a synthesis to rival the defunct one I have labeled Parringtonian? First, my suggestions do not dispose of the idea that the intellectual history of the United States is a story of the movement from Calvinism through various kinds of liberalism to secularism. This organization holds roughly true if one defines intellectual history as dealing with an articulate elite, and perhaps this is how it should be defined. Such a definition need not be damaging. No one would be more hostile than I to any suggestion that it is somehow immoral to study elites. I would hate to think that students in the future would cease to have to come to terms with Jonathan Edwards, Ralph Waldo Emerson, the James brothers, or Henry Adams. But those who deal with these fascinating figures and others like them

HENRY F. MAY

will find them even more interesting if they deal with them in the full context of American culture, and a large part of this context must be provided by religious history. Were these great figures really, as some of them thought they were, spokesmen for the people as a whole? This cannot be assumed, and the argument will prove a tricky one.

For those who deal with religious history it has become apparent that a progressive synthesis, running from Calvinism to liberalism, will not do. This again works only when one deals with the most verbally articulate sections of American religion. As Sydney Ahlstrom's impressive summary demonstrates, that is only a small part of the story.

I do not intend to abandon intellectual history for religious history. Rather I am suggesting that to move back and forth between these two fields makes a stimulating and fruitful trip, provided one is conscious of the movement. To take into account both intellectual and religious history will help us understand the relation between words and other kinds of symbols, between organized ideas and those only partly organized. It will therefore help students of American culture with what I think is their hardest and most important problem, the special and unique relation between elites and masses in this country. It will open questions one does not think of otherwise. In fact it has already done this: think of the problem of civil religion and also the history of all kinds of millennialism. It may provide categories for investigating phenomena that have proved perennially elusive, including the springs of social reform in many periods.

I hope that in my enthusiasm—the enthusiasm of a convert—I am not telling anyone what he should work on, or still less what he should like. I do not think one need admire something either because it is big, or because it is as American as apple pie—or evangelical Protestantism. There is nothing wrong, for instance, with finding Ralph Waldo Emerson more admirable and interesting than Jospeh Smith. But I am suggesting that it will make the study of either more interesting if one remembers constantly that the other was also powerfully present.

Notes

1. Clifford Geertz, *The Interpretation of Cultures: Selected Essays* (New York: Basic Books, 1973), especially "Religion as a Cultural System," pp. 87–125; and "Ethos, World View, and the Analysis of Sacred Symbols," pp. 126–41.
2. David D. Hall, *The Faithful Shepherd* (Chapel Hill: University of North Carolina Press, 1972); J. W. T. Youngs, *God's Messengers: Religious Leadership in Colonial New England, 1700–1750* (Baltimore, Md.: The Johns Hopkins University Press, 1976).

INTELLECTUAL HISTORY AND RELIGIOUS HISTORY

3. See John William Ward, *Andrew Jackson: Symbol for an Age* (New York: Oxford University Press, 1955).
4. The main ingredients in the kind of liberalism I am talking about here were divine immanence and evolutionary progress, sometimes associated with a social interpretation of the New Testament promises.
5. For a valuable new survey of Christian semisocialism, see Peter J. Frederick, *Knights of the Golden Rule* (Lexington: The University Press of Kentucky, 1976). A useful beginning is made in the neglected subject of Populism and religion by Robert C. McMath, *Populist Vanguard* (Chapel Hill: University of North Carolina Press, 1975), esp. pp. 62–76, 133–37.
6. A representative early example is Harold E. Stearns, whose *Civilization in the United States* (New York: Harcourt, Brace, 1922) looks at that subject from the point of view of the young intellectuals. In his preface Stearns tells us that when he tried to procure an article on religion his prospective contributors told him "almost unanimously" "that real religious feeling in America had disappeared, that the church had become a purely social and political institution, that the country was in the grip of what Anatole France had aptly called Protestant clericalism, and that, finally, they weren't interested in the topic" (p. vi).
7. Bellah's much discussed essay on civil religion and a number of the essay's critics are presented in Russell E. Richey and Donald G. Jones, eds., *American Civil Religion* (New York: Harper & Row, 1974).
8. A helpful taxonomy of recent evangelical religion is offered by Richard Quebedeaux in *The Young Evangelicals* (New York: Harper & Row, 1974). This is brought up to date by the same author's "The Evangelicals: New Trends and New Tensions," *Christianity and Crisis* 36, no. 14 (20 September, 1976): 197–202.

THE LIBERAL TRADITION REVISITED
AND THE REPUBLICAN TRADITION ADDRESSED

⊂▭▭▭ ◖ ◗ ▭▭▭⊃

DOROTHY ROSS

The reason for returning to the liberal tradition in America some twenty years after Louis Hartz published his book by that name is the recent publication of J. G. A. Pocock's *The Machiavellian Moment*.[1] Pocock explicitly offers an alternative tradition to Hartz's in which to ground the American mind and historical experience. In this paper I would like to examine some of the strengths of Pocock's work as a guide to American intellectual history.

Hartz's analysis of the liberal tradition narrowed and simplified the American mind. Hartz claimed that America is a "fragment society," a society formed and forever shaped by the transfer to this continent of the liberal fragment of seventeenth- and eighteenth-century European society. Without any substantial implantation of feudalism and aristocracy, America never developed its nineteenth-century counterforce, socialism. Assuming that the American mind and the American society were mirror images, Hartz denominated that mind Lockean "in the classic . . . sense."[2] Since he made no further reference to Lockean texts or specific chains of intellectual transmission, however, the American mind appeared simply as individualistic and oriented toward capitalism. Hartz permitted the antebellum south to stand as an exception, but everything else collapsed into this flattened landscape. Federalism and Whiggery disappeared into the same sort of liberal politics and entrepreneurial impulses the Jacksonians displayed; Bryan and McKinley, New Nationalists and Wilsonian liberals, were not essentially different; the Progressive intellectuals who tried to escape the bonds of consensus succeeded merely in confusing themselves. Only the New Deal involved real departures, but it did so disguised as pragmatic liberalism.

Pocock, like Hartz, grounds the American mind in a single tradition, but the effect of his work is to broaden and complicate our view. He shows how the ancient tradition of civic humanism was recalled and developed in Renaissance Italy, then in seventeenth- and eighteenth-century Britain, and finally in revolutionary America. Although American republicanism thus appears as a late and provincial flowering of a Renaissance and early modern political dialogue, Pocock examines the

116

THE LIBERAL AND REPUBLICAN TRADITIONS

logic and social nuance of that dialogue in such depth that American thought takes on new richness and complexity.

The ideal of the republic the Americans inherited rested on the assumption that man attained his full humanity through participation or citizenship in a republic, where government was balanced among the one, the few, and the many. Only in such a balanced polity could each man play the part for which he was suited; only when all citizens were animated by the public good as well as their own, were capable that is, of virtue, could the balance be sustained. Pocock argues that when Machiavelli and his contemporaries took up this ideal, it was profoundly affected by their conception of time. The ancient view that only the timeless was rational and real and the Christian view that meaning lay in the sacred realm outside the natural world combined to give Renaissance men a restricted understanding of human change in time. They tended to understand change as the degeneration or corruption of ideal initial forms, and the history of republics passed on to them confirmed the specific kinds of corruption to which republics eventually succumbed. "The Machiavellian moment" is the name Pocock gives to the point when Machiavelli confronted the fragility of the republic in time.

Harrington and his successors not only inherited this body of thought, they were still largely constrained by similar conceptions of time. Protestant millennialists could believe that an ideal republic could be established in England; after the Glorious Revolution more traditional Englishmen came to think that their mixed constitution had embodied and perpetuated these ideal principles since time immemorial. But millennialists and traditionalists continued to fear the ravages of earthly time. During the eighteenth-century rule of Walpole, those who retained these earlier ideals—the Commonwealthmen and the adherents of a "Country" ideology—feared that in fact Britain's balanced Constitution was threatened by corruption. Their anxious, vivid restatement of the republican ideal passed directly to the Founding Fathers, and the premodern view of historical time it embodied took root in America's Protestant millennial mentality.

Pocock shows that while civic humanism at one level perpetuated ancient and Renaissance conceptions of time, it also stimulated its adherents to begin to think analytically about historical conditions that could maintain virtue and about the historical changes that bred corruption; in effect, they began to develop a "sociology of virtue" and move toward an understanding of historical change as genuinely creative, toward historicism. Harrington had asserted that citizenship must be based on independent freehold in land if the individual was to possess sufficient independence to maintain republican virtue, and the "Country" party of landholders perpetuated that belief. But Englishmen were

DOROTHY ROSS

aware from the beginning of the eighteenth century that commerce was rapidly growing, creating more wealth, greater dependence on the unstable mechanisms of credit, and greater specialization and diversification in function and interest. Within the framework of civic humanism these changes appeared as corruption: luxury, selfishness, dependencies between man and man, and in collusion with government, bribery, placemen, speculation, and debt. Unlike the purist "Country" party, those in control of the government and allied to it, the "Court," were willing to live with corruption, to postpone the day of reckoning, perhaps indefinitely, and meanwhile to enjoy the diverse fruits of wealth and national power. Some theorists, particularly the Scottish moralists, began to understand the development of commerce as progress and to examine history as a realm of genuine creativity. But both the Court and Adam Smith, Pocock argues, developed their views in dialogue with civic humanism and retained its fear that ultimately the very mechanisms of progress could go too far and corrupt men and the polity.

While England abandoned her millennial identity after the seventeenth century, defeated the "Country" party in the eighteenth century, and in the nineteenth century developed a spectrum of political thought and historicist consciousness of time from largely "Court" sources, America, Pocock suggests, retained her "Country" mentality. The millennial hope with which the nation established a republic wedded America to the timeless morality of "Country" ideals. Engaged nonetheless in the avid pursuit of commerce, Americans continued to be moved by the dialectical conflict between virtue and commerce, from the struggles between Jefferson and Hamilton, to Jackson and the Bank, through Populist battles against plutocracy. At the same time, Americans sought to escape the conflict by constructing a utopian vision of time. The continent of virgin land would counter the corrupting effects of industrial growth with the moral strength of an agrarian yeomanry and fend off the decadence of increasing civilization with the dynamic energies bred in the conquest of nature. Yet uneasiness remained, repeatedly calling forth fears for the survival of the virtuous republic. As the frontier disappeared, Americans clung to the belief in their millennial mission, now codified by Turner in historical writing, and penetrating as myth into the modern American political and literary imagination.[3]

Even so brief a recital of Hartz's theory and Pocock's complex work suggests that Pocock more adequately takes account of the evidence historians have accumulated over the past two decades. The central issue he sees in American history—the survival of the virtuous republic—reinforces the findings of many recent studies of the Revolution, the early republic, and the antebellum decades.[4] His dialectic between virtue and commerce not only gives reality to the partisan political voices Hartz

THE LIBERAL AND REPUBLICAN TRADITIONS

silenced, but also places in perspective the kind of ambivalence that Marvin Meyers discovered in Jacksonian, and Richard Hofstadter in Populist, rhetoric.[5] Pocock's theory also gives partial historical grounding to some of the work produced by American Studies analysts of myth and symbol. Unlike David Noble, for example, who has reduced the American mind to a single gesture (presumed to be Lockean), a utopian flight from the past into nature, the classic works of American Studies have long recognized that the myths of the American mind were generated by a dialectic between nature and civilization, and that each term was anchored in both past and future.[6] Pocock describes a complex political mentality that intersects the popular and literary imaginations.

There are other reasons why Pocock's theory deserves more serious attention from intellectual historians today than Hartz's received in the past. Hartz wrote just as American historians were leaving behind progressive historiography and beginning to explore sophisticated techniques of social and intellectual analysis that made them suspicious of synthetic efforts, particularly political ones. Despite Hartz's castigation of the Progressive historians, he merely drew different conclusions from the simplified Marxist premises the Progressives had adopted. Where Progressives had seen class conflict, Hartz saw bourgeois consensus. Where Progressives reduced conflicting ideas to conflicting economic interests, Hartz reduced conflicting ideas to false consciousness. Hartz thus tried to explain away the ideas of his subjects as confusions and mistakes, just as intellectual historians were learning to analyze ideas as coherently explicable responses to intellectual and historical problems. On the level of grand theory, Hartz did provide brilliant insight into the consequences of the absence of feudalism and the resulting liberal inclination of American thought. On that level, he found wide ideological support among both liberal and New Left historians. But it is my impression that his analysis of the American mind in various periods of its history has been much less used.[7]

Historians of our own day, and particularly intellectual historians, ought now to be ready to return their attention tó political ideology and its long-term continuities. The power a study of political ideology can bring to political history has already been demonstrated by historians of the Revolution like Bernard Bailyn and Gordon Wood, and Pocock's theory extends the reach of that analysis. Despite the high level of abstraction on which he works, his categories can be traced in the actual ideologies of practical politics. A recent stunning attempt to map the main ideological lines of American politics by Robert Kelley suggests how two-party conflict has retained the phenotypic traits of republican ideology. The eighteenth-century alignment of "Country" versus "Court," provinces versus center, transposed into the regional and ethnic

DOROTHY ROSS

diversity of America, Kelley suggests, has shaped political alignments to the present day.[8] In recent decades the range and resonance of what we have been accustomed to think of as political thought also has expanded. The republican ideology as it took root in America was a specifically Puritan mentality, suggesting that religious and political consciousness were fundamentally intertwined. Republicanism thus offers an intellectual framework in which to examine more fully the ties between religion and politics that so much recent research has uncovered.[9]

Intellectual historians ought also to return to an examination of American political thought to correct a failing that Pocock and Hartz share. Neither Pocock's complex dialectic nor Hartz's simple consensus recognizes the existence in American politics of a radical, egalitarian strain. Yet there is considerable evidence that an "equal rights" ideology made its appearance during the Revolution and gathered force during the antebellum decades. Linked to antimonopoly doctrines, it took specific root in Locofoco politics and labor, currency, and agrarian movements through most of the nineteenth century. Though the connection has hardly been investigated, this egalitarian strain of American politcs was sometimes linked to the ideal of a cooperative commonwealth, and like its counterpart in England, it sometimes developed in the post–Civil War decades into native varieties of democratic socialism.[10] If Progressive historians exaggerated the coherence and importance of this egalitarian strain, more conservative recent historians have mistaken and overlooked its significance.[11] Pocock's work, however, allows us to return to the problem of American radicalism with more penetrating questions. To what extent was the "equal rights" ideology different in origin and separate in thrust from the republicanism sown by the Founding Fathers? How and when was it drawn into the dialectic between virtue and commerce? Did it, unlike the republican view of individual citizens and public duty, carry the possibility of supporting a radical class consciousness? And what was the relationship between "equal rights" and the "equal opportunity" of the capitalist market? The ideal of a cooperative commonwealth suggests that the two doctrines, if sometimes subsumed under the umbrella of entrepreneurial individualism, also diverged. With the lineaments of republican ideology in plain view, we can begin to explore the subtle oppositions and convergences of American political thought with greater accuracy than heretofore.

For the moment, however, I would like to explore a final aspect of Pocock's work which points the way to a more sophisticated understanding of American political thought. He demonstrates that historical consciousness—how a people locates itself in time—is a basic dimension of political and social thought. American historians have sometimes noted this dimension but have not fully explored its implications for

THE LIBERAL AND REPUBLICAN TRADITIONS

intellectual history.[12] In many ways this aspect of Pocock's work is the most original, and for the remainder of the paper I would like to focus my attention on it. I believe Pocock's view of historical consciousness can clarify not only the early republic, but also those decades at the end of the nineteenth and beginning of the twentieth centuries when American social thought was consciously recast.

It has been common to recognize that Europeans in the early nineteenth century began to apprehend time in a historicist mode. Whether seen through German idealism or the positivism of Spencer and Comte, history was understood as a creative process: culture, society and human nature itself were seen to change fundamentally over the course of secular time. The timelessness of American thought during the same period has also been recognized, but Pocock links this characteristic to the prehistoricist logic of the republican tradition.[13] Believing in the Providential guidance and millennial mission of the American republic, Americans sought utopian conditions that would stave off the corruption of historical change and keep secular time frozen in its original and predetermined course.

When I encounter popular social thought in the 1880s it is still explicable in the terms Pocock has discovered. The most widely read social thinkers of the eighties, like Josiah Strong, Henry George, and Edward Bellamy, still held a millennial view of the course of republican history. Their perception of historical time was fixed in the ambivalent movement of progress and the threat of corruption Pocock traced to eighteenth-century thinkers in the civic humanist tradition. So long as time remained on its original upward course, the millennial and secular planes could remain locked in concert, and corruption could recede from view. By the 1880s, however, as political scandal, plutocracy, and class conflict raised the fear of historical decay, the republican metahistory was clearly visible.

The persistence of this pre-historicist consciousness of time through the nineteenth century should not be surprising. Although intellectual elites centered in Boston and New York had absorbed and disseminated more modern European ideas, for many in the native middle and working classes, evangelical Protestantism perpetuated a powerful belief in the millennial mission of America. Strong, George, and Bellamy all were thoroughly schooled and heavily influenced by this tradition. In addition, though the ancient and Renaissance premises of republican theory may have grown vague, classical education and American political instruction repeated the themes of the fragility of the republic, its dependence on virtue, and its liability to corruption.[14]

The principal text for republican metahistory in the eighties is Strong's *Our Country*, an analysis of the contemporary crisis historians have

DOROTHY ROSS

found difficult to categorize. The work of a Congregational clergyman writing for his church's Home Missionary Society, *Our Country* exploded the confines of the traditional missionary tract. Over half a million copies were ultimately circulated, and its impact has been compared to that of *Uncle Tom's Cabin*.[15] When placed in the context of the civic humanist tradition, *Our Country* announces the arrival of another "Machiavellian moment" in American history, and its odd configurations suggest the final poverty of the republican historical imagination.

Strong announced at the outset that the "closing years of the nineteenth century" were one of the "great focal points in history . . . second in importance to that only which must always remain first; viz, the birth of Christ." America faced an apocalyptic moment, one that would either fulfill her destiny as the last and permanent home of liberty in its westward march ("There are no more New Worlds") or crush her beneath the mounting perils that threatened her virtue. The historic scene, therefore, was the scene constructed by republican visionaries since the seventeenth century whenever the virtuous republic was threatened. The perils America faced were nineteenth-century evangelical versions of corruption: the immigration of alien peoples, Roman Catholicism, intemperance, socialism, great wealth, and the development that magnified the effects of all the others—the city. In each case, these perils threatened to undermine the independence, the virtue, and the relative equality required by citizens in a self-governing community. And the response Strong urged to these perils was the familiar call for the assertion of virtue against history, in this case, a call to give money, pure and simple, so that the Society could plant virtue where peril threatened.[16]

The oddity of the analysis stems from the conclusions to which this republican logic led when it had to digest the conditions of late–nineteenth-century historical development. The logic of the westward course of liberty, to which the Home Missionary Society had long been dedicated, had singled out the American West as the critical area in which virtue must supplant vice. Yet the perils Strong described were the perils of civilization and of rapid industrial development, in the minds of his audience as surely as in the minds of later historians, the perils of the eastern city and not those of the western frontier. Strong's elaborate statistical projections of the future growth of the West could not quite erase the incongruity.

More important, Strong, like the Augustan analysts of emerging commercial society, could only attribute the growth of these perils to the progress of civilization itself. Time after time, when explaining the causes of the great increase in immigration or intemperance, socialism or excessive wealth, he was forced to show that they resulted from the fundamental processes of modernization. The graphic power of Strong's statistics accentuated the underlying paradox by which the tremendous forces of nineteenth-century historical development were linked to corruption in time. Strong did not consciously analyze that looming contradiction, but he surely felt it: he tells us that "the western world in its progress is gathering momentum like a falling body."[17] There could be no better image of the fundamental impasse to which the republican historical imagination had come.

The final oddity is Strong's hope to purify this immense force by donations to the Home Missionary Society. By 1886 the traditions of missionary charity and of republican jeremiad were clearly inadequate to cope with unprecedented historical change. The threat to virtue called forth in Strong, as it had in anxious republican theorists earlier, an apocalyptic mood.

There is a great deal of evidence to suggest that the sense of crisis of the 1880s was a crisis of the still-republican mind of the Protestant middle class. According to a recent study, the burgeoning utopian literature published in the eighties and nineties was structured on the image of the apocalypse with its threat of fiery destruction and its promise of the Kingdom of Christ. In all that literature, what precipitated the apocalyptic moment was the rapid historical change of the late nineteenth century, change that created the spiraling corruption, inequality, class conflict, and moral decay announcing the end of republican liberty.[18]

Analogies to the end of the Roman republic abound in the literature of the eighties. "Whence shall come the new barbarians?" Henry George asked. "Go through the squalid quarters of great cities, and you may see, even now, their gathering hordes!" In the last section of George's *Progress and Poverty* he showed that the law of rent derived from the larger laws of historical progress, and that these laws described the familiar republican trajectory of progress and progressive decay. The work was controlled by the same apocalyptic perception as was Strong's and Bellamy's work: "The civilized world is trembling on the verge of a great moment. Either it must be a leap upwards . . . or it must be a plunge downward which will carry us back toward barbarism."[19] The signs of corruption that had perennially set off Puritan and republican jeremiads seemed to advance at a speed that escaped the traditional republican remedies. The very term—"the social problem"—by which these massed corruptions were known suggests the vague way in which the new facts of social history had to take shape outside the boundary of the wholly political and religious republican mentality.

The constraints of this mentality are seen more clearly when we note the kind of historical analysis that emerged within, but did not break out from, the republican metahistory. George articulated his historical theory as a revision of Spencer's law of progress. What Spencer did not recognize, he argued, was that "the obstacles which finally bring progress to a halt are raised by the course of progress." George found the key to decay in the historical tendency toward unequal distribution of wealth and power, and it is worth quoting at some length the one paragraph in which he tried to conceptualize the paradoxical historical relationship between progress and corruption:

> Now, this process of integration, of the specialization of functions and powers, as it goes on in society, is, by virtue of what is probably one of the deepest laws of human nature, accompanied by a constant liability to inequality. I do not mean that inequality is the necessary result of social growth, but that it is the constant tendency of social growth if unaccompanied by changes in social adjustments which, in the new conditions that growth produces, will secure equality. I mean, so to speak, that the garment of laws, customs, and political institutions, which each society weaves for itself, is constantly tending to become too tight as the society develops. I mean, so to speak, that man, as he advances, threads a labyrinth, in which, if he keeps straight ahead, he will infallibly lose his way, and through which reason and justice can alone keep him continuously in an ascending path.

The repeated "so to speaks" suggest the difficulty George had in conceiving this relationship.[20]

Had George been dealing on the purely phenomenal level of history he would have had no problem: in a complex society, historical causes produce unintended and antagonistic results. That was the chief message of Spencer's *The Study of Sociology*, which George knew and quoted. George was not dealing with merely phenomenal history, however, but with millennial American history, whose laws of historical progress were ordained by God and nature. His problem was therefore as difficult, George noted himself in the next paragraph, as "the problem of the genesis of evil." The logical consequence of the "tendency of social growth" toward inequality, as his metaphors suggested, was a view of history in which vice is constantly generated by historical change and constantly hedged about by changes in "social adjustments," by human management. It was an embryonic historicism, and according to Pocock's theory, more likely to emerge from the "Court" Whiggism of the eighteenth century than the "Country" mentality of America, with its determination to fix virtue eternally against the ravages of time.[21] The larger logic of George's "single tax" and his millennial hope was still "Country," to avert history and restore the virtuous republic, once and for all. Bellamy's historical imagination, too, which turned evolving economic trusts all at once into the utopian commonwealth, incorporated a span of evolutionary historicism into a millennial view of time.[22]

Apparently George was led to historical analysis by reading the historical theories that had emerged in Europe during the course of the century. He was familiar with Comte as well as Spencer. He argued at length against Bagehot. The emerging historicism of these British and Continental thinkers had begun to erode George's millennial historical imagination, but it had not yet come to dominate that imagination. Even Strong was familiar with nineteenth-century English histories, like those of Macaulay and Lecky, and used them to discuss the consequences of industrialization—the logical point for Americans to begin to see themselves as following the same historical course as that of modern Europe.[23] Before we can properly assess the historical consciousness of the 1880s we need to know much more about such influences, particularly the influence of the British historians, Comte, and Spencer during the middle decades of the century. I know of no study of Comtian influence in America written since 1938, and that one is highly fragmentary.[24] Spencer's influence has unfortunately been viewed almost exclusively in relation to "social Darwinism," when his major impact on social thought may have been a heightened perception of society's historical interconnectedness.[25]

The development of historicist thinking in the nineteenth century is important because a shift in historical consciousness may well be the underlying ground for the major intellectual changes that occurred in American social thought between the 1880s and 1920. Historians of these decades have noted that the mentality of the eighties was typically "utopian" and in basic ways characteristic of thought earlier in the nineteenth century, while the Progressive intellectuals who followed are often seen to have adopted evolutionary and historicist insights, or to be centrally concerned with the problem of historical change.[26] Pocock now allows us to see that conjunction in coherent terms. The "utopian" thought of the eighties was apocalyptic, the response to industrialization of a republican mentality still fundamentally millennial in its conception of time and thus still unable fully to grasp an historicist understanding of historical change. The Progressive intellectuals, however, the first American generation raised amidst the industrial crisis to feel fully the impact of science and positivism, could not believe in a millennial frame for American history or in an apocalyptic salvation for the dying republican order. They were thus forced for the first time to gauge the course of America's future in historical time, and they were free to appreciate for the first time the historicist understanding of change in time that European thinkers had developed during the nineteenth century. The erosion of the millennial vision of America after the 1880s made the nature and

DOROTHY ROSS

direction of historical change the central concern of the Progressive intellectuals and historicism the new insight they brought to American social thought.

We can see the value of this interpretation more clearly if we reexamine Robert Weibe's influential discussion of these decades in *The Search for Order*. Wiebe denotes three patterns of thought: utopian, characteristic of the eighties; idealist, which characterized most of the Progressive intellectuals; and bureaucratic, which emerged slowly after 1900 but did not triumph until after 1920. Wiebe recognizes a multitude of intellectual traditions that combine to compose these three mentalities, but he traces their source not to ideas but to the social reality in which they arose and which they are presumed to reflect. Utopian thought is linked to the "distended society" America had become in the eighties; thinking still in the personalistic terms characteristic of older face-to-face relations, the utopians sought desperately to preserve the communal America. Bureaucratic thought is linked to "the fluidity and impersonality of an urban-industrial world"; these thinkers "pictured a society of ceaselessly interacting members and concentrated upon adjustment within it, . . . stressed techniques of constant watchfulness and mechanisms of continuous management." The idealists, left without a specific social referent, are presumed to arise from the transitional stage between communal and industrial society; their major theme was a "historically rooted sense of progress by stages . . . to a final goal inherent in and predetermined by the process of social evolution itself."[27]

While thought clearly arises from experience, it is also true that experience is apprehended through categories of thought, and Wiebe's analysis ascribes the shape of these mentalities to social conditions alone. We have seen that the "distended society" was also the American republic and that its apocalyptic impulse was no mere invention of communal desperation, but the natural resort of anxious millennial republicans. It can also be shown that both the idealist and the bureaucratic thought Wiebe describes were reflections of the new historicism and were related phases in the Progressive intellectuals' effort to discover its implications for the fate of American society.

Wiebe recognized that the idealists, the bulk of the Progressive intellectuals, were fundamentally concerned with the historical evolution of modern society and were intent on finding in the last stage of evolution the basis for an ideal society. But he stressed the rigid quality of their three-stage historical theories and the utopian quality of their final stage as an attempt finally to "step outside of history." In this he followed the seminal work of David Noble, who saw the Progressive intellectuals as merely reformulating an American utopia.[28] But this is to miss the novelty of the Progressives' goal, for their purpose was to find a basis for a

THE LIBERAL AND REPUBLICAN TRADITIONS

moral society *within* history, to ground *in* history and society the values previously guaranteed to America by God and nature. It is thus appropriate that they turned to the major historical thinkers of the nineteenth century for insight into the evolution of human society, for they were engaged in the same enterprise that Hegel, Marx, Comte, and Spencer had begun in Europe much earlier. They were belatedly addressing the problem of secular change in time, and seeking, like the historical philosophers, to find social forms or historical matrices in which values could find a permanent ground, a task America's Protestant millennial mentality and massive agrarian reservoir had protected American intellectuals from facing through most of the nineteenth century.

Nor was the recognition of history as a process of continuous change, interaction, and human management—Wiebe's bureaucratic thought—fundamentally discontinuous with this idealistic historicism. Wiebe notes with some surprise that most of the Progressive intellectuals displayed a penchant for bureaucratic thought within their idealist systems and concludes that they were "eclectic," inadvertently adopting a kind of fluid thinking, which the advent of a bureaucratic society would carry to dominance.[29] But the perception of historical change, as Pocock describes its emergence against the backdrop of Christian and Renaissance conceptions of time, was an awareness that human change in time was creative and carried within itself rational causes of change. It thus included a heightened perception of both qualitative change over the course of human history and natural causes active in the processes of social change. The multi-stage analysis of human society sketched by Adam Ferguson and the attempt by Adam Smith to pick out the moving variables of economic activity and analyze their interaction developed from the same matrix of emerging historicism. It should not therefore be surprising that Progressive intellectuals could develop theories of historical evolution and fluid analyses of social processes.

Arthur F. Bentley is the only Progressive intellectual Wiebe finds wholly given over to bureaucratic thought. His 1908 study, *The Process of Government*, is indeed a thoroughgoing attempt to conceptualize politics as the interaction and adjustment of group pressures. Bentley, however, was schooled in, and developed his perceptions within, Progressive historicism. While still an undergraduate at Johns Hopkins he came under the influence of the historical economist Richard T. Ely and published his first paper, "The Condition of the Western Farmer as Illustrated by the Economic History of a Nebraska Township." Bentley purposely studied only one township so he could penetrate to "the actual economic life of the individual." He took for granted that such a study would be both historical and analytical. In his doctoral dissertation published two years later, Bentley differentiated between genetic and static

DOROTHY ROSS

studies but recognized that the distinction "is a purely logical one . . . made only for purposes of convenience in treatment." Both methods study the same social units and both are legitimate parts of social science; they involve "looking but the opposite ways along the stream of time." Indeed, in his *Process of Government*, he often shifted focus, tracing group formation and pressures back to historically earlier forms in a manner that still bore the marks of three-stage evolutionary history. He attributed his insight into group process to such German historicist thinkers as Marx, Simmel, and Gumplowicz. And he stated that his largest purpose was to construct the "backbone of history":

> We can easily conceive of a solid structure of group relationships as they have developed in historic times becoming known to us, which must inevitably define the fundamental shapes which the history writing that varies with the generations must take, if it is to have meaning and value at all beyond the meaning and value of the most narrowly partisan outcry.

Bentley used a historicist perception of historical process to fashion a solution to the historicist's problem of historical relativity.[30]

If the central impulse of Progressive thought, idealist and bureaucratic alike, was historicist, Wiebe is nonetheless correct to suggest that American social thought was taking a new direction by the end of the period. And Bentley's disenchanted probing for objective units of social process forecast that direction. According to Wiebe, bureaucratic thought was not only fluid and process oriented, it was exclusively so; an ideal direction of history, fixed laws of development, often articulate ends of any kind beyond social process itself, disappeared. I would also emphasize that in the focus on social process, social thought largely severed its connection with the analysis of long-term historical change over time. Although there were important exceptions, like institutional economics and political philosophy, the social science disciplines that emerged by 1920 were largely ahistorical in focus. The real paradox of Progressive thought is that historicism, with its desire to secure values within history, ended in an ahistorical social science that had adopted the objective voice and strove to be value-free. The turn to European historicism ended in an ahistorical and scientistic approach to social thought that has distinguished American social science ever since from the European sciences of man.[31]

The solution of this paradox is hardly within the scope of this paper, but I can point briefly to some of the directions in which the solution may lie. As Wiebe indicated, bureaucratic industrial society lends itself to the production of specialized, technical bodies of thought. It was groups of professionalizing academics who turned social thought into the social sciences. On the intellectual side of the ledger we must take into

THE LIBERAL AND REPUBLICAN TRADITIONS

account the great influence of scientism. If the growing authority of science originally opened the Progressive intellectuals to historicism, the scientific demand for objectivity could ultimately have undermined it. There is also the fact that besides historicism, there already existed strong native traditions of classical economics and philosophical psychology; most of the social science that took firm hold in early–twentieth-century America grew out of these foundations of static social analysis.

Behind these reasons, however, it is tempting to see the shadow of the "Country" mentality stretching into the twentieth century. For it may be no accident that the contracted spheres of technical, process-oriented knowledge left space for the idea of American mission to flourish as myth; that the quest for objectivity echoed the "Country" demand for timeless values, inverting dogmatic moralism into value-free social science; that social scientists chose to pursue lines of ahistorical analysis that had developed during America's millennialist past. There is a great deal more in the American mind than the Atlantic republican tradition, but Pocock's explication of the logic of that tradition projects a long light.

Notes

1. Louis Hartz, *The Liberal Tradition in America: An Interpretation of American Political Thought since the Revolution* (New York: Harcourt, Brace, 1955); J. G. A. Pocock, *The Machiavellian Moment: Florentine Political Thought and the Atlantic Republican Tradition* (Princeton, N.J.: Princeton University Press, 1975).
2. Hartz, *Liberal Tradition*, p. 4.
3. Pocock also assays the impact of the civic humanist tradition on America in "Civic Humanism and Its Role in Anglo-American Thought," in *Politics, Language, and Time: Essays on Political Thought and History* (New York: Atheneum, 1971), and "Virtue and Commerce in the Eighteenth Century," *Journal of Interdisciplinary History* 3 (Summer 1972): 119–34.
4. I will mention only a few of many possible antecedent works: Bernard Bailyn, *The Ideological Origins of the American Revolution* (Cambridge: Harvard University Press, 1967); Gordon S. Wood, *The Creation of the American Republic, 1776–1787* (Chapel Hill: University of North Carolina Press, 1969); Richard Buel, Jr., *Securing the Revolution: Ideology in American Politics, 1789–1815* (Ithaca, N.Y.: Cornell University Press, 1973); and Fred Somkin, *Unquiet Eagle: Memory and Desire in the Idea of American Freedom, 1815–1860* (Ithaca, N.Y.: Cornell University Press, 1967).
5. Marvin Meyers, *The Jacksonian Persuasion* (Stanford, Ca.: Stanford University Press, 1957); Richard Hofstadter, *The Age of Reform* (New York: Alfred A. Knopf, 1955).
6. For example, Henry Nash Smith, *Virgin Land: The American West as Symbol and Myth* (Cambridge: Harvard University Press, 1950); Leo Marx, *The Machine in the Garden: Technology and the Pastoral Ideal in America* (New York: Oxford University Press, 1964); Perry Miller, "The Romantic Dilemma in American Nationalism and the Concept of Nature," (1955) reprinted in Miller, *Nature's*

DOROTHY ROSS

Nation (Cambridge: Harvard University Press, 1967), pp. 197–207. See David W. Noble, *The Eternal Adam and the New World Garden* (New York: Braziller, 1968).

7. Two studies on the Left that claim direct descent from Hartz's analysis of the American liberal mind are Michael Paul Rogin's *Fathers and Children: Andrew Jackson and the Subjugation of the American Indians* (New York: Alfred A. Knopf, 1975), and N. Gordon Levin's *Woodrow Wilson and World Politics: America's Response to War and Revolution* (New York: Oxford University Press, 1968). For this influence, and for an excellent discussion of the historiographical theme of consensus and conflict, see Pope McCorkle, "Getting Right with American Historical Writing" (Senior thesis, Princeton University, June 1977).

8. Robert Kelley, "Ideology and Political Culture from Jefferson to Nixon," *American Historical Review* 82 (June 1977): 531–62.

9. I will mention only three seminal works: Timothy L. Smith, *Revivalism and Social Reform in Mid-Nineteenth Century America* (New York: Abingdon Press, 1957); Alan Heimert, *Religion and the American Mind from the Great Awakening to the Revolution* (Cambridge: Harvard University Press, 1966); and Paul Kleppner, *The Cross of Culture: A Social Analysis of Midwestern Politics, 1850–1900* (New York: Free Press, 1970).

10. Joyce Appleby, "The Social Origins of American Revolutionary Ideology," *Journal of American History* 64 (March 1978): 935–58; Chester McArthur Destler, *American Radicalism, 1865–1901* (New London, Conn.: Connecticut College, 1946); Dorothy Ross, "Socialism and American Liberalism: Academic Social Thought in the 1880's," *Perspectives in American History* 12 (1977–78).

11. For example, Robert Wiebe, *The Search for Order, 1877–1920* (New York: Hill and Wang, 1967), reads the goal of a cooperative commonwealth advocated by such groups as the Knights of Labor and the Nationalists in a wholly retrospective light.

12. See H. Trevor Colbourn, *The Lamp of Experience: Whig History and the Intellectual Origins of the American Revolution* (Chapel Hill: University of North Carolina Press, 1965); David W. Noble, *The Paradox of Progressive Thought* (Minneapolis: University of Minnesota Press, 1958); and idem, *Historians Against History* (Minneapolis: University of Minnesota Press, 1965).

13. Pocock, *Machiavellian Moment*, pp. 523–48.

14. See, for example, David Hall, "The Victorian Connection," *American Quarterly* 27 (December 1975): 561–74; Arthur E. Morgan, *Edward Bellamy* (New York: Columbia University Press, 1944); Charles A. Barker, *Henry George* (New York: Oxford University Press, 1955); Ross, "Socialism and American Liberalism," sections 1, 2, 3.

15. Josiah Strong, *Our Country*, ed. Jurgen Herbst (Cambridge: Harvard University Press, 1963). On the book's influence, see the Herbst introduction, p. ix, and Wiebe, *Search for Order*, p. 44.

16. Strong, *Our Country*, pp. 13–18, 53, 56, 60–65, and *passim*.

17. Ibid., p. 18.

18. Kenneth M. Roemer, *The Obsolete Necessity: America in Utopian Writings, 1888–1900* (Kent, Ohio: Kent State University Press, 1976).

19. Henry George, *Progress and Poverty* (1879; reprint ed., New York: Modern Library, 1938), pp. 538 and 506–43.

20. Ibid., pp. 488, 514.

21. Pocock, *Machiavellian Moment*, pp. 459–60, 493–504.

22. Edward Bellamy, *Looking Backward* (1888; reprint ed., New York: Modern Library, 1942).

23. Strong, *Our Country*, pp. 144, 147.

24. Richmond Laurin Hawkins, *Auguste Comte and the United States (1816–1853)* (Cambridge: Harvard University Press, 1936); idem, *Positivism in the United States (1853–1861)* (Cambridge: Harvard University Press, 1938).

25. See recent British views of Spencer's influence: J. D. Y. Peel, *Herbert Spencer*

THE LIBERAL AND REPUBLICAN TRADITIONS

(New York: Basic Books, 1971), ch. 7; Willard Wolfe, *From Radicalism to Socialism* (New Haven, Conn.: Yale University Press, 1975), pp. 188–92, 262–64, 268–70.

26. John L. Thomas's "Utopia for an Urban Age: Henry George, Henry Demarest Lloyd, and Edward Bellamy," *Perspectives in American History* 6 (1972): 135–66, discussed the utopian cast of mind of this period as "the product of a romantic liberalism *in extremis* and on the defensive." Morton White's *Social Thought in America: the Revolt Against Formalism* (Boston: Beacon Press, 1957) noted the progressive intellectuals' new insight into historicism and organicism.

27. Wiebe, *Search for Order*, ch. 6 and pp. 140–41, 145.

28. Noble, *Paradox of Progressive Thought* and *Historians Against History*.

29. Wiebe, *Search for Order*, pp. 145, 151–52.

30. Bentley, "The Condition of the Western Farmer . . ." in *Johns Hopkins University Studies in Historical and Political Science* 11th ser., nos. 7–8, 1893, p. 9; idem, "The Units of Investigation in the Social Sciences," (Ph.D. diss., The Johns Hopkins University, 1895), pp. 107, 113; idem, *Process of Government* (Chicago: University of Chicago Press, 1908), pp. 319–20, 465–76, 481–82.

31. John Higham with Leonard Krieger and Felix Gilbert, *History* (Englewood Cliffs, N.J.: Prentice-Hall, 1965); Dorothy Ross, "The Development of the Social Sciences," in *Knowledge in American Society, 1870–1920*, ed. Alexandra Oleson (Baltimore, Md.: The Johns Hopkins University Press, 1979).

DETERMINISTIC IMPLICATIONS
OF INTELLECTUAL HISTORY

⊂══⊃ ◖ ◗ ⊂══⊃

THOMAS L. HASKELL

To have no opinion on the question of free will and determinism is nowadays thought to be a sign of mature professionalism among historians and social scientists. Tolstoy thought all serious minds would be drawn toward this eternal puzzle, but we prefer to leave such intractable problems to the professional philosophers, on the one hand, or to college sophomores, meeting in late-night dormitory bull sessions, on the other. Try as we may, however, we can never really escape the question, for one cannot say anything about human affairs without making statements about causation and responsibility that imply an opinion about the extent and character of human freedom. Those who read our books and hear our lectures form an impression of our opinion, and perhaps adopt it for their own, however little thought we may have given to it.

The tacit lessons about freedom and determinism that we all teach are as diverse as our individual intellectual temperaments, but some rough generalizations seem in order. If all historians and social scientists could be placed on a spectrum running from "most deterministic" at one end, to "most voluntaristic" at the other, no doubt historians would be found scattered all along its length, but the scattering probably would not be random: historians would tend to cluster near the voluntaristic end of the spectrum. The tendency of historians to convey tacitly to their students a comparatively voluntaristic message, and social scientists a more deterministic one, follows naturally from the prominence that historians give to narration and the unique or nonrecurring aspects of human affairs, and from the stress that social scientists typically place on lawlike regularities.

Not all historians are voluntarists, though, and within the ranks of historians it would not be surprising to find that some of those closest to the deterministic end of the spectrum were practitioners of intellectual history. Moreover, it seems likely to me that the field of intellectual history will take on an even stronger deterministic cast in the years ahead, as many of its practitioners follow the path that Thomas S. Kuhn staked out in his *The Structure of Scientific Revolutions*. Just exactly where that path lies is open to debate, but, as I will try to show, those

132

DETERMINISTIC IMPLICATIONS

who follow it can scarcely avoid casting human affairs in a decidedly deterministic light. My purpose in this paper is not to oppose this deterministic current in intellectual history or to offer any extended defense of it, but simply to show that it exists, to show that Kuhn's influence is likely to reinforce it, and to examine both its sources and the dangers that it may entail.

Determinism is not a comfortable doctrine and we intellectual historians had better be aware of its dangers before we embrace it any more firmly than we already have. A full flowering of the deterministic implications of intellectual history is likely to strain the already somewhat fragile relations between intellectual historians and the fundamentally voluntaristic mainstream of their profession, and to disappoint those practitioners of intellectual history who have celebrated the autonomy of ideas and conceived of their discipline as a bastion against materialism and behaviorism. Even those of us who are not greatly moved by considerations such as these may find that determinism drives a bitter wedge between our double roles as researchers and teachers. A deterministic frame of mind comes most easily when we are pursuing the causes of events through ever-deeper layers of historical context, but when we leave our studies and enter the classroom, thereby assuming a degree of responsibility for the attitudes and conduct of our students, we may wish to retreat from the fatalistic implications of our research.

The dangers posed by determinism were poignantly illustrated in an article titled "No-Fault Guilt-Free History" that appeared not long ago on the opinion and editorial page of the *New York Times*. The author, Professor Richard M. Hunt, had recently taught a course called "Moral Dilemmas in a Repressive Society: Nazi Germany" to 100 Harvard undergraduates. He was horrified by the depressingly fatalistic conclusions that his students expressed in their papers and exams. "I read comments and questions such as these," said Hunt:

> "In the last analysis what else could the average citizens of these little towns have done but vote for a dynamic leader like Hitler?" "Given the desperate circumstance of 1930 it was inevitable that the Nazis would come to power." "After all nobody in 1933 believed the Nazis would really lead the country into war." "When the regime succeeded in controlling public opinion through censorship of the press, radio and public speeches, how could anyone disbelieve Hitler's promise of peace, full employment, a "reborn Germany"?" "And with the ever present threat of Gestapo terror, who would dare to speak out and resist? Would you? Would I? Probably not!"[1]

This, said Hunt, is "deterministic thinking." It leads to what Hunt calls a "no-fault" view of history: "Since most choices of many people were wrapped up in extenuating circumstances, since the entrapments of the

THOMAS L. HASKELL

regime took place so slowly and so reasonably, and since the ultimate confrontation with the Nazi evil came so late in the day, then who is to say where and when and with whom real responsibility lies?" When he began to suspect that his students might have pardoned or even aquitted most of the defendents at Nuremburg, Hunt resolved that he was "through teaching no-fault history." Next time he teaches the course, he says, he hopes "to stress more strongly my own belief in the contingencies, the open-endedness of history. Somehow I have got to convey the meaning of moral decisions and their relations to significant outcomes. Most important, I want to point out that single acts of individuals and strong stands of institutions at an early date do make a difference in the long run." What he wishes at all costs to defeat is the "despairingly deterministic view of the past and the present" that too many students now hold.[2]

Hunt, like most historians, seems to have in mind no very exact doctrine when he calls a particular view of human affairs "deterministic." Distressing though such imprecision may be to philosophers, the problem of determinism that historians face really does hinge on basic impressions rather than on fine logic. The issue is always one of degree: it is simply whether a particular account of events does or does not have an air of inevitability about it, whether events are or are not seen to flow mainly from the conscious choices of thinking individuals who might have chosen other than they did. As Hunt's plans for revising the tone of the course suggest, the impression conveyed by a particular account derives as much from its rhetorical or dramaturgical structure as from the evidence it cites or the causal relations it specifies. A philosopher of the "compatibilist" school might advise Hunt to acquaint his students with any of the various arguments that seek to show that determinism is compatible with, or even indispensable to, the idea of moral responsibility.[3] But one suspects that this would not satisfy Hunt, for no delicate argument could overcome the primary impression of events moving out of individual control.

The case against determinism is not hard to make, and I imagine that most historians will enthusiastically endorse Hunt's condemnation.[4] The charges are serious, and they may in fact be unanswerable; in any case, my purpose is not to answer them here, but rather to show in the coming pages that we intellectual historians who work along Kuhnian lines will be vulnerable to similar charges, and had better begin preparing our answers. One brief observation about the alleged evils of determinism suggests itself at this juncture, however.

The danger that students will draw fatalistic conclusions from a deterministic account of human affairs is genuine. But there is an equally

DETERMINISTIC IMPLICATIONS

serious danger that a more voluntaristic account will lull them into a false confidence that their capacity to act morally is independent of circumstance. Certainly we would be doing them no favor if we left them with the cocksure impression that if they had been citizens of Nazi Germany they would have seen clearly what to do and would easily have found the strength to do it. As teachers, all of us want to do what we can to prepare our students to act responsibly in crisis, but it is not obvious that we insure this result by avoiding determinism.

Do we prepare our students best by stressing the openness and contingency of history, by lingering over the critical moments when an individual act of heroism might have turned the tide? Or is it conceivable that we would prepare them better by presenting a darker picture, stressing the extreme difficulties of resistance and asking them to recognize that under the pressure of circumstance people no worse than themselves have consented to unspeakable crimes? Do we accomplish our goal best by using history to persuade students of the transforming power of the moral act? Or by teaching them that the moral act ought to be undertaken, not because of its probable success, but sometimes in spite of its almost certain failure? Does not the very idea of courage entail determinism in the historian's loose sense of a flow of events running contrary to the actor's will?

I feel sure that Professor Hunt would agree that the answers to these questions are not self-evident; yet to the extent they are not, determinism (as distinct from fatalism) is not quite the bogyman he makes it out to be. Sartre gave us the name "bad faith" for the exaggeration of necessity, the pretense that one's conduct is determined when in fact it is freely chosen. We need a more, memorable label than "unrealistic" for the opposite error, the exaggeration of man's freedom. If intellectual history has consistently deterministic implications, as I shall argue it does, that is a problem, and it is one worth our careful attention, but it need not deprive our work of redeeming value.

Sixteen years have gone by since *The Structure of Scientific Revolutions* was published and we seem now to be on the trailing slope of the wave that carried it so far. The naysayers who never saw what the fuss was about are growing bolder, and I even know enthusiasts whose eyes now glaze over at the name "Kuhn" and whose throats constrict involuntarily when they try to say *paradigm*. Kuhn's critics have exposed important limitations of his thesis. But if provocativeness and wide influence are signs of importance, as I suppose they undeniably are, I see

THOMAS L. HASKELL

no alternative but for all of us—yeasayers and naysayers alike—to admit that this book remains one of the two or three most important works in intellectual history of our time.

Admittedly, Kuhn does not call himself an intellectual historian, and his book is so heavily analytical that by some strict definitions it is not a *history* of anything, not even of scientific revolutions. But for my present purpose neither objection seems germane. The book is certainly about the historicity of ideas, even if it is not a history of any particular set of them, and if Kuhn's allegiance is to the history and philosophy of science, that field is logically, if not institutionally, part and parcel of the larger field of intellectual history. As to the ability of the book to provoke fruitful debate, I need not spell out the remarkable impact that Kuhn has had on the history, philosophy, and sociology of science; on the history of economics, political science, psychology, and the other social scientific disciplines; on any number of different fields of historical investigation; and now even on social thought. Few works in intellectual history have ever been so widely read and discussed both inside and outside the discipline.[5]

The extraordinary reception given the book suggests that Kuhn has done something right, and we fellow workers in intellectual history ought to ask what it is. The point of ascertaining the essential nature of his achievement is not simply to follow him, but also to learn where not to follow. Kuhn's fragile and delicately balanced thesis has proven unusually susceptible to misinterpretation by foes and to heavy-handed misuse by ardent friends. It is a difficult question of interpretation to know which aspects of his achievement are of general relevance and which are specific to the history of science or to the particular questions he addressed. His book probably will exert a lasting influence on the writing of intellectual history whether we wish it to or not; selecting what is suitable for emulation is the task that all of us now face.

My own conviction is that the most essential and broadly relevant aspects of Kuhn's achievement are a good deal more primitive and elementary than has sometimes been thought. What he did, he did elegantly, but for the most part his novelty consists in carrying some of the conventional predilections and techniques of intellectual history to a new extreme and applying them where they seemed least applicable. Emulating these aspects of Kuhn's work will come easily to most intellectual historians, for we can pretty much continue doing what we have always done. In fact, intellectual historians of all methodological persuasions ought to be cheered by this book's success, for it not only demonstrates the indispensability of intellectual history to other realms of scholarship, it also reaffirms the explanatory fruitfulness of the field's most conventional practices. What is most problematic in Kuhn's work lies in its

DETERMINISTIC IMPLICATIONS

deterministic implications, but in this regard, too, Kuhn has merely forced to the surface an aspect of intellectual history that ought to have been obvious from the start.

To isolate the essential nature of Kuhn's achievement we must begin with his now-familiar notion of the paradigm, though we shall not want to end there. By *paradigm* Kuhn originally meant a concrete scientific achievement on the order of Copernicus's heliocentric theory or Newton's *Principia* that is sufficiently unprecedented and open-ended to serve as "a locus of professional commitment," a seed about which there crystallizes a community of researchers and a research tradition.[6] The paradigm is the achievement itself, which logically precedes and is a good deal more mysterious in its functioning than any of the specific rules, concepts, laws, theories, or points of view that may be derived from it. It supplies the consensual basis for a community of researchers and guides their " normal" work by posing problems for solution and assuring them that a solution exists. But no paradigm can master the richness of reality. Normal scientific research undertaken in accordance with a paradigm necessarily generates anomalies, the accumulation of which leads to a sense of crisis and eventually perhaps to a "scientific revolution," which is the wholesale shift of community loyalty from one paradigm to another. A new tradition of normal research then begins on the basis of the new paradigm, and practitioners who cling to the older one are ignored or dismissed as cranks.

As Kuhn originally formulated the concept, a paradigm was a rare and exalted thing. Real scientists possessed them, but laymen and the practitioners of immature fields of science did not. Kuhn has since backed away from this rigorous formulation, and he now invites us to use the word loosely so that even immature fields of inquiry, or unscientific ones like art and philosophy, may also be said to have paradigms. "What changes with the transition to maturity is not the presence of a paradigm, but rather its nature," Kuhn now says.[7] Moreover, he has proposed that paradigms be regarded as only one of several elements in the "disciplinary matrix" that provides the consensual basis for a community of inquiry.[8]

If virtually all fields of knowledge may be said to possess paradigms, then it seems doubtful to me that the term can any longer serve a good purpose (except, paradoxically, in the history of natural science, because there the existence of a "succession of tradition-bound periods punctuated by non-cumulative breaks" is still debatable, as it is not in other fields).[9] Intellectual historians presumably have always known that explanations can make sense only within a given framework of assumptions; that in most fields there exist competing "schools of thought"; and that both orthodoxy and innovation play an important role in the development of knowledge. If the notion of paradigm is so diluted that it becomes merely a rubric under which we subsume all of our familiar "frameworks," "schools," and "orthodoxies," then we invite the just complaint of Paul Conkin that we are pretentiously applying new labels to old bottles.[10]

But looking for paradigms is not the only, or the most penetrating, lesson to draw from Kuhn's work. More important, I believe, are three quite elementary insights that may be disentangled both from the concept of paradigms and from the history of science and put to use quite generally in intellectual history. None of them is foreign to the customary ways of intellectual historians.

First there is Kuhn's radical contextualism. History has always cultivated a stronger sensitivity to context than its more abstractive sister disciplines in the social sciences, but Kuhn goes further than usual and insists on the importance of contextual considerations where they hitherto have seemed irrelevant. By doing so he throws down the gauntlet to those historians who persist, in spite of what would seem to be the inherent tendency of their discipline, to read the past as no more than a series of imperfect approximations to the present. If, as he says, discarded views of nature such as "aristotelian dynamics, phlogistic chemistry, or caloric thermodynamics . . . were, as a whole, neither less scientific nor more the product of human idiosyncrasy than those current today," then surely all of us must adopt an equally tolerant and respectful attitude—though not necessarily an admiring one—toward discarded social theories, antiquated lifestyles, and abandoned frameworks of moral and ethical judgment.[11] Kuhn presents us with a limiting case that seems to me quite impossible to circumvent: if Whiggishness does not work in the history of science, it works nowhere, for science is the name we give to those fields of human endeavor that seem most unambiguously to progress.

To carry out in all areas of intellectual history the "historiographic revolution" of contextualism that Kuhn hoped to stimulate in the history of science would be no easy task. It would require major changes in the way we approach our work and could result in drastic revisions to our understanding of the past. Historians might well have to subordinate their role as moral critics to the mission of sympathetic understanding, whenever the two came into conflict, as often they would. And while it is one thing to suspend judgment in order sympathetically to reconstruct the intellectual system of which caloric thermodynamics was a part, it will be quite another to do the same for ideas justifying slavery or the patriarchal household.[12]

Bland neutrality in the face of evil is not what we want, and if that were the upshot of Kuhnian contextualism I would reject it. But as long

DETERMINISTIC IMPLICATIONS

as Kuhn's example encourages historians to suspend moral judgment long enough to achieve full understanding of alien viewpoints, and discourages them from being provincial boosters of their own politics or moral code, I applaud it.

Another aspect of Kuhn's work that seems suitable for importation into other areas of intellectual history is his refusal to segregate intellectual from social history. I deliberately phrase this cautiously, saying "refusal to segregate" rather than "insistence on the unification of" social and intellectual history, because Kuhn's legacy in this respect seems to me divided and ambiguous. Just how ambiguous can be shown by trying to classify *The Structure of Scientific Revolutions* according to those tired but unavoidable stereotypes that pit Lovejoy, internal analysis, and the "history of ideas" against Curti, external analysis, and "intellectual history." One's first impulse is to classify Kuhn as an unabashed externalist, for only this label would seem to accord with his radical contextualism. Moreover, Kuhn's analysis is in fact profoundly sociological. A main purpose of his book is to shift emphasis away from the purely intellectual confirmation/falsification procedures that control our usual image of science, and to stress instead a brute social fact: "Competition between segments of the scientific community is the only historical process that actually results in the rejection of one previously accepted theory or in the adoption of another."[13] Now in our unguarded, unsophisticated moments, even if we know better, we like to think that scientists are people whose thought is controlled almost entirely by its object, and hardly at all by such seeming irrelevancies as the social situation in which the thinker happens to find himself. So it might seem that Kuhn has offered us another limiting case: if, in order to understand the thought of scientists, we must take into account the internal dynamics of the communities in which they work, then surely we must pay the same close attention to social relations when we try to understand the thought of nonscientists.

Though I am inclined to believe that this proposition is true, I do not believe that Kuhn can be cited as evidence for its validity. The history of science cannot serve as a limiting case on this occasion because of the peculiar nature of a scientific community. Such communities are extraordinarily insulated from the rest of society by virtue of their esoteric concerns.[14] They are at the same time intensely competitive internally, so that anything approaching a consensus within them wields unusual power over the mind of each individual member. If there is anything that Kuhn has taught us, it is to appreciate the uniqueness and the efficiency of these social engines for the suppression of idiosyncrasy and the generation of consensus. Where such dense communities do not exist (and there are none in most areas of thought) it is not at all clear that

THOMAS L. HASKELL

Kuhn has any useful message for us about the relation between thought and social setting. And where such communities *do* exist, Kuhn seems quite content to study the dynamics of the community in almost complete isolation from the surrounding society.[15] This is not a Lovejoyean "internalism," for certain social facts are held to be highly relevant—but the range of relevant ones is not large. I conclude, then, that Kuhn's example sensitizes us to the fact that ideas, like politicians, cannot survive without constituents, and that ideas can, in some cases, be constitutive of human communities, but he leaves wide open all the most difficult questions about the exact ways in which social circumstances may influence thought.[16]

What makes Kuhn so important to intellectual historians is not his notion of the paradigm or his strategy of radical contextualism or his openness to the possibility that conceptual change in science is shaped by social factors. Rather, his chief importance lies in a still more primitive insight: namely, that mankind's most fundamental assumptions—the "paradigmatic" ones—are normally immune to the experiential evidence that might modify or falsify them.

Intellectual history has repeatedly taught that the deepest layers of assumption in human belief systems are so tenacious that they shape experience far more often than they are shaped by it. The lesson is not new, but never before has it been taught so forcefully.

Kuhn's demonstration of the superior power that preconception and assumption ordinarily wield over the supposed "brute facts" of experience carries special force because he applied it where it would seem least applicable: to scientists, those members of society who most deliberately and systematically submit their preconceptions to the tests of experience. There is no act more characteristic of the scientist than the experiment, the controlled experience deliberately contrived to bring the full weight of empirical evidence to bear upon a specific assumption. Yet during periods of "normal science," says Kuhn, the scientist relies totally on the operative paradigm in his field. From it he deduces hypotheses for empirical examination that, if found wanting, are freely modified or discarded; here theory dutifully submits to experience. But the overarching paradigm that generates theory and confers meaning on the scientist's experimental enterprise normally remains impervious to experience. Except in revolutionary moments, it is not tested. It controls experience rather than being controlled by it. It determines what the scientist will construe as falsifying evidence, but it is not itself susceptible to falsification.

No other member of society is as eager as the scientist to risk his assumptions against potentially falsifying experience. Even the scientist is open to reversals of opinion only in comparatively impersonal, tech-

DETERMINISTIC IMPLICATIONS

nical matters. If even the scientist is normally prisoner of his most fundamental assumptions, and if his intellectual confinement persists even in those technical areas that he most conscientiously exposes to criticism and to empirical testing, then what of the rest of us, in the everyday routines of life? How free are we, really, to change our minds and to learn from experience?

These questions bring into sharper focus the source of the extraordinarily deterministic undercurrents that flow through *The Structure of Scientific Revolutions* and account, I suspect, both for the book's great popularity and the fierce repugnance felt toward it in certain quarters. These questions also point up the principal relevance of the book to intellectual historians working in fields other than the history of science. Kuhn's achievement consists mainly in providing us with two limiting cases: (1) if a strongly anti-Whiggish contextualist program is appropriate in the history of science, then we must conclude that it is utterly indispensable in other fields, and (2) (and still more fundamentally), if even scientists are firmly tethered to their deepest-lying assumptions, as Kuhn suggests, then so is everyone else. It follows that historians ought to assign a high priority indeed to the exploration of these controlling presuppositions that shape thought, and thus behavior, in every sphere of life.

Now there is nothing new about the kind of inquiry into presuppositions that is made to seem so important by Kuhn's limiting cases. Kuhn's major contribution has been to "freshen the charter" for the enterprise that intellectual historians have been engaged in for a long time. In 1957, when John C. Greene tried to sum up the best advice about "Objectives and Methods in Intellectual History," drawing especially on the precepts of Weber, Whitehead, Lovejoy, and Perry Miller, he concluded that "a capacity to penetrate to implicit major premises" was the talent intellectual historians needed most. "The primary function of the intellectual historian," said Greene, "is to delineate the presuppositions of thought in given historical epochs and to explain the changes which those presuppositions undergo from epoch to epoch. . . . It is the peculiar province of the intellectual historian to search for and describe those most general ideas, or patterns of ideas, which inform the thought of an age, define its intellectual problems, and indicate the direction in which solutions are to be sought."[17] One could go on for pages showing that intellectual historians have always tried to "read between the lines," to pick out those assumptions that seemed so fundamental to contemporaries that they were taken for granted and required little or no explicit comment. This objective has been pursued with varying intensity and success by all the warring schools in intellectual history. Loyalty to it cuts across the internalist-externalist divide; it unites the myth and symbol school of

THOMAS L. HASKELL

literary historians with their most skeptical critics; and it is relevant to students of both low and high culture.

Although quarrying for presuppositions is old hat to intellectual historians, I am not aware that they have ever devoted much attention to the method itself. Given our penchant for this particular approach, it is curious that we have never asked what the method of presuppositions itself presupposes about the nature of thought and conceptual change. Nor—as far as my hasty search discloses—have intellectual historians before Stephen Toulmin and Quentin Skinner even cited the philosophical work that bears most directly on this question: R. G. Collingwood's *An Essay on Metaphysics.*[18] By taking a quick look at Collingwood's work and Toulmin's criticism of it, we can put some finishing touches on this portrait of the deterministic implications of intellectual history.

Collingwood set out in the *Essay* to redefine metaphysics as a "science of absolute presuppositions."[19] If metaphysics is ever reformed along the rather idiosyncratic lines that Collingwood laid out, it will become a historical discipline that, up to a point, corresponds closely with the practices of intellectual historians. Collingwood began by observing that although we are not ordinarily aware of it, "every statement that anybody ever makes is made in answer to a question."[20] To say of a horizontally stretched rope that "it is a clothesline" is, it appears on thoughtful analysis, to answer the question "What is that thing for?" Having noted that statements necessarily stem from questions (seldom consciously asked at the time, though logically obvious on reflection), Collingwood next observed that "every question involves a presupposition."[21] Indeed, every question stems directly from one and only one presupposition, though indirectly it may involve many more that are sequentially related to it. So to ask "What does that mark mean?" directly presupposes that the inscription on the paper "means something," and indirectly presupposes that the mark is "not accidental" and that it is a mark rather than an imperfection in the paper or a speck of dirt. The questions one asks depend on the presuppositions one makes, and a given question cannot arise without the logically and temporally prior existence of the appropriate presupposition. "To say that a question 'does not arise'," said Collingwood, "is the ordinary English way of saying that it involves a presupposition which is not in fact being made."[22]

The power of a presupposition to cause certain questions to "arise" Collingwood called its "logical efficacy." The notion of logical efficacy is a distinctive feature of Collingwood's analysis, for he held that the "logical efficacy of a supposition does not depend upon the truth of what is supposed, or even on its being thought true, but only on its being supposed."[23] As Stephen Toulmin points out, this notion gives Collingwood's analysis an unorthodox character: "Most recent philosophers had

DETERMINISTIC IMPLICATIONS

thought of our concepts as organized into axiomatic' systems: that is, into systems the *truth* of whose general principles implies—and is in turn reinforced by—the *truth* of the specific propositions deduced from them."[24] But Collingwood thought that this image of the way we think did justice only to pure mathematics. Toulmin summarizes Collingwood's rival scheme as follows:

> Our concepts form not axiomatic systems, but systems of "presuppositions"; and the logical relations between propositions on different levels of generality are not truth-relations but meaning-relations. Thus specific questions either "arise" or "do not arise" depending on what more general principles are assumed, and broader assertions are related to narrower ones, not as axioms to theorems, but rather as presuppositions to consequential questions. So it is not the truth of general principles that determines—or is determined by—the truth of particular statements; instead, specific statements rely on the validity and applicability of more general doctrines for their *meaning*.[25]

The task of the metaphysician in Collingwood's scheme is to untangle the jumbled chains of statements, questions, and presuppositions that appear in everyday thought—to straighten them out, separately articulate each link in its logical, not natural, sequence, and to proceed upwards through the conceptual hierarchy, finally reaching its summit, the "absolute presuppositions," from which these chains of thought spring.

The absolute presupposition, unlike all the ones subordinate to it in the chain, presupposes nothing. All the others, which Collingwood calls "relative presuppositions," stand "relatively to one question as its presupposition and relatively to another question as its answer."[26] But an "absolute presupposition is one which stands relatively to all questions to which it is related, as a presupposition, never as an answer."[27] Like Kuhn's paradigm, it is constitutive of the meaning of all questions asked under its auspices, but there is no way in normal discourse meaningfully to ask whether it is true or false. It is a supposition on the order of "light ray" in optics or "inertia" in dynamics, which neither admits nor requires verification.[28] If you aggressively interrogate a worker in any field of inquiry, forcing him back on his most fundamental assumptions, he may finally "blow up right in your face," said Collingwood, "because you have put your finger on one of his absolute presuppositions, and people are apt to be ticklish in their absolute presuppositions."[29]

The highest part of the metaphysician's work is the most historical. Having isolated several different clusters of absolute presuppositions, says Collingwood, he should compare and contrast them, and then finally go on "to find out on what occasions and by what processes one of them has turned into another."[30]

Provoked by a friend who complained that his scheme based all in-

THOMAS L. HASKELL

tellectual endeavors on irrational "changes of fashion," Collingwood observed in an illuminating footnote that

> People are not ordinarily aware of their absolute presuppositions . . . and are not, therefore, thus aware of changes in them; such a change, therefore, cannot be a matter of choice. Nor is there anything frivolous or superficial about it. It is the most radical change a man can undergo, and entails the abandonment of all his most firmly established habits and standards for thought and action.
>
> Why, asks my friend, do such changes happen? Briefly, because the absolute presuppositions of any given society, at any given phase of its history, form a structure which is subject to "strains" . . . of greater or less intensity, which are "taken up" . . . in various ways, but never annihilated. If the strains are too great, the structure collapses and is replaced by another, which will be a modification of the old with the destructive strain removed; a modification not consciously devised but created by a process of unconscious thought.[31]

The similarity of Collingwood's and Kuhn's accounts of conceptual change is readily apparent, and both are sharply condemned by Stephen Toulmin for their determinism.[32] Toulmin's zeal to vindicate the rationality of science has led him to be rather strident in his criticism of Kuhn, but surely he is correct to raise the issue of determinism, and his criticism of Collingwood throws that issue into bold relief.[33] The problem with Collingwood's account is this, says Toulmin:

> Do we make the change from one constellation of absolute presuppositions to another because we have reasons for doing so; or do we do so only because certain causes compel us to? Are questions about the "modifications" in our intellectual "structures" to be answered in terms of reasons, considerations, arguments, and justifications—that is in terms of rational categories? Or must they be answered, rather, in terms of forces, causes, compulsions, and explanations—that is, in terms of "causal" categories?[34]

Collingwood supplies no clear answer to these questions. Their either-or character does not do justice to the subtlety of Kuhn's position in regard to them, but they nonetheless point to a nagging difficulty at the heart of his analysis. When all is said and done, Kuhn really does not claim to know exactly why people shift their loyalties from one paradigm to another. How paradigmatic assumptions can withstand anomalous and contrary evidence for so long, and then so suddenly fall, remains a mystery. There is therefore more than a grain of truth to Toulmin's claims that Kuhn's analysis really is not a theory of conceptual change at all (at least, it sheds more light on continuity than change) and that Kuhn's book could have been titled not *The Structure of Scientific Revolutions*, but *Revolutions in Scientific Structure*.[35] Although developments leading up to paradigm shift may possess a structure, the mysterious revolutionary moment itself would seem by definition to lack it.

The possibility of accounting either for Kuhn's paradigm shifts or Collingwood's changes in absolute presuppositions mainly by reference to "reasons" rather than "causes" seems quite remote. Of course the two categories are not mutually exclusive, and most accounts will refer to both. But it appears likely that what the method of presuppositions itself presupposes is profoundly deterministic, at least in the historian's loose sense of the word, and perhaps in a more rigorous sense as well.[36]

⊂⊃ ◗ ◖ ⊂⊃

As Professor Hunt's vow to avoid historical determinism suggests, our revulsion over the horrors of Nazi Germany is one of the principal anchors of the twentieth-century mind. However strong the currents of relativism may run, however tempting it may be to accommodate oneself to them, we know that we cannot permit that anchor to break loose: that evil was not relative, but absolute, its perpetrators not merely determined reflexes of their environment, but also morally responsible human beings.

Our eagerness to keep the anchor firmly set should not, however, lead us to admire only voluntaristic accounts of human affairs. The primary obligation of the history profession is to make sense of the past, and in carrying out that mission we ought to be concerned not only to sensitize our readers and students to the dangers of "bad faith," but also to the dangers of unrealistic exaggerations of individual autonomy. If intellectual historians tend toward a comparatively deterministic view of human affairs, that may be no defect but an advantage if it lends balance to a profession otherwise inclined toward voluntarism. One might on that account even welcome a broader alliance under the rubric of "social and intellectual history" of all those historians whose curiosity centers not on events, but on the circumstances underlying and shaping events, regardless of whether the circumstances are social or intellectual in character.

Historians specializing in the more deterministic aspects of human affairs may have to come up with better replies to their critics than I am now able to supply, but the very least we can ask for is tolerance. Tolerance is not always a virtue, especially in intellectual matters, where it often masks shoddy thinking. But when people disagree about something so far-reaching and so unlikely of final resolution as the problem of free will, tolerance and coexistence are the best we can hope for.

Niels Bohr speculated that the rival accounts of human affairs given by voluntarists and determinists reflected a complementarity no less pro-

THOMAS L. HASKELL

found and no less insoluble than the rival accounts that physicists give of the nature of light as a wave and as a particle phenomenon.[37] Alfred North Whitehead seems to have thought the dilemma less deeply fixed in the nature of things and more a product of transient confusion. In Western thought, he said, "A scientific realism, based on mechanism, is conjoined with an unwavering belief in the world of men and the higher animals as being composed of self-determining organisms. This radical inconsistency at the basis of modern thought accounts for much that is half-hearted and wavering in our civilization. It would be going too far to say that it distracts thought. It enfeebles it, by reason of the inconsistency lurking in the background."[38]

If Bohr was right, the voluntaristic and the deterministic perspectives are equally worthy of respect, and the historical profession would seem therefore to be obliged to offer the public both kinds of interpretation in equal measure. Even if Bohr was wrong and we can look forward with Whitehead to the ultimate resolution of this "radical inconsistency," we can be confident that the resolution will not come from the pen of an historian. Consequently, regardless of who was right, Bohr or Whitehead, the worst error for the historical profession would be to close the door prematurely on either voluntarism or determinism.

Notes

1. Richard M. Hunt, "No-Fault Guilt-Free History," *New York Times*, 16 February 1976, p. 19.
2. Ibid.
3. See, for example, Moritz Schlick, "When Is a Man Responsible?" and R. E. Hobart (pseud. for Dickinson Miller), "Free Will as Involving Determinism and Inconceivable without It," in *Free Will and Determinism*, ed. Bernard Berofsky (New York: Harper & Row, 1966). Especially relevant for historians are the discussions of causation in H. L. A. Hart and A. M. Honoré, *Causation and the Law* (London: Oxford University Press, 1959), and Joel Feinberg, "Causing Voluntary Actions," in his *Doing and Deserving: Essays in the Theory of Moral Responsibility* (Princeton, N.J.: Princeton University Press, 1970).
4. A powerful hostility toward determinism would seem to be the basis for Jacques Barzun's popular tirades against psychohistory, though I must report that when I suggested as much to Professor Barzun at the end of a public lecture at Rice University in 1976, he denied it and labeled the suggestion "ad hominem." See Jacques Barzun, *Clio and the Doctors: Psycho-History Quanto-History and History* (Chicago: University of Chicago Press, 1974).
5. David A. Hollinger's article, "T. S. Kuhn's Theory of Science and Its Implications for History," *American Historical Review* 78 (April 1974): 370–93, contains—in addition to its valuable discussion of Kuhn's "sense of development" and his "sense of validity"—a splendid guide to the literature spawned by Kuhn up through 1972. See also Martin Bronfenbrenner, "The 'Structure of Revolutions' in Economic Thought," *History of Political Economy* 3 (Spring 1971): 136–51; R. D. Collison Black, A. W. Coats, and Craufurd D. W. Good-

DETERMINISTIC IMPLICATIONS

win, eds., *The Marginal Revolution in Economics: Interpretation and Evaluation* (Durham, N.C.: Duke University Press, 1973); Richard J. Bernstein, *The Restructuring of Social and Political Theory* (New York: Harcourt Brace Jovanovich, 1976); Anthony Giddens, *New Rules of Sociological Method: A Positive Critique of Interpretive Sociologies* (New York: Basic Books, 1976).

6. Thomas S. Kuhn, *The Structure of Scientific Revolutions*, rev. ed. (1962; Chicago: University of Chicago Press, 1970), p. 11. This paragraph and several other passages in the following pages appear in slightly different form in Thomas L. Haskell, *The Emergence of Professional Social Science: The American Social Science Association and the Nineteenth-Century Crisis of Authority* (Urbana: University of Illinois Press, 1977), pp. 19–23.

7. Kuhn, *Structure*, p. 179.

8. Ibid., p. 182.

9. Ibid., p. 208.

10. Paul K. Conkin, "Intellectual History: Past, Present, and Future," in *The Future of History: Essays in the Vanderbilt University Centennial Symposium*, ed. Charles F. Delzell (Nashville: Vanderbilt University Press, 1977), p. 121.

11. Kuhn, *Structure*, p. 2; Hollinger, "Kuhn's Theory of Science," p. 389.

12. John Higham, "Beyond Consensus: The Historian as Moral Critic," in his *Writing American History: Essays on Modern Scholarship* (Bloomington: Indiana University Press, 1970), pp. 138–56. John Dunn suggests that history may be Whig as to choice of subject, while Tory as to truth: "The Identity of the History of Ideas," *Philosophy* 43 (April 1968): 98.

13. Kuhn, *Structure*, p. 8.

14. Ibid., p. 164.

15. T. S. Kuhn, "The Relations between History and History of Science," in *Historical Studies Today*, ed. Felix Gilbert and S. R. Graubard (New York: Norton, 1971), pp. 158–92, esp. pp. 168–70; idem, "Mathematical vs. Experimental Traditions in the Development of Physical Science," *Journal of Interdisciplinary History* 7 (Summer 1976): 3.

16. Kuhn is credited with somewhat more than this by other scholars. See Robert F. Berkhofer, Jr., "Does History Have a Future? The Challenge of New Ways of Understanding Past Human Behavior for Traditional Historical Analysis," (Paper delivered at the Annual Meeting of the Organization of American Historians, April 1974), p. 11; and J. G. A. Pocock, *Politics, Language, and Time: Essays on Political Thought and History* (New York: Atheneum, 1971), pp. 14–41.

17. John C. Greene, "Objectives and Methods in Intellectual History," *Mississippi Valley Historical Review* 44 (June 1957): 60, 59.

18. Stephen E. Toulmin, *Human Understanding*, (Princeton, N.J.: Princeton University Press, 1972), 1: 65–85; Quentin Skinner, "Meaning and Understanding in the History of Ideas," *History and Theory* 8 (1969): 7n.

19. R. G. Collingwood, *An Essay on Metaphysics* (London: Oxford University Press, 1940), p. 41.

20. Ibid., p. 23.

21. Ibid., p. 25.

22. Ibid., p. 26.

23. Ibid., p. 28.

24. Stephen Toulmin, *Human Understanding*, p. 68.

25. Ibid., p. 69.

26. Collingwood, *Essay on Metaphysics*, p. 29.

27. Ibid., p. 31.

28. Ibid., pp. 33, 42; Toulmin, *Human Understanding*, pp. 70–71.

29. Collingwood, *Essay on Metaphysics*, p. 31.

30. Ibid., p. 73.

31. Ibid., p. 48n.

32. The similarity of the two accounts should not be exaggerated, of course. Kuhn's paradigms are concrete achievements and as such are more nearly events than presuppositions, although they presumably are intimately associated with the

THOMAS L. HASKELL

latter. Moreover, Collingwood's sharp distinction between relative and absolute presuppositions has no counterpart in Kuhn's account, nor does it seem a useful distinction in general: see Toulmin, *Human Understanding*, pp. 71–80. Even assuming that there is a meaningful distinction between relative and absolute presuppositions, intellectual historians presumably would devote most of their attention to the relative ones and leave the absolute ones to metaphysicians.

33. Toulmin's extraordinary book *Human Understanding* should become a basic text for all intellectual historians in spite of the rough treatment it has received from reviewers: see David Bloor, "Rearguard Rationalism" *Isis* 65 (June 1974): 249–53; David L. Hull, "A Populational Approach to Scientific Change," *Science* 182 (14 December 1973): 1121–24; Richard S. Westfall, "Toulmin and Human Understanding," *Journal of Modern History* 47 (December 1975): 691–98; L. Jonathan Cohen, "Is the Progress of Science Evolutionary?" *British Journal of the Philosophy of Science* 24 (1973): 41–61; Norman Daniels, review of *Human Understanding*, *Philosophical Review* 83 (January 1975): 108–12.

34. Toulmin, *Human Understanding*, p. 76.

35. Ibid., pp. 117, 127.

36. I do not mean by this statement to dismiss Kuhn as an "irrationalist," of course. He has a "sense of validity," as Hollinger says, and he successfully "sidesteps" relativism, as Berkhofer says. But these defenses hinge on subtle and fragile distinctions. Throughout this essay I have tried to focus not on the fine logic of arguments but on the basic (even crude) impressions they create in the minds of an imperfect audience. Perhaps the question comes down to this: Are scholars responsible only for what they say, or also for what their audiences hear? Hollinger, "Kuhn's Theory of Science," pp. 378–93; Berkhofer, "Does History Have a Future?" p. 16. See also David Bloor, "Two Paradigms for Scientific Knowledge?" *Science Studies* 1 (1971): 101–15.

37. Leon Rosenfeld, "Niels Bohr in the Thirties," in *Niels Bohr: His Life and Work as Seen by His Friends and Colleagues*, ed. S. Rozental (Amsterdam: North-Holland Publishing, 1967), p. 132.

38. Alfred North Whitehead, *Science and the Modern World* (Middlesex: Penguin, 1938), p. 110.

III

HISTORY OF CULTURE

THE PLACE OF BELIEFS
IN MODERN CULTURE

MURRAY G. MURPHEY

Thirty years ago intellectual history occupied an envied place in the American university; its courses were full to overflowing and its practitioners—men such as Merle Curti, Ralph Gabriel, and Perry Miller—were famous throughout the profession, and indeed beyond. But thirty years have brought a marked change. Students no longer see intellectual history as the place "where the action is," and the profession seems to concur that the "cutting edge" of historical scholarship lies elsewhere. An explanation of this change in attitude would involve many factors: the impact of the behavioral revolution in social science, the rise of quantitative history, the student uprisings of the 1960s and the related rise of interest in the history of the inarticulate and the oppressed—all of these and more have played a role. But the upshot is that intellectual history is now perceived as the study of the esoteric productions of an elite or elites. How those productions relate to society—particularly to modern society—is for contemporary historians unclear, and even the students of Miller and Curti seem not to have seen ideas as the vehicle through which the culture is best understood. Whether or not there was a New England mind in the seventeenth century the understanding of which could illuminate the whole of Puritan culture, most historians seem convinced that there is no such American mind today.

The significance of intellectual history depends upon the importance of belief for the functioning of society. If beliefs have little importance in society, their history will tell us little about society. The question therefore is one of the function of belief considered as a part of the culture. And the attempt to answer this question confronts us at once with an anomaly, for if we examine the typology by which we presently categorize the field of belief, we find that different types of beliefs are assigned quite different statuses, and functions. Thus we categorize the field by rubrics such as religion, science, philosophy, history, and the like, or, even more broadly, as the sciences and the humanities. This typology is a traditional one with deep historical roots, and it is embedded in the structure of our academic institutions as well as having a pervasive hold over our thinking about beliefs and our conceptualization of research. But this typology involves much more than a classification of

MURRAY G. MURPHEY

beliefs by subject matter; it also involves differential ways of describing and analyzing beliefs. Thus on the one hand we say of scientific beliefs that they are true or false, that they are based upon empirical evidence, and that they are confirmed by observation. But we never speak of religious beliefs in this way; they are never said to be true or false and are never said to rest on empirical evidence. On the other hand, we speak of religious beliefs as a projective system determined by emotional needs; but we never speak of scientific beliefs in this fashion. The treatment of philosophic beliefs is again distinct; while the emotional foundation of philosophic belief is admitted, empirical verification is also sometimes claimed, yet both of these factors are made secondary to the criterion of consistency. Our typology therefore reflects more than the claim that beliefs should be classed by their subject matter; it also involves the claim that beliefs dealing with different subject matters are different kinds of beliefs, subject to different standards of truth, evidence, and acceptability. Using this typology, we cannot talk about belief in general, or functions of belief in general, because these are conceived to vary radically by type. And so we are unable to formulate any theory about how belief relates to other components of culture, or even to think intelligently about how such a question might be approached.[1]

Given these drawbacks to our classification of belief, it behooves us to look more closely at our classification. It is easy to show that this typology has little utility either cross-culturally or historically, and that it represents a development of our own intellectual tradition. Moreover, the assumption that these categories distinguish different sorts of belief —different in kind—is modern, and the presence of this assumption in our cultural system is a problem requiring explanation—a point to which I will return. What must be stressed here is that this assumption has no epistemological warrant. Epistemologically considered, all belief systems, religious and scientific alike, are attempts to give order and coherence to experience. As Quine has put it

> As an empiricist I continue to think of the conceptual scheme of science as a tool, ultimately, for predicting future experience in the light of past experience. Physical objects are conceptually imported into the situation as convenient intermediaries—not by definition in terms of experience, but simply as irreducible posits comparable, epistemologically, to the gods of Homer. For my part I do, qua lay physicist, believe in physical objects and not in Homer's gods; and I consider it a scientific error to believe otherwise. But in point of epistemological footing the physical objects and the gods differ only in degree and not in kind. Both sorts of entities enter our conception only as cultural posits. The myth of physical objects is epistemologically superior to most in that it has proved more efficacious than other myths as a device for working a manageable structure into the flux of experience.[2]

THE PLACE OF BELIEFS IN MODERN CULTURE

The Homeric theory of the gods is no less a cognitive theory seeking to account for experience than is modern physics; both may be assessed in terms of their success or failure in making sense out of the chaos of experience. That is to say, all belief systems have the function of giving order and stability to experience.

The claim that religious systems are empirically based may seem odd at first, but the oddness comes from a failure to appreciate that *empirical* here means based upon experience considered as evidential, and that what experience is considered as having evidential value is defined by the theory in question. Thus it is still debated in psychology whether or not the results of introspection are to be considered as evidence. According to how this question is answered, one or another theory of psychology will be found to be "empirically confirmed" or "without empirical warrant." Once it is seen that any experience may have evidential value if a given theory so defines it, it is obvious that the domain of experience available to serve as evidence is vastly larger than is dreamed of in positivist metaphysics. Thus if one looks at the writings of New England Puritans, one finds there voluminous records of concrete experiences that are accounted for by their theological systems. The fact that a positivist would attribute these experiences to intrapsychic disturbances shows only that the same experiences can be explained by alternative hypotheses; it in no way diminishes the explanatory power of Puritan theology with respect to such experiences. All systematic thought has some experiential basis.[3]

Such a functional approach to the understanding of belief systems has existed for some time in anthropology. Introduced by Redfield[4] and Hallowell,[5] the concept of the world view has been widely used to characterize the way in which a society constructs its world. The term *construct* is crucial here, for the anthropological use of *world view* deliberately avoids the assumption that the external world is given; it rather sees the construction of the world—the definition of what there is and how it is—as a work of the human imagination operating collectively in societies. What is given are the neural stimulations that form the basis of sensation. The interpretation of sensation as indicative of a world of objects, the characterization of such objects, the differentiation of the self from other objects, the definition of the relations among these objects and the self, the location of the self and other objects in relation to space and time—all of these are constructed by the mind as interpretations of experience. Cultures can therefore differ on any one or all of these dimensions, and the known variability among human societies is breathtaking. Man lives in a world he himself creates, and different cultures inhabit different worlds.

If cultures differ in their world views, it is also true that there is no

MURRAY G. MURPHEY

culture without a world view. Indeed, it is impossible to conceive of a human level of existence without the orientations and guides provided by a world view. Man is so underendowed with instinct, so lacking in genetically determined guides to action, that he would be unable to survive without the elaborate symbolically mediated cognitive systems that constitute the world view. Human action at the voluntary level is action guided by belief, appraised and evaluated by norms; without the conceptual systems that provide such beliefs and norms, wants could not be satisfied and effective action would be impossible. The world view is thus the system of belief in terms of which human action is planned and executed. In fact, so crucial is the role of belief in human adjustment that some recent definitions of culture have come close to identifying it with the system of belief held by the group, and while others strongly disagree, all admit that human culture intrinsically involves systems of belief.[6]

The world view does more than define what there is and provide a basis for action; it also provides the individual with a set of orientations toward himself and the world around him that are of fundamental significance for his psychological well-being. Without some stability and order in experience and without normative and motivational orientations toward himself, other humans, and his natural environment, the human individual could have no security, no satisfying interpersonal relations, and no moral worth. Who may be loved and who must be hated, what one may be proud of and what one must be ashamed of, who is a friend and who is an enemy—these and hundreds of similar questions are answered for us by the world view. Our ideas can domesticate the world and make us at home there, or they can leave us terrified strangers on an alien shore.[7]

On the basis of these reflections, we may conclude that belief systems or world views have at least the following functions: they define the nature and characteristics of the self and the behavioral environment, and by so doing provide an explanation of experience that affords order and predictability; they provide a basis upon which action may be planned and executed, and they satisfy a variety of important human needs. Systems of belief are therefore not only relevant to the functioning of society, they are indispensable both to society and to its individual members. Miller was right to approach New England society through its "mind"; why then do we not do similar studies of the American mind today?

The beginnings of an answer to this question may emerge if we look to the way in which systems of belief change. Because belief systems provide a means of accounting for experience, it is fairly clear that they will change as our experience changes, or at least that changes in our

THE PLACE OF BELIEFS IN MODERN CULTURE

experience will produce stresses that will motivate change. Were this not so, the system of belief would soon cease to be functionally adaptive. But such changes are always constrained by a second factor—the need for consistency* with already established beliefs. How severe this constraint is seems to depend upon the particular culture in question. Indeed, there is ample evidence that the degree of consistency that exists in the world view is highly variable, both between cultures and within cultures over extended periods of time. Students of ancient Egypt, for example, have remarked the fact that the Egyptians had various accounts of the origin of the separation of earth and sky—accounts that were inconsistent in our sense yet were evidently all equally acceptable within the culture.[8] But we also know of cultures in which all beliefs are expected to form a consistent whole, although we may doubt that such consistency has ever been fully achieved. How difficult such an integration will prove of course depends upon the standard of consistency employed. Logical consistency is but one such standard, and obviously one limited to those cultures in which some sort of logical calculus has been developed, but even there the meaning of logical consistency will vary between a culture employing, say, the logic of Ramus, and one employing the logic of Whitehead and Russell. Clearly, the more rigorous the criteria of consistency the more difficult its attainment will be, and the greater the constraints upon intellectual innovation the culture will impose.

How does consistency affect innovation? Consider a world view in which a high standard of consistency is demanded, for example, logical consistency in the sense of Whitehead and Russell. Let this world view consist of the propositions $p_1 \ldots p_n$. Let us furthermore suppose that this world view is axiomitized, that $p_1 \ldots p_5$ are the axioms and that $p_6 \ldots p_n$ are theorems. What sorts of changes are possible for this world view? Two types of change can be made with relative ease: we may add further propositions, $p_{n+1} \ldots p_{n+k}$, which are logical consequences of the axioms $p_1 \ldots p_5$, or we may add propositions, $q_1 \ldots q_m$, which are independent of $p_1 \ldots p_5$, and any further propositions derivable from $p_1 \ldots p_5$ together with any of the q's. But what we cannot do is delete any p that is a logical consequence of $p_1 \ldots p_5$, or add any proposition inconsistent with $p_1 \ldots p_5$, and these restrictions are extremely severe. Indeed, the system described is quite rigid, and if any of the propositions $p_1 \ldots p_n$ turn out to be incompatible with experience, the system is in trouble. Not only must the troublesome theorem be rejected, but, since it

---

* I use the term in a popular rather than a logical sense to refer to a felt coherence or compatibility among ideas or statements—where logical consistency is meant, the adjective is used.

MURRAY G. MURPHEY

is a theorem, changes must be made in the axioms, and these changes may ramify through the whole body of theorems. Moreover, some new principles must be introduced to account for the anomalous experiences that made the trouble, and the old world view must be revised to be consistent with these new principles. In some cases these modifications can be made with relative ease, and the bulk of the old world view can be retained. In other cases, however, the result is a rejection of the old system and the substitution of a new one that, while it may contain some propositions of the old theory, is yet a fundamentally new conceptualization of the subject.

This hypothetical example is misleading because it takes into account only the logical relations among propositions and leaves out the historical and psychological factors that have led such logically independent propositions as Newton's laws of motion and the law of universal gravitation to be regarded as inseparable parts of the Newtonian paradigm. But the effect of adding these psychological and historical factors is to accentuate even further the rigidity of such systems and to clarify the reason why fundamental change is likely to take the form of a revolution in which one complete theory replaces another. T. S. Kuhn's book has of course made these notions familiar, at least in their application to change in science.[9] But a similar process of change appears to be involved in what Wallace has called revitalization movements—a type of change that applies to entire cultures.[10] The process that generates such movements begins, according to Wallace, when some group within the society finds that the established ways no longer provide a satisfactory mode of life. If the crisis so created becomes severe enough, members of the group will begin to distort the established ways into new forms, which they hope will prove adequate. Then, if revitalization occurs, a particular reformulation of the culture will be advanced that does offer a successful solution to the crisis situation, and that gains sufficient support within the society so that it is substituted for the older system. This new cultural configuration then becomes the established culture of the society, to endure until it in turn is found wanting. Clearly, what Wallace is describing here is a more general form of the process described by Kuhn, but the generalization is hardly surprising. To the extent that the world view has the form of a consistently integrated set of propositions, it is structurally similar to a specific theory of science and can be expected to behave in a similar fashion, and what is true of the world view is also true of the culture as a whole.

Now it is quite clear that American history does contain instances of the sort of change described by Kuhn, and it is equally obvious that it does not contain an instance of the sort described by Wallace. One may well ask how this can be so; why does the process apply to subfields of

THE PLACE OF BELIEFS IN MODERN CULTURE

the world view but not to the world view itself? If the consistency criterion applied to the world view as a whole, we would certainly expect change by revolution to apply to the entire world view. The fact that this is not so shows that the consistency criterion has been limited to subdomains of the world view—to what we usually designate as specialities. We have, in other words, substituted a social structural solution for an intellectual one, with the result that the extreme rigidity of a fully consistent world view has been traded for a marvelously dynamic structure of specialities.

That all the praises of the division of labor which Adam Smith sang apply to the division of labor in intellectual pursuits is a proposition that hardly needs belaboring at this date.[11] We all know that intellectual specialization has been the secret of the progress of modern science, and the process is constantly accelerating. But it is important to ask what labors are being divided, and how the separate divisions relate to each other. Specialities may be defined in several ways: by subject matter, by method, by instrumentation, by theories held, or by any combination of these. But what seems always to be involved is a resolution to seek within some more or less vaguely circumscribed substantive domain for an integration of belief, method, and instrumentation without worrying how that particular integration will affect those achieved in other fields. In other words, the division of intellectual labor into separate domains limits the demand for consistency to beliefs within that domain, and allows the question of consistency between domains to be sidestepped. The dynamism that results from such specialization is then due, not only to the often remarked inverse relation between the depth and breadth of knowledge, but also to the fact that the demand for consistency with all its conservatism can be, to some degree, avoided.

To avoid misunderstanding, the above discussion must be qualified by pointing out the difference between what is presupposed and what is postponed. Biochemistry is a subfield of chemistry; it presupposes chemistry, and its results must be consistent with those of chemistry in general. Linguistics is a field independent of chemistry; its results have nothing to do with those of chemistry and the problem of consistency does not arise. The theory of electromagnetism in physics developed independently of mechanics and evolved along a path that, at the hands of Faraday and Maxwell, led to a formulation that was not only conceptually radically different from that of mechanics (for example, the field concept), but that, taken in conjunction with the discovery that Maxwell's equations were invariant under transformations of the coordinates from one Galilean frame to another, was actually inconsistent with that of mechanics. Similarly, quantum mechanics before Dirac developed along lines very different from relativity theory and in a manner

MURRAY G. MURPHEY

that created considerable doubt that the two could be harmonized. What is crucial then is that the range of consistency can be limited to a particular area so that innovations can be worked out and developed there that would have had to be rejected at the outset if consistency with results in other areas had been required.

What then becomes of the problem of consistency among fields? There seem to be three stages to the handling of this problem. In the first, the problem of consistency is seen as simply postponed. The lack of consistency is regarded as a fault, but one due to our limited knowledge to date, and so one that will be remedied in due time. In other words, the consistency criterion for all knowledge is maintained, but whereas within fields the demand for consistency is immediate, its attainment between fields is regarded as a problem to be solved at a later time. The faith in consistency, however, remains. It is affirmed that nature cannot contradict itself, that knowledge is one. But the revelation of that oneness is put off until tomorrow.

A second stage arises when the question of interfield consistency is taken up directly as a research problem. This usually results in the reduction of theories of one field to theories of the other, or in the subsumption of theories from both fields under some broader conceptualization. The reduction of thermodynamics to statistical mechanics and the reduction of mathematics to logic are instances of the first type of synthesis; the absorption of mechanics and electromagnetic theory into general relativity is an instance of the second. In these cases the question of interfield consistency is solved by the substitution of one theory for the several disparate ones that preceded it.

There is, however, a third stage that is not a sequel to the second but an alternative to it. This third stage appears to begin when the disagreements between fields become so serious that faith in the eventual attainment of consistency begins to wane. It is at this point that we begin to hear of different kinds of knowledge—that is, that attempts are made to rationalize the fact that consistency cannot be attained in a way that avoids the imperative to reject all but one of the inconsistent theories. The division of intellectual activities into the various types remarked at the beginning of this paper is an indication that such a situation now obtains with respect to certain categories of our own culture. Thus science and religion may both be accepted because their respective propositions are "different in kind" and so cannot conflict. This strategy is a difficult one to sustain, however, because the abandonment of the consistency requirement is difficult to justify. The justifications that have actually been used in our culture are: (1) different standards for believing propositions obtain in the separate categories, and (2) the propositions of different areas have different kinds of mean-

THE PLACE OF BELIEFS IN MODERN CULTURE

ing.[12] Since the proponents of these claims have also insisted that the set of standards and type of meaning characterizing one area are superior to those characterizing the other, acceptance of these claims has been limited and uneasy. One may therefore suspect that this third stage is a temporary one, which will end either in a reintegration of the disparate areas or with some of them being denied the status of knowledge.

The social development of intellectual activity in the United States over the past century has been characterized by the continual proliferation of specialities. But it is obvious that the knowledge so produced must be integrated if it is to serve the social and psychological functions of the world view, and it is necessary to examine how this integration takes place. We may distinguish here two levels of integration of belief to form a basis for effective action—the individual and the institutional. Since the human individual is always an actor, he must always have available an integration of beliefs sufficient to provide those orientations toward himself and his behavioral environment upon which successful action depends. But society and its institutions are also actors and they too must base action upon some sort of integrated set of beliefs. Where specialization is minimal and all members of the society subscribe to pretty much the same system of belief, that system will have to suffice as a basis for action for individuals and institutions alike. What the church or the state or the guild should do will be determined by an appeal to the beliefs all members of the society share. But where specialization is well advanced there become available bodies of knowledge that are too vast to be understood by any one individual but that, in due combination, may offer a basis for action far superior to the knowledge of even the most gifted member of the society. The question arises therefore as to how such a combination arises at either the institutional or the individual level, and what the consequences of such modes of integration are.

At the institutional level such an integration seems to involve at least four elements. First, there must be a well-developed structure of specialities in which knowledge is fragmented into a large number of autonomous or semiautonomous fields. It matters not at all how arcane the research of a particular specialist may be or how much unremitting dedication to that speciality may limit the perspectives of the individual. The scientist who devotes himself to the search for quarks with charm or the proof of the four-color theorem need not, and indeed cannot, master other fields as well. And the same is true of the Romance philologist who specializes in Portuguese past participles in the Azores in the fifteenth century or the philosopher who specializes in the graphic logic of C. S. Peirce. What one finds there is continually proliferating specialization with ever more people in ever narrower fields.

MURRAY G. MURPHEY

The second element is, of course, the bureaucratic apparatus that is necessary to achieve the integration of these specialities. This complex structure is itself one of the supreme achievements of mankind. Consider for example the way in which the findings of research chemists are translated into a new cosmetic. There are first the research chemists themselves—specialists who know their particular field within chemistry but little else. Then there are the chemical engineers who design the actual production process, the financial analysts who estimate the costs, the marketing experts who estimate the market, the patent lawyers who ensure the company's control over the process, the managers who direct the entire process, and all the seried ranks of clerks, bookkeepers, workmen, and technicians who contribute their special mite to the process whereby a newly synthesized chemical eventually finds its way to Lord and Taylor's in a $6.95 jar of face cream. But most important of all is the organizational structure itself, which allots each specialist his place and combines the sundry outputs of all the specialists to achieve the final product. While this structure utilizes the knowledge of each group, no member of the organization ever knows, or could ever know, the full range of knowledge that is involved in the process. The synthesis of knowledge that is embodied in the process is not intellectual; it is social structural.

The third element concerns the reliability of the results achieved in the particular specialities. Because these results will be used by others who are able neither to check them nor to understand fully the processes by which they were reached, it is essential to the success of the institution that some method be found of assessing their reliability. One such test is, of course, the success of the process, but this is not a sufficient test because failure would only indicate that some results were wrong somewhere without indicating which results were at fault. In view of the specialized character of the knowledge involved, it is necessary that appraisal be done by members of the speciality. This right (and duty) of peer review is usually seen as a protection of the freedom of the specialists from outside interference, but it may with equal justice be regarded as a mark of their subjection to the demands of the institution.

The fourth element is the code of professionalism that enables the specialist to speak with authority within his own field and renders him impotent beyond it. From the professional's standpoint, the emphasis falls upon his authority within the domain of his expertise. From the institution's standpoint, it is no less important that his authority be limited to that domain, for it is this limitation that permits the institution to separate the production of technical results from the control over their use. It is the specialist who makes the decisions involved in generating the technical results; it is the managers who decide how these results will

THE PLACE OF BELIEFS IN MODERN CULTURE

be used, and it is the professional code that legitimizes this division of responsibility.

As we have seen above, the world view provides the individual with a set of orientations that permits him to relate himself meaningfully to himself and his behavioral environment and that forms a foundation for planning and executing action. In societies with minimal specialization, this integration of knowledge at the individual level also provides the basis for social action. Where the integration of belief occurs at the institutional level and specialization is well developed, however, it follows that the range of knowledge available for institutional action is not available at the individual level. The individual will have available that knowledge which pertains to his own speciality, but he will not have available that which pertains to other specialities. What, then, is to provide the knowledge basis necessary for individual adjustment?

Such a situation would appear to place the individual at a severe disadvantage, but this is not necessarily so. In the first place, in modern society the individual will often have access to the results of specialization in fields in which he is not himself a specialist. An obvious example of this situation is provided by medicine. No individual possesses the whole of modern medical knowledge. Yet by hiring the services of physicians and hospitals an individual can obtain the benefits of that complex body of knowledge. Precisely the same phenomenon is true in a host of other areas. Few individuals know the law, but they can get legal assistance for action by hiring a lawyer. Few individuals know enough about the economy to invest money intelligently, but they can hire investment counselors to tell them what to do. Thus the individual actually has available (at a price) a wide range of specialists whose function it is to translate the results of advanced investigations into forms relevant to the individual as a basis for decision-making and action, and there is no reasonable doubt that the individual so served has actually a better basis for action than he could possibly have, no matter what his intellectual gifts, if he were dependent upon his own knowledge alone. Indeed, what the individual so circumstanced needs to know is not how the experts come to their conclusions but how to access and manage the experts.

In the second place, the individual may not need to know or use the same knowledge that is utilized by institutions. It is not clear that a knowledge of advanced economics will significantly improve one's ability to manage household finances, or that expertise in particle physics will improve one's ability to fix the front doorbell. The problems facing the individual are not the same as those facing institutions, and the bodies of knowledge relevant to individual action are correspondingly different. It is entirely possible that what the individual needs to know

MURRAY G. MURPHEY

can be adequately furnished to him by public education, by the media, by hired experts, and by organizations such as his political party and his church.

Finally, it should be remarked that the relation between beliefs operative as a basis for individual action and those operative at the institutional level may be one of contradiction. Consider for example the role of astrology in contemporary American society. For many people, astrology forms an important body of belief that provides significant guidance for their everyday activities. The fact that experts in celestial matters regard astrology as poppycock in no way inhibits the attachment of these people to their doctrine or interferes with its functioning in their lives. Similarly, different individuals within the society may well hold radically contradictory systems of belief, each of which provides for its adherents an adequate basis for action. This has long been true in the United States in the area of religion, and it is true in other areas as well.[13] As Wallace has shown, cognitive nonsharing is no bar to complementarity of action, and it is complementarity of action that is essential to the operation of society.[14]

It thus appears that within a complex modern society it is possible to achieve integrations of belief adequate as a basis for action at both the individual and the institutional levels. Yet it is far from clear that such integrations are adequate to fulfill the psychological functions of the world view. What these complex integrations of specialized beliefs involve is not an intellectual synthesis but a managerial synthesis; one knows how to create the necessary combinations of results to achieve a goal of action just as one knows how to combine the ingredients to form a cake. One does not, however, know why the synthesis works in any intellectual sense any more than the cook knows why these ingredients, mixed thus and baked so, form a cake. The cook, of course, does not care why so long as the cake is baked, and to a considerable extent neither does modern man care, so long as the goal is attained. Yet for the individual in a complex society, there are clear costs. For one thing, he is rendered utterly dependent upon others whose advice he must follow whether he can understand it or not. What is more helpless than a sick man in the hands of his doctor, or a defendant in the hands of his lawyer? This fact emphasizes the crucial importance of professionalism in our society; the individual's security against exploitation rests largely upon the reliability with which he can expect the code of the professional to be adhered to. And this dependence is a cause of concern and resentment for the dependent; how else are we to explain the mixture of respect and hostility with which such experts are regarded in our society? Dependence bespeaks inadequacy, and inadequacy is always a

THE PLACE OF BELIEFS IN MODERN CULTURE

source of fear and anxiety. If under this system individual action is more effective, the individual is less so, and the sense of felt inadequacy is intensified when one has to deal with the larger society beyond one's own sphere. For most Americans, the problems of American society as a whole appear simply overwhelming and, indeed, beyond comprehension. The apathy of the people toward issues such as welfare reform, tax reform, energy conservation, and unemployment arises in no small part from a felt inadequacy to cope with such matters.

Beyond these inadequacies there lies a deeper problem. Even though operational adequacy is achieved by the mode of belief integration currently in use, meaningfulness is not. Knowing how to do something does not confer meaning upon the activity, does not set the action in a wider context in which its worth can be assessed. Such a wider perspective can only be furnished by a world view that relates man to time and space in some meaningful fashion and provides a way of assigning significance to individual life and achievement. Religious systems, of course, do this for their adherents; so too do ideologies such as those now prevalent in China and Russia, although with what success over the long run remains to be seen. At present, neither type of belief system can be said to do this effectively in the United States, although the babel of religions clearly comes closer to the mark than any extant ideology. We have thus the paradox of a society in which the capacity to do is developed beyond any historical example, but in which no one is certain what is worth doing.

We have then in modern complex societies a vast body of knowledge that is utilized by the individuals and institutions of that society as a basis for action. But the complete body of this knowledge, or indeed any significant part of that body, is not known to any individual in that society. What knowledge is available to the individual will be a function of his own position in the social structure, his education, and the expert opinion he can command. But there will certainly be areas in which his views will diverge from those of others in his society, including the specialists. It follows that the actual distribution of knowledge in such a society will assume a peculiarly complex form: not only will command of particular specialties be limited to a small number of people, but the views of the nonspecialists, who are numerically the larger group, may be inconsistent with those of the specialists. The attempt to characterize the world view of such a society becomes extraordinarily difficult. The number of beliefs common to the whole society will turn out to be relatively small, and these will usually be vague and ambiguous—that being, in fact, the price of being widely held. Any inventory of beliefs held by the members of the society will yield flagrant inconsistencies and

MURRAY G. MURPHEY

radical variation in the degree of technical sophistication. Indeed, those beliefs which are most sophisticated will turn out to be held by numerically insignificant groups.

If this is the character of the world view, what follows for the study of intellectual history? First, those who are interested in the study of complex or sophisticated ideas must pursue that history through the specialities in which they are now developed. This means that the intellectual historian interested in physics must become a historian of physics, and correspondingly for other fields. This trend is already well advanced; we now have historians of physics, historians of chemistry, historians of anthropology, and so on. Even subspecialities are often so technical that they require their own historians with distinctive training, for example, the history of logic as opposed to the history of philosophy generally. As specialization becomes the order of the day in intellectual endeavors, so it must also be in the history of intellectual endeavors. Second, it is clear that the grand synthesis, as developed by men such as Miller, simply cannot be applied to so complex an entity as modern society; whether or not there was a New England mind in the seventeenth century, there is no American mind today. An inventory of American beliefs today would yield not a system but a mass of inconsistent fragments. Third, the grand synthesis cannot be replaced by studies of beliefs common to the bulk of the society or those advanced by so-called "spokesmen" whose ideas happen to be particularly appealing to the historian. What common beliefs there are are insufficient to provide an understanding of American life, and the significant feature of intellectual elites today is not who they speak for but who uses their ideas and for what ends.

If we would overcome the fragmentation implicit in the histories of specialities, we must look to the ways in which in fact these diverse sets of beliefs are integrated, and this means that we must focus on the social and psychological functions of ideas and on the social structures through which they are combined and utilized. This will mean a very different type of intellectual history than we have traditionally done. It will involve the history not only of ideas and men but of roles and institutions. It will mean analyzing a man's thought not only as the expression of a time and a place but as a socially useful product generated by an appropriately positioned actor and consumed by others for ends of their own. In short, the synthesis at which intellectual historians aim will not be found in the realm of ideas; it will be found by relating ideas to action, experience, psychological need, and social structure as components of a complex functioning sociocultural system.

THE PLACE OF BELIEFS IN MODERN CULTURE

Notes

1. Murray G. Murphey, "On The Relation between Science and Religion," *American Quarterly* 20 (1968): 275–95.
2. Willard V. Quine, *From a Logical Point of View* (New York: Harper & Row, 1961), p. 44.
3. Murphey, "Science and Religion."
4. Robert Redfield, *The Primitive World and Its Transformations* (Ithaca, N.Y.: Cornell University Press, 1953).
5. A. I. Hallowell, "The Self and Its Behavioral Environment" in *Culture and Experience* (Philadelphia: University of Pennsylvania Press, 1955), pp. 75–110.
6. Ward Goodenough, *Culture, Language, and Society* (New York: Addison-Wesley, 1971); Clifford Geertz, *The Interpretation of Cultures: Selected Essays* (New York: Basic Books, 1973), ch. 1. See, however, Marvin Harris, *The Rise of Anthropological Theory: A History of Theories of Culture* (New York: Crowell, 1968).
7. Hallowell, "The Self and Its Behavioral Environment." Erik Erikson, *Young Man Luther* (New York: W. W. Norton, 1962).
8. H. and H. A. Frankfort, eds., *Before Philosophy* (Baltimore, Md.: Penguin Books, 1946), pp. 53–55.
9. Thomas S. Kuhn, *The Structure of Scientific Revolutions*, rev. ed. (1962; Chicago: University of Chicago Press, 1970).
10. Anthony F. C. Wallace, "Revitalization Movements: Some Theoretical Considerations for Their Comparative Study," *American Anthropologist* 58 (1956): 264–81.
11. Adam Smith, *The Wealth of Nations* (New York: Modern Library, 1937), ch. 1. Smith was not, however, blind to the stultifying effects of such divisions upon those involved.
12. Both justifications were used by the logical positivists.
13. How true it is we have yet to recognize. Belief clearly varies among different ethnic groups, among different social strata, and among various other sociocultural categories. A consideration of these types of variation and of how the culture deals with them lies beyond the scope of this paper.
14. Anthony F. C. Wallace, *Culture and Personality* (New York: Random House, 1961), ch. 1.

THE WORLD OF PRINT
AND COLLECTIVE MENTALITY
IN SEVENTEENTH-CENTURY NEW ENGLAND

DAVID D. HALL

A twelve-year-old boy, precociously alert to the literary marketplace, writes a ballad (in "Grubstreet" style) on the capture of a pirate. Printed as a broadside, the poem is hawked in the streets of Boston and sells "wonderfully." An old man retells a family legend of how, in the persecuting times of "Bloody Mary" more than two centuries earlier, his ancestors hid their Protestant Bible in a stool. A young minister, ambitious as a writer, dreams of hiring a peddler who will carry cheap religious tracts from town to town.[1]

These are gestures that draw us into the world of print as it was experienced by Americans in the seventeenth century. I begin with this world because it is a useful starting point for rethinking the limitations and possibilities of intellectual history. A starting point, but not the means of answering every question, because the world of print is an imperfect mirror of intellectual experience, a partial reflection of all that is thought and believed. My evidence is taken from the seventeenth century, but I mean to contribute to a more general debate. This is the debate between social and intellectual historians about the distance that exists between elites or intellectuals and other groups; between "high" culture and that which is usually described as "popular"; between books and collective belief.

If we feel uneasy with the intellectual history of seventeenth-century New England, the explanation is our renewed sense of distance in any or all of these forms. It is the felt distance of the ministers from the rest of society that limits them to being spokesmen for an elite. It is the distance between the ministers, who live in the world of print, and the mass of the people, who retain "peasant" ways of thinking.[2] This last distinction has been enormously reinforced by the work of Keith Thomas, which shows that in seventeenth-century England formal systems of religious belief competed with alternative, more "primitive" beliefs, and, more generally, by the work of French historians of *mentalité*, which uncovers for early modern France a mental world of superstition and folk belief apparently quite separate from the mental world of the literate.[3] In

THE WORLD OF PRINT AND COLLECTIVE MENTALITY

effect, the discovery of collective mentality is being used as a weapon against intellectual history, a means of restricting it within narrow boundaries.

In taking up the world of the book, I mean to explore the possibilities for extending these boundaries. There are many limitations to what can be accomplished by the history of the book, one of which is intrinsic in the complexity of any verbal statement: how much or what parts of that complexity is transmitted to any reader?[4] Many assumptions must be made, the chief one being that those books which sold in largest quantity reflect collective ways of thinking. Nonetheless, I want to use the history of print as a means for reappraising the relationship between the ministers and society as a whole in seventeenth-century New England, and in doing so, to point the way toward a broader understanding of intellectual history.

The world of print in seventeenth-century New England was broadly continuous with that of Europe. Shortly after the discovery of printing, the book in Europe assumed the form it would have for centuries to come, even as techniques for the book trade also became standardized. In the early years, and especially in England for much of the sixteenth century, individual patrons played an important role in deciding what was published. Early and late, the state attempted to control the world of print by restrictive licensing and censorship. But every effort at restraint was undercut by the lure of the marketplace. Printers produced whatever readers would buy. One-third of the books published in sixteenth-century England were not entered in the Stationer's Register, and in France, taking into account both what was printed within its borders and what was made available from outside, the actual world of print was far larger than any official version.[5] The entrepreneur reigned. What Robert Darnton says of publishers in Paris on the eve of the French Revolution, though colored by legal conditions, reflects the situation everywhere:

> "Innovation" came through the underground. Down there, no legalities constrained productivity, and books were turned out by a kind of rampant capitalism. . . . foreign publishers did a wild and wooly business in pirating [books officially licensed in France]. . . . They were tough businessmen who produced anything that would sell. They took risks, broke traditions, and maximized profits by quantity instead of quality production.

Almost as soon as printing began, printer-publishers were reaching out for the widest possible audience.[6]

DAVID D. HALL

The printing technology of the day was amazingly responsive to demands for quantity and speed.[7] But speed and innovation were not the only rhythms of the marketplace. For every Nathanael Butter (a London printer of the early seventeenth century who specialized in domestic intelligence, murders, cases of treason, and adventure stories, all requiring rapid publication before they fell out of date),[8] there was a printer who catered to needs that seemed unchanging, a printer who marketed the same product year in and year out. Provincial booksellers in eighteenth-century France published catechisms, liturgical hand-books, books of devotion, and similar steady sellers in far greater quantity than anything else; these were books, moreover, for which the copyrights had lapsed.[9] Their lack of glamour should not betray us into ignoring the significance of such steady sellers and the audience they served. In effect two major rhythms crisscrossed in the marketplace: one of change, the other of repetition. A constant recycling of tried and true literary products accompanied the publication of new styles and genres.

These rhythms offer clues to the relationship between modes of print and modes of thinking. But before pursuing them further, we must turn to evidence about literacy and book ownership in order to gain a clearer understanding of the marketplace. Figures on literacy vary from country to country and within each country by region. National averages can conceal the crucial difference in France between the North (literate) and the South (illiterate). What seems true of early modern Europe is that each country had its "dark corners of the land," regions in which the book was rare, few printers set up shop, and illiteracy (at least in the national language) was high. These were regions, moreover, where cosmopolitan travelers could barely make themselves understood.[10] In more integrated communities, literacy and book ownership varied with social and economic rank. By the early seventeenth century, professionals (clergy, lawyers) in England were completely literate, the aristocracy nearly so, with the rate descending to approximately 50 percent for yeomen and small tradesmen. Thereafter the decline is rapid, to a low of a few percent for laborers.[11] As for book ownership in England, a careful study of probate inventories in three towns in Kent has shown that by the early seventeenth century, between 40 and 50 percent of males owned books. This figure conceals immense variances: no laborer owned any books, but close to all professionals did.[12]

These estimates for literacy and book distribution are perplexing. It is possible to interpret them as meaning that a chasm separated the culture of the elite, who lived in the world of print, from that of the poor, who did not. Since the printed book was something new in European culture, historians have also argued that a "traditional oral" culture remained intact among "peasants" even as the world of print came into being in

THE WORLD OF PRINT AND COLLECTIVE MENTALITY

urban areas and among the upper classes.[13] But the evidence about literacy and reading may really indicate that these categories of elite and nonelite are too limiting. Every social group contained a certain percentage of persons who could read, even if their doing so defies our expectations. To us there is a mystery about the ways and means by which a French peasant in the sixteenth century taught himself to read the Bible he had acquired. Yet it happened.[14] In the sixteenth- and seventeenth-century Cambridgeshire towns Margaret Spufford has studied, books were read with extraordinary care by persons of every description, including many women. Her evidence, which goes beyond quantitative estimates of literacy to consider how print was put to use, indicates that social, economic, and sexual boundaries all yielded to the book.[15] As for "oral" culture, it too was entwined with the world of print. The culture of the European peasant may be likened to a river full of debris. That debris had various origins and qualities. Some of it arose from communal experience and was therefore "folk" in nature. But much of the rest of it is easily recognized as bits and pieces of literary culture extending from Christianity as far back as classical civilization. By the early seventeenth century this accumulation of materials effectively meant that there was nothing immaculate about "oral" culture. We must speak instead of a continuum between print and oral modes.[16]

That the boundaries of print were fluid and overlapping is apparent from books themselves. The reach of some books in the early modern period was extended visually by the woodcuts that embellished broadsides, primers, almanacs, emblem books, and the like. Collectively these pictures transmitted ideas beyond the reach of print. Iconography carried ideas downward into social milieux where the book may not have widely penetrated. It also seems true that certain kinds of books circulated in ways that touched even the apparently illiterate—the Bible, naturally, but also the cheapest of pamphlet literature, such as the "many old smokie paperbacks" on astrology complained of by a late-sixteenth-century English writer, and the equally inexpensive "Bibliotheque Bleue" of Troyes, a series of books designed to be read aloud.[17] We must also bear in mind that the illiterate participated in communal gatherings (fairs, festivals, church services) that functioned as occasions for the exchange of knowledge among different social groups. For all of these reasons it should be "obvious that illiteracy does not mean stupidity or mental blankness." The illiterate in early modern France, Pierre Goubert has observed, "are Christians, if unaware of the controversies over the nature of grace; . . . all of them receive an oral culture and even a bookish culture, by way of a reader or story-teller, since there is a whole printed literature designed especially for them." In England the same fluidity prevailed. There as elsewhere, illiteracy can-

DAVID D. HALL

not be equated with a "peasant" mentality cut off from the world of print.[18]

To be sure, some boundaries do cut through the world of print. Most of the literate could not read Latin, but a large (though after 1600, a steadily decreasing) percentage of books were published in that language. In some sense books in Latin bespoke a separate culture. But as translations multiplied in the late sixteenth century,[19] and as the classics were redacted in popular formats, Latin lost most of its significance as a carrier of ideas or as a cultural code. Meanwhile printer-entrepreneurs were responding to the needs of professional groups, publishing law books and manuals of church practice that had little circulation beyond their immediate audience.

But over all such categories of books stand others that, to judge from the number of editions and the quantities produced, reached a general audience. That such books bear witness to shared beliefs and common ways of thinking seems apparent from two kinds of evidence. One is the marketplace rhythm of long duration, the continuous production of certain literary genres and formulas over centuries. The other is evidence about quantity: the sheer number of books that were printed. Together, these types of evidence point to three major categories as dominant in the marketplace.[20] Let me consider each in turn.

Religious books outnumber all other kinds. This fact, like others in the history of print, may perplex historians who think of religion solely as a system of doctrine. H. S. Bennett, describing the situation in pre-Reformation England, brings us closer to actuality:

> The religious houses required works of spiritual instruction and consolation in the vernacular. . . . The reader of pious legends, such as those contained in that vast compilation, *The Golden Legend*, or in smaller collections, . . . was catered for. Volumes of pious stories; handbooks of practical help in church worship; books of systematized religious instruction; volumes of sermons and homilies; allegorical and lyric poems. . . .

Still closer is the anecdote repeated by Keith Thomas of an "old woman who told a visitor that she would have gone distracted after the loss of her husband but for the *Sayings* of the Puritan pastor John Dod, which hung in her house." Similarly, the wife of John Bunyan thought so much of Arthur Dent's *The Plaine Mans Pathway to Heaven*, a book that went through twenty-five editions between 1601 and 1640, that she included it in her dower, together with Lewis Bayly's *Practice of Piety*. Such devotional manuals flourished beneath the level of doctrinal controversy. Medieval *fabula* reappeared in Protestant guise, just as emblems were freely exchanged between Catholic and Protestant moralizing tales. Given this intermingling, it comes as less of a surprise that in 1667 a

THE WORLD OF PRINT AND COLLECTIVE MENTALITY

printer in Cambridge, Massachusetts, published an edition of Thomas a Kempis's *Imitation of Christ*.[21]

Romances—fairy stories, chivalric poems, light fiction—tell of " 'Superman': the Paladin who splits Saracen skulls with a single blow; the crusader knight on his way to liberate Jerusalem and pausing to do the same for 'Babylon'; . . . the good giant Gargantua, coolly removing the bells of Notre-Dame; the artful righters of wrongs, straight or comic, Lancelot or Scaramouche; the invincible good enchanters and powerful fairies whose miracles almost outshine the saints'." A recurring thematic structure of danger and rescue can be said to have appealed to the wish to escape. In the "Bibliotheque Bleue," a paradigm of the literature of escapism, there is nothing of everyday reality, no poor people, no artisans, merely the sensation of entering, however briefly, a glittering world of miracle and magic. Allied to these romances were those kinds of print, especially broadsides, which played upon spectacular events such as murders and acts of treason. In Protestant England and Catholic France the genre was identical. The London printer Nathanael Butter printed news sheets and broadsides catering to "the public's innate curiosity in the strange, the supernatural, the gruesome, the intrepid and the splendid." Meanwhile in France the news sheets were telling of "juicy crimes sung in interminable lays, one *sou* per sheet, incendiarism, maned stars, weird, contagious ailments," all perhaps serving, as one historian has suggested, to provide "useful employment for the bemused minds of the . . . poor."[22]

Books of history range from travel narratives that verge on being sensational to the most ponderous of chronicles. Little of what passed as history was critical, in the sense of detaching legend from fact. Rather, legend was the stuff of historical writing. Most of these legends had to do with the history of the Christian church or the Christian community. The great example in English is Foxe's *Book of Martyrs*. Its structure as myth, providing a sacred interpretation of community origins and community destiny, together with its symbolism of light (the saints) warring against dark (the devil), were characteristic of popular history as a whole, though in any particular example the symbolism was adapted to partisan purposes.[23]

Books of history, romance, and religion as I have described them constituted a special kind of literary culture. The rhythms of this culture were slow, for what sold in the marketplace were formulas that did not need changing. Equally slow was the pace of reading, as the same books were read and reread. This practice may be designated "intensive," in contrast to the "extensive" style of persons wanting novelty and change.[24] Some readers in early modern Europe wanted new ideas from books or regarded them as objects of fashion, valuable for a season but

DAVID D. HALL

then falling out of style. Not so the booksellers and their patrons in provincial France who sought books that had long since passed out of copyright. Not so the Franklin family or John Bunyan's wife, for whom Scripture and books of devotion gained in meaning as time went by. Such examples suggest the power of a world of print in which certain formulas had enduring significance.

Let me call this the "traditional" world of print. By doing so, I mean to emphasize the continuities between oral and print modes of culture, and among social groups. Class is certainly a factor in the making of the world of print, but the literary formulas that comprised "traditional" culture had appeal across class lines. I find it interesting that many of the stories in the "Bibliotheque Bleue" of Troyes, a true peddlers' literature, were derived from classical authors, or from "high culture" authors of a century earlier. Motifs, both literary and iconographic, seem to circulate among milieux and levels, some starting "high" and descending, others starting "low" and moving upward. What this means I do not know, but it surely suggests that all readers in early modern Europe, and many of the illiterate, participated in a common culture.[25]

Keith Thomas and Robert Mandrou argue differently. In *Religion and the Decline of Magic*, Thomas says that the reach of Protestantism extended only so far in post-Reformation England, leaving untouched an area of culture that included belief in magic, astrology, and witchcraft in ways that were contrary to orthodox religion. Adapting the view of Christopher Hill, Thomas suggests that this clash of cultures links up with the hostility between the middle class and social groups placed beneath it. An aggressively Protestant middle class preferred rationality, while groups lower in the social scale, suffering from dispossession and never in control of things, turned to magic and astrology for their world view. This world view is a survival from earlier times; it is "traditional" in the sense of having been around for ages, and also in not depending on books (though manifesting itself in the world of print) for transmittal. A kindred argument is made by Robert Mandrou, who believes that "French popular culture of the ancient regime constituted a separate category of culture, characterized by a literature of colportage portraying an unchanging wonderland of magic and miracles."[26]

These efforts to describe the mental world of the lower classes may help to correct the distortions inherent in labels like the "Age of Reason," and they teach us to take seriously the most casual of literary productions. But in the case of French popular culture an alternative interpretation is easily available, as I have already indicated.[27] And in the case of Thomas's "traditional" culture, the argument depends upon a sociology of religion (that marginal groups, or groups hard pressed by the environment, turn to "magic" for relief), or on assumptions about "ritual"

THE WORLD OF PRINT AND COLLECTIVE MENTALITY

(meaning a more "primitive" form of religion, appealing to lower classes) that cannot be borne out. Nor does the concept of a "rational" middle class take adequate account of the sloppy reading tastes of the literate, at once serious and sentimental, realistic and escapist. The case for separate and segregated cultures is yet to be made.[28]

The exception may be the milieu of the urban avant-garde. Here, two worlds of print coexist: the world of slow and repetitive rhythms, and that concerned with the new and critical. In ways we perhaps know little of, this latter had its own formulas and rituals bound up with distinctive cultural agencies (the literary salon, the Royal Society) and distinctive modes of communication (the *Journal des Savants*, the *Proceedings* of the Royal Society).[29] Yet the line between readers of these journals and readers of "traditional" books cannot be drawn too sharply. There was always an intermediary group interpreting the one to the other. And there came moments when the need for reassurance could only be satisfied by returning to the formulas that never changed.

In the storybook version of New England history, every one in Puritan times could read, the ministers wrote and spoke for a general audience, and the founding of a press at Cambridge in 1638 helped make books abundant.[30] The alternative, argued most strenuously by Kenneth Lockridge, is that illiteracy shackled half of the adult males and three-fourths of the women, with consequences for the whole of culture.[31] Any of these statistics is suspect. More to the point, they do not really define the relationship between the colonists and the world of print. In thinking about that broader problem, it is important to recognize that the "dark corners of the land" that figure in the European landscape failed to reappear in New England. A considerable number of seventeenth-century Europeans had to contend with three languages: Latin, a formalized version of the vernacular, and a local dialect. In New England these distinctions became insignificant. While allowing for minor variations, we can say that a common language linked all social groups. We can also say that the colonists lived easily in the world of print. In part this was owing to Puritanism, a religion—and here I repeat a cliché—of the book. In part this sense of ease was merely a consequence of the times, for by the mid-seventeenth century the book had lost its novelty. But whatever the reasons, the marketplace of print in New England was remarkably complex and mature.

Throughout the seventeenth century the colonists depended upon imports for the bulk of their reading. In buying from abroad, these Puritans acted much like the typical patron of print in early modern Europe.

DAVID D. HALL

Religious books dominated, forming nearly half of the imports of Hezekiah Usher, a Boston bookseller, in the 1680s. Schoolbooks, the staple of many a bookseller then and now, ranked second. Aside from books in law, medicine, and navigation, all of which catered to professional needs, the next largest category was belles-lettres—romances, light fiction, modern poetry.[32]

Already, then, we know from Hezekiah Usher's records that two of the three basic types that made up the "traditional" world of print recurred in New England. And once printer-entrepreneurs began to publish locally, their imprints round out a picture of remarkable continuity between old world and new. In its early years the Cambridge press was responsive to state patronage, publishing books for the Indians, law codes, and public documents. But by the 1640s the imprint list was reflecting the entrepreneurial instincts of printers and booksellers. Almanacs and catechisms (all written locally) made their appearance.[33] History became important, as did a closely related literature of disasters. *The Day of Doom* struck a popular nerve, an edition of 1800 copies selling out within a year. Other popular books followed, like Mary Rowlandson's captivity narrative and Cotton Mather's execution sermon for the pirate Morgan. That the American marketplace was like the European in catering to "intensive" readers and the rhythm of long duration is stunningly suggested by the reprinting in 1673 of John Dod's *Old Mr. Dod's Sayings; or, a posie out of Mr. Dod's Garden.* Here too it must have become a familiar household object as, sixty years before, it had been in England.

The Cambridge press did not publish any romances, but almost from the outset included works of history in responding to colonial needs. A familiar structure reappears in the history published locally. All of these books taught either a generalized version of the Protestant myth or a version tied more closely to the founding of the colonies. Some of this literature dealt with the millennium and the Last Judgment (for example, Samuel Whiting's *Discourse of the Last Judgment*); some of it was about enemies of the saints, not only Catholics, but also those Protestant groups who wandered from the truth.[34] Local publications, chiefly election- and fast-day sermons, drew the colonists themselves into the drama of a chosen people warring against their enemies.

Judging by the qualities of what sold and the interaction of the local press with the marketplace, the world of print in seventeenth-century New England bespeaks collective mentality. As in Europe, the "traditional" literary culture reached out to and engaged every social group. There is other evidence as well of how certain ways of thinking extended across the levels of society. The case is clearest, perhaps, with anti-Catholicism, always a "popular" form of belief, and one that found expression in the iconography and rites of street festivals such as the celebration of Guy Fawkes Day.[35] The iconography of gravestones is something of a parallel case, for various of the symbols circulated from emblem books through poetry to carvings done by untrained artists.[36] The extraordinary publishing history of *The Day of Doom* grows out of the fact that all the basic themes of the "traditional" marketplace converged in a single text, a text that also borrowed its literary form from the ballad by which current events ("sensations") were announced to a popular audience. The event itself is sensational, the return of Christ to earth amid thunder and convulsions of the natural world. And in Wigglesworth's vivid pictures of heaven and hell his readers could find the excitement of adventure and assurance that the faithful would triumph over pain, disorder, and their enemies. All these forms of sustenance recur in Mrs. Rowlandson's captivity narrative. The book as artifact, the literary marketplace, the "intensive" reader, and collective ways of thinking all are joined in the history and substance of such texts.

What, then, of the ministers and their relationship to collective mentality? It is worth noting that no New England minister ever complained of having parishioners who could not understand his diction. The "dark corners of the land" in England and France were alien territory to persons speaking the English or French of the city. By comparison, the whole of New England constituted a reasonably uniform language field, a circumstance that helps us understand how deeply the culture was bound up with print as a medium of communication.[37]

We err greatly in thinking of the ministers as intellectuals, if by that we mean they formed a coterie, dealt in abstractions, and were interested in new ideas or criticism. Leaving aside all the other ways in which the ministers mingled with a general audience, their relationship to the literary marketplace would alone disprove this view. The ministers who entered the marketplace as writers offered a wide range of fare, from almanacs and poetry to works of history and popular divinity. They published in every size and format, from the cheapest broadside to the folio. Some of their publications sold well, others poorly. In nearly all, the contents were conventional, as were their intentions. The author in seventeenth-century New England did his writing in harmony with the modes of collective mentality. A "traditional" relationship, one ensuring the widest possible audience, existed between the ministers and the world of the book.

Two brief examples must do as illustrations of this argument: Cotton Mather and the Antinomian controversy.

DAVID D. HALL

Mather, like Franklin, seems to have arrived in the world with a full-blown awareness of the literary marketplace. The intensity of his life as reader and writer is obvious from the extraordinary number of books he owned, and equally from the number he wrote. The *Diary* makes it clear that this intensity flowed in traditional channels.[38] The marketplace in Mather's Boston was competitive (nineteen booksellers and seven printers were at work by 1700), pluralistic, and patterned to meet certain kinds of cultural needs. When Mather began his career as a minister, each week preaching sermons to an audience in Second Church, he simultaneously launched himself as a writer who with each book felt his way toward a popular audience. The two roles of minister and writer were really one. As minister-writer he spoke to and for collective needs, appropriating in his turn the formulas and genres of the traditional marketplace. Like the precocious Franklin, a youthful Mather took advantage of the formulas of "sensation" literature in his first publication, *The Call of the Gospel*, a sermon preached "to a vast Concourse of People" prior to the execution of the criminal James Morgan in 1686. Here is Mather speaking for himself about his literary endeavors and the marketplace: "Now it pleased God, that the people, throughout the Country, very greedily desired the Publication of my poor Sermon. . . . The Book sold exceedingly; and I hope did a World of Good . . . There has been since, a second Edition of the Book, with a Copy of my Discourse with the poor Malefactor walking to his Execution, added at the End." That is, Mather told the world the conversation he had had with Morgan as the criminal walked to the scaffold. This mating of morality with sensation, one that endures into our own day, was thereafter a formula Mather used frequently, and, unfortunately, he used it when it came to witchcraft. The literature of remarkable providences and the literature of captivity narratives are related formulas, which he and his father produced in abundance and with excellent success in the marketplace. Cotton Mather was a popular writer alertly responsive to audience needs and audience tastes.[39]

At a certain point every student of the Antinomian controversy comes to appreciate John Winthrop's rueful remark that no one at the time could understand what separated the parties in terms of doctrine. Winthrop's point is really that the controversy had become rhetorical, a controversy that revolved around popular catchwords more than issues of Christian doctrine. Although the controversy included both, my purpose is to suggest why it expanded outside the circle of ministers to engage the anger and interests of all the colonists. The explanation lies in the rhetoric of the controversy. It is a rhetoric built around simple contrasts that invoke the symbolism of collective identity. On the part of the Antinomians, the basic pairing is that of light (Christ, the gospel, free

THE WORLD OF PRINT AND COLLECTIVE MENTALITY

grace, freedom) against dark (Adam, the law, bondage, captivity), a pairing that John Wheelwright, in a fast-day sermon that is a remarkable example of popular speech, applied to the nature of history: the ultimate struggle between the children of light and the children of darkness is occurring right here and now in New England. The "legal" preachers, Wheelwright made clear, were threatening figures, not because they misinterpreted the exact position of faith in the order of salvation, but because they represented, they were agents of, a gigantic conspiracy against the saints. The "legal" preachers were equally rhetorical in linking Anne Hutchinson with the Familists, a shadowy but monstrous group, as though "free love" were really at issue in 1637. But the ministers themselves on either side of the controversy could conceive of the situation in no other terms. Their rhetoric was not a matter of expediency, but was intrinsic to a collective mentality they shared with ordinary people. The Antinomian controversy had its roots in and drew energy from ways of thinking that united ministers and laymen.[40]

I do not mean to simplify the position of the ministers. University educated and at ease in the world of Latin, they stood apart from the general population. As writers and readers they participated in a wider range of literary culture than most of their parishioners, moving from formulas and proverbs that are very nearly "folk" in character to more esoteric prose, and back again. The contradictions in Cotton Mather's character exaggerate but also accurately reflect the complexity of roles: at once a pedant and a popularizer, Mather was also a man who eagerly read new books while continuing to publish in old forms. After this complexity is acknowledged, however, the fact remains that Mather was primarily engaged with the formulas of popular religion, and with the forms of print most suited to them.[41]

Leaving aside the ministers and their relationship to the "traditional" world of print, I want again to warn against the presumption that ordinary people think in different ways, or possess a separate culture, from the modes of an "elite." It does us little good to divide up the intellectual world of seventeenth-century New England on the basis of social class, or even, for that matter, of literacy. Rather, we can move from the world of print, with its fluid boundaries and rhythms of long duration, to an understanding of intellectual history as itself having wider boundaries than many social historians seem willing to recognize. How precisely to describe the formulas, the assumptions, that comprise collective mentality in seventeenth-century New England is a task that lies ahead. Another task is to locate the breakdown of "traditional" literary culture, a process that may well have been underway in Mather's time, and that was certainly occurring in the eighteenth century as upper-class groups began to detach themselves from popular culture.[42] But change came

DAVID D. HALL

slowly. It is really the continuities that impress. In taking them seriously, we free ourselves from distinctions that seem to have restricted the scope and significance of intellectual history.[43]

Notes

1. *The Autobiography of Benjamin Franklin* (New Haven, Conn.: Yale University Press, 1964), pp. 50, 59–60; *The Diary of Cotton Mather*, 2 vols., ed. W. C. Ford (New York: Frederick Unger, n.d.), 1: 65.
2. Kenneth Lockridge, *Literacy in Colonial New England* (New York: W. W. Norton, 1974). Important arguments correcting Lockridge appear in Lawrence Cremin, "Reading, Writing and Literacy," *Review of Education* 1 (November 1975): 517–21.
3. Keith Thomas, *Religion and the Decline of Magic* (London: Weidenfeld and Nicolson, 1971); Robert Mandrou, *De la culture populaire aux xvii and xviii siècles: La Bibliotheque Bleue de Troyes* (Paris: Stock, 1964).
4. "Mais à propos de chaque image et de chaque theme reste posée la question pour qui étaient-ils comprehensibles?" Georges Duby, "Histoire des mentalités," in *L'Histoire et Ses Méthodes*, ed. Charles Samaran (Paris: Gallimard, 1961), p. 923.
5. H. S. Bennett, *English Books & Readers, 1475 to 1557* (London: Cambridge University Press, 1969); idem, *English Books & Readers, 1558 to 1603* (Cambridge: At the University Press, 1965), referred to hereafter as Bennett, *English Books & Readers*, 1, and Bennett, *English Books & Readers*, 2. The importance of patronage is argued in Bennett, *English Books & Readers*, 2, ch. 2, and the figure concerning the Stationer's Register is given in Bennett, *English Books & Readers*, 2, p. 60. The situation in eighteenth-century France is described in the essays brought together in *Livre et Societe dans La France du xviii siècle*, 2 vols. (Paris: Mouton, 1965, 1970). See also Lucien Febvre and Henri-Jean Martin, *The Coming of the Book* (Atlantic Highlands, N.J.: Humanities Press, 1976).
6. Robert Darnton, "Reading, Writing, and Publishing in Eighteenth-Century France: A Case Study in the Sociology of Literature," in *Historical Studies Today*, ed. Felix Gilbert (New York: W. W. Norton, 1972), pp. 261–62.
7. Bennett, *English Books & Readers*, 2, p. 244.
8. Butter's career is described in Leone Rostenberg, *Literary, Political, Scientific, Religious & Legal Publishing, Printing & Bookselling in England, 1551–1700* (New York: Burt Franklin, 1965), ch. 3.
9. Julien Brancolini and Marie-Therese Bouyssy, "La vie provinciale du livre à la fin de l'Ancien Régime," in *Livre et Société*, 2: 3–37.
10. Thomas, *Religion and the Decline of Magic*, p. 165; Eugen Weber, *Peasants into Frenchmen: The Modernization of Rural France, 1870–1914* (Stanford: Stanford University Press, 1976), pt. 1, especially chs. 1 and 6 (on language).
11. John Cressy, "Literacy in Seventeenth-Century England: More Evidence," *Journal of Interdisciplinary History* 8, no. 1 (Summer 1977): 141–50; Lawrence Stone, "Literacy and Education in England, 1640–1900," *Past and Present* 42 (February 1969): 69–139. The methodological limitations in reckoning literacy on the basis of signatures are underscored in Cremin's review of Lockridge, "Reading, Writing and Literacy," and in Margaret Spufford, *Contrasting Communities: English Villagers in the Sixteenth and Seventeenth Centuries* (Cambridge: At the University Press, 1974). Spufford demonstrates that persons who signed their wills with an *x* had written out their names on other documents (ch. 7).
12. Peter Clark, "The Ownership of Books in England, 1560–1640: The Example of Some Kentish Townsfolk," in *Schooling and Society*, ed. Lawrence Stone (Baltimore, Md.: The Johns Hopkins University Press, 1976), pp. 95–111. The situation

THE WORLD OF PRINT AND COLLECTIVE MENTALITY

in sixteenth-century France is touched on in Natalie Zemon Davis, *Society and Culture in Early Modern France* (Stanford: Stanford University Press, 1975), pp. 195–97. Probate inventories record holdings at the time of death, not the flow of experience with print over time. Since books get used up and discarded, the inventories are at best a partial record of encounters with the world of print. That no copies survive of the first edition of *The Day of Doom* or of any of the *New England Primer* published before 1729 are cases in point of books that were widely owned and used but that do not often turn up in inventories simply because they perished from so much use.

13. Davis, *Society and Culture*, ch. 7. Davis (and also Kenneth Lockridge) invokes the work of the anthropologist Jack Goody in drawing a sharp line between oral and literate experience. But how useful is this distinction when applied to European culture two millennia after the emergence of writing? Goody's point of view is presented in *Literacy in Traditional Societies* (Cambridge: At the University Press, 1968). But see the review by Daniel McCall, "Literacy and Social Structure," *History of Education Quarterly* 11 (Spring 1971): 85–92.

14. Davis, *Society and Culture*, p. 203.

15. Spufford, *Contrasting Communities*, pt. 2, ch. 8; pt. 3.

16. The most substantial demonstration of this point is Peter Burke, *Popular Culture in Early Modern Europe* (New York: Harper Torchbooks, 1978). The "oral" culture of the French peasants who proved impervious to Protestantism was rich in Catholic ideas and images; see Davis, *Society and Culture*, pp. 203–8.

17. Bennett, *English Books & Readers*, 2, p. 204; Mandrou, *De la culture populaire*.

18. Pierre Goubert, *The Ancien Regime* (New York: Harper Torchbooks, 1974), p. 263, generalizing from Mandrou, *De la culture populaire*. "If it is true that the parish meeting did not yet involve the kind of collective guidance of the community's spiritual life which it became at the end of the seventeenth century, the parish was nevertheless alive in the form of the Sunday gathering for mass, when for a long time the priest . . . communed with his flock" (Robert Mandrou, *Introduction to Modern France, 1500–1640: An Essay in Historical Psychology* [New York: Harper Torchbooks, 1976], p. 91).

19. Bennett, *English Books & Readers*, 2, ch. 4.

20. There are tables quantifying production by types in *Livre et Société*, 1: 14–26. Less precise information is in Bennett, *English Books & Readers*, 1 and 2.

21. Bennett, *English Books & Readers*, 1, p. 8; Thomas, *Religion and the Decline of Magic*, p. 82; Spufford, *Contrasting Communities*, p. 210.

22. Goubert, *Ancien Regime*, pp. 267–68, relying on Mandrou, *De la culture populaire*; Genevieve Bolleme, "Littérature populaire et littérature de colportage au xviii siècle, in *Livre et Société*, 1: 61–92; Rostenberg, *Literary Publishing, Printing & Bookselling*, p. 78.

23. William Haller, *Foxe's Book of Martyrs and the Elect Nation* (London: Jonathan Cape, 1963).

24. This distinction between types of reading was drawn to my attention by Norman Fiering. The original source is Rolf Engelsing, *Analphabetentum und Lektüre: Zur Sozialgeschichte des Lesens in Deutschland zwischen feudaler und industrieller Gesellschaft* (Stuttgart: J. B. Metzler, 1973). It is Fiering's view that the experience of reading romances and other fiction was not like the experience of reading devotional manuals, the difference being the novelty of successive works of fiction.

25. Duby, "Histoire des mentalités," p. 923. I am sympathetic to Alan Gowans's argument that "no consistent pattern of styles related to social class can be ascertained; in every one of these [American nineteenth- and twentieth-century] popular arts every sort of form can be found, from the most abstract to the most photographically literal." Gowans, *The Unchanging Arts* (Philadelphia: Lippincott, 1970), p. 53.

26. Thomas, *Religion and the Decline of Magic*, pp. 76, 111–12, 145, and *passim*; Robert Mandrou, "Cultures ou niveaux culturels dan les sociétés d'Ancien Régime," *Revue des études Sud-Est européenes* 10, no. 3, pp. 415–22, as sum-

DAVID D. HALL

marized in Traian Stoianovich, *French Historical Method* (Ithaca, N.Y.: Cornell University Press, 1976), p. 170n.

27. See the work of Genevieve Bolleme on the "Bibliotheque Bleue" in "Littérature populaire."

28. Hildred Geertz, "An Anthropology of Religion and Magic, I," *Journal of Interdisciplinary History* 6, no. 1 (Summer 1975): 71–89; Mary Douglas, *Natural Symbols* (New York: Vintage Books, 1973), ch. 1. The most impressive demonstration of the circulation of motifs and the wholeness of popular culture (meaning without class boundaries) is Burke, *Popular Culture in Early Modern Europe.*

29. See Jean Ehrard and Jacques Roger, "Deux périodiques francais du xviii siècle: 'le Journal des Savants' et 'des Mémoires de Trévoux,' Essai d'une étude quantitative," *Livre et Société*, 1: 33–59.

30. As found in Samuel Eliot Morison, *The Intellectual Life of Colonial New England* (New York: New York University Press, 1956).

31. Lockridge, *Literacy in Colonial New England.* Apart from its methodological limitations, Lockridge's argument proceeds in complete disdain of what was printed and read in New England, and the relentless opposing of "traditional" or "peasant" modes of thinking to others, which are denoted "modern," can only be regarded as a sad case of being trapped in abstract categories. For further comments, see my "Education and the Social Order in Colonial America," *Reviews in American History* 3 (June 1975): 178–83.

32. Worthington C. Ford, *The Boston Book Market, 1679–1700* (Boston: Club of Odd Volumes, 1917); books are analyzed according to subject categories in James D. Hart, *The Popular Book: A History of America's Literary Taste* (New York: Oxford University Press, 1950), p. 8.

33. The early almanacs were commissioned by the first Boston bookseller, Hezekiah Usher.

34. For example, a translation of a French history of the Anabaptists, published in 1668 as the Baptists in Boston were challenging the orthodoxy.

35. "Samuel Checkley's Diary," *Publications* of the Colonial Society of Massachusetts 12 (1908–9): pp. 288–90.

36. As demonstrated in Allan Ludwig, *Graven Images* (Middletown, Conn.: Wesleyan University Press, 1966).

37. Lebvre and Martin, "Printing and Language," in *The Coming of the Book*, pp. 319–32.

38. It is also true that Mather and his father were attracted to, and tried to create in New England, an urban avant-garde culture, their model being the Royal Society.

39. *The Diary of Cotton Mather*, 1: 54, 65, 106, 122–23.

40. David D. Hall, ed., *The Antinomian Controversy: A Documentary History* (Middletown, Conn.: Wesleyan University Press, 1968), *passim.*

41. Burke, *Popular Culture in Early Modern Europe*, pp. 133–36.

42. Ibid., chs. 8 and 9.

43. I am indebted to James McLachlan for a number of the references in this paper, and to Norman Fiering, James Henretta, James McLachlan, Elizabeth Reilly, and Harry Stout for thoughtful advice.

THE CULTURES OF INTELLECTUAL LIFE: THE CITY AND THE PROFESSIONS

⸺ ◖ ◗ ⸺

THOMAS BENDER

Men and women of ideas work within a social matrix that constitutes an audience or public for them. Within this context they seek legitimacy and are supplied with the collective concepts, the vocabulary of motives, and the key questions that give shape to their work. These communities of discourse, which I am here calling cultures of intellectual life, are historically constructed and are held together by mutual attachment to a cluster of shared meanings and intellectual purposes. They socialize the life of the mind and give institutional force to the paradigms that guide the creative intellect.[1]

A consideration of the historical development of these cultures of intellectual life brings us to an insufficiently studied but vital point where intellectual history and social history touch. To discern the character of these networks of intellectual discourse, to assess their relative significance over time, and to discover their pattern of interaction promises to illuminate the social foundations of intellectual life in America.

The public culture that intellectual historians seek to explicate and understand is the product of an exceedingly complex interaction between speakers and hearers, writers and readers. Reality is created out of this dynamic interplay.[2] "Men of knowledge," writes Robert Merton, "do not orient themselves exclusively toward their data nor toward the total society, but to special segments of that society with their special demands, criteria of validity, of significant knowledge, of pertinent problems, etc. It is through anticipation of these demands and expectations of particular audiences, which can be effectively located in the social structure, that men of knowledge organize their own work, define their own data, seize upon problems."[3]

Merton obviously has in mind the disciplinary peers so prominent in contemporary intellectual life, but his point can be applied to earlier periods, when the social organization of knowledge took different forms. Before the rise of modern professionalism, there were identifiable audiences that judged and affected the work of American thinkers. Until the middle of the nineteenth century, in fact, the city provided the primary context for the life of the mind. Since the "social frameworks of knowl-

THOMAS BENDER

edge" that give shape to relationships between thinker, audience, and that which is to be explained are historically variable, they are properly the subject of sociological and historical inquiry, as is the interaction between these particular cultures of intellectual life and the larger society.[4]

Intellectual historians are beginning to consider the professions as a context for intellectual life, but neither they nor urban historians have so far devoted much attention to the importance of the local community as a context and audience for intellectual life.[5] If the modern professions can be described as community without locality, it is important to recall that before 1850 locality provided an important sense of "we-ness" to intellectual life. I aim in what follows to suggest the changing significance of two fundamental and contrasting foundations of intellectual community: the city and the professions.

⊂══⊃ ◑ ◐ ⊂══⊃

Questions of legitimacy and hegemony apply to intellectual life as well as to politics. Different cultures of intellectual life may succeed each other; they may also vie for hegemony within a given society. An adequate account of the life of the mind in America requires an understanding of why and how one or another of these cultures achieves hegemony. The way in which the scientific professionals founded disciplinary associations and ensconced themselves in research universities at the end of the nineteenth century provides an example of the kind of problem that must be resolved. They succeeded in appropriating and institutionalizing science within the context of a culture of professionalism. They persuaded many of their contemporaries (and historians since) that they stood for the advent of "real" science in America. Yet they actually represented a particular kind of scientific inquiry. They were able to achieve hegemony by discrediting an alternative pattern of science based upon different assumptions about the nature of reality and rooted in civic, as opposed to disciplinary, institutions.[6]

Several obvious questions flow from the perspective suggested here. We must ask what failures in the older organization of intellectual life (and what new intellectual needs) prepared the way for such shifts in intellectual hegemony. How did the differing social organizations of knowledge affect or relate to the way "reality" was perceived? Did particular frameworks of knowledge, whether because of their structural characteristics or their acquired traditions, emphasize mystical over rational knowledge, positive over reflective approaches, symbolic over concrete understanding?[7] How did different patterns of social relation-

THE CULTURES OF INTELLECTUAL LIFE

ships within particular cultures of intellectual life affect intellectual style and strategies? Felix Gilbert rightly notes that "whether a manuscript [was] circulated among a small number of people with education and interests similar to those of the writer, or whether a manuscript might be read by a great number of people unknown to the author creates necessarily a great difference in the attitude of an author."[8] Does it make a difference that locality-based intellectual life was overwhelmingly face-to-face interchange, while in the modern professions communication is mediated by the printed word?[9] What analytical capacities were strengthened (or weakened) by a shift from one culture of intellectual life to another? How was society's need for general explanatory ideas affected? What was the effect on the prospects for a shared public culture and for a socially responsible intelligentsia?

Professionalism in the eighteenth- and early–nineteenth-centuries differed profoundly from what emerged in association with the graduate school. The scientific professionals who led the way in defining the new professionalism did not take the traditional professions as their model. They created something original.[10] In stressing this discontinuity in the history of the professions, I make a conceptual distinction between what I call "civic professionalism" and "disciplinary professionalism." The former pattern has a historic association with the commercial city and the Florentine tradition of civic humanism, while the latter coincides with the emergence of industrial and corporate capitalism.[11] During the course of the nineteenth century in America, civic professionalism declined in significance and even the traditional professions of law, medicine, and the ministry began to associate themselves with the model provided by the rising disciplinary professions.

The outlines of the change can be sketched in a quick comparison of professionalism revealed in the careers of two men remembered for their contributions to the development of medical training: Samuel Bard and William H. Welch.[12] Bard's reputation rests on his advocacy of a hospital that could be made part of the medical instruction offered at Kings College. His campaign led to the founding of the New York Hospital in 1771, and most commentators have assumed that he thus anticipated "the modern structure of academic medicine."[13] But a superficial similarity with the Johns Hopkins idea of a university hospital should not be allowed to obscure a profound difference between eighteenth- and twentieth-century medical professionalism. Early American professionals were essentially community oriented. Entry to the professions was usually through local elite sponsorship, and professionals won public trust within this established social context rather than through certification. While specialisms were recognized, disciplinary professions did not exist.

THOMAS BENDER

Medicine, like other professions and learned avocations, represented an emphasis within a shared and relatively accessible public culture that was nurtured by general associations of cognoscenti.

Although eighteenth-century professionals were cosmopolitan in their interests, this did not compromise their attachment to localities. They participated avidly in the trans-Atlantic "Republic of Letters," but this union was decentralized and federalized, and not, to use the eighteenth-century political term, consolidated. The cosmopolitanism of intellectuals and professionals often took the form of city-boosting. Bard, who studied in Edinburgh, wanted New York City to have the medical institutions that major European cities had. His advocacy of a hospital was linked to his work in behalf of a whole network of civic institutions. He was active in the effort to rebuild Trinity Church after it was damaged in the Revolutionary War, he was a leader in the reorganization that transformed Kings College into Columbia, and he was one of the initiators of the New York Society Library, the New York Historical Society, and the New York Society for Promoting Useful Knowledge. These efforts in civic improvement were the product of the combined energies of the educated and powerful in the city, and they integrated and gave shape to its intellectual life.[14]

In contrast, the Johns Hopkins of Daniel Coit Gilman and Welch was a product of professional, disciplinary communities. To that extent it was an alien presence in Baltimore. It was created, President Eliot of Harvard stiffly observed, not because of any civic ambition in Baltimore, but because one man, a bachelor Quaker, willed it. The original faculty of philosophy included no Baltimoreans, and no major appointments in the medical school went to members of the local medical community. William Welch, who moved from New York to Johns Hopkins, identified with his profession in a new way; it was a branch of science—a discipline—not a civic role. Bard had been involved, as Welch was not, in a civic culture reminiscent of the traditional role of cities in directing intellectual life.

Other examples of early American civic culture come easily to mind as further illustrations. In antebellum Boston, the intellectual leadership provided by George Ticknor did not depend upon his disciplinary accomplishments or his Harvard professorship. For all of his cosmopolitan awareness and interest in the German model of academic life, Ticknor was enmeshed, socially and intellectually, in the life of the city. He wanted most to be a gentleman of Boston whose civic activities included being a Harvard professor and promoter of the public library. Hence, he took his intellectual cues from his fellow citizens, and their respect made him a preeminent and influential intellectual.[15]

This embrace of civic culture was not merely an eastern seaboard

THE CULTURES OF INTELLECTUAL LIFE

phenomenon. One of the most striking facts of the movement of people and institutions west during the first half of the nineteenth century, at least in the North, was the replication of this civic institution pattern of urban culture in locality after locality. Because intellectual and cultural historians have been careless about specifying the setting for intellectual activity, they have failed to note the surprisingly dense networks of institutions supporting intellectual life in nineteenth-century provincial towns and cities.[16] Even places with small populations aspired to a full intellectual life and established a full complement of urban institutions to nourish it.[17]

Western towns organized their intellectual life on the "principle of mutual instruction."[18] Within the context of this broadly inclusive culture of intellectual life, townspeople discussed the leading scientific and literary publications of the day. In larger towns and cities the key institution giving form to this culture might be a local institute of arts and science; the structure of discourse might, however, be quite informal in small towns. William Dean Howells recalled that in his father's printing office in a small Ohio town about 1850,

> there was always a good deal of talk going on. . . . When it was not mere banter, it was mostly literary; we disputed about authors among ourselves and with the village wits who dropped in. There were several of these who were readers, and they liked to stand with their back to our stove and challenge opinion concerning Holmes and Poe, Irving and Macaulay, Pope and Byron, Dickens and Shakespeare. Any author who made an effect in the East became promptly known in that small village of the Western reserve. . . . Literature was so commonly accepted as a real interest, that I do not think I was accounted altogether queer in my devotion to it.[19]

If Howells emphasized literary interests, other commentators, from Tocqueville, to Martineau, to Lyell, remarked upon the extent of scientific activity they found in American towns. Lyell also noticed how remarkably inclusive intellectual life was. In Cincinnati, he commented, the joining of literary and scientific men, lawyers, clergymen, physicians, "and principal merchants of the place forms a society of a superior kind."[20]

While these townspeople were certainly aware of the greater accomplishments of the metropolises of the East and of Europe, they were not intimidated. In an address before a local literary society in 1814, Daniel Drake of Cincinnati observed:

> Learning, philosophy and taste, are yet in early infancy, and the standards of excellence in literature and science is proportionably low. Hence, acquirements, which in older and more enlightened countries would scarcely raise an individual to mediocrity, will here place him in a commanding station.

THOMAS BENDER

Those who attain to superiority in the community of which they are members are relatively great. Literary excellence in Paris, London, or Edinburgh is incomparable with the same thing in Philadelphia, New York, or Boston: while each of these, in turn, has a standard of merit, which may be contrasted, but cannot be compared, with that of Lexington or Cincinnati.[21]

To a certain extent provincial intellectual life benefited from the same difficulties of transportation and communication that stimulated manufacturing in the small towns of the trans-Appalachian West. There was enough communication with the metropolis to maintain cultural aspirations, but not enough to stifle local activity through domination by metropolitan products, whether in manufacturing or in intellectual life.[22] The large-scale social and economic transformations that would ultimately undermine local life were becoming apparent as early as the 1830s, but it was not until after the Civil War that Americans began to realize their implications. The consequences for civic professionalism were noted by Henry W. Bellows in 1872:

Thousands of American towns, with an independent life of their own, isolated, trusting to themselves, in need of knowing and honoring native ability and skill in local affairs—each with its first-rate man of business, its able lawyer, its skilled physician, its honored representative, its truly *select-men*—have been pierced to the heart by the railroad which they helped to build. . . . It has annihilated their old importance . . . removed the necessity for any first-rate professional men in the village, destroyed local business and taken out of town the enterprising young men, besides exciting the ambition of those once content with a local importance, to seek larger spheres of life.[23]

Bellows, I suspect, expected the establishment and ultimate hegemony of trans-local structures of intellectual life and standards of competence to be accomplished through the ascendancy of an urban-based metropolitan system. In such a cultural model, which implies the legitimate concentration of elites, local organizations of intellectual life would be "federated" under metropolitan auspices. Americans, for example, might have followed the contemporary model of the British Association for the Advancement of Science, which united local, provincial societies in a national framework. American scientists were familiar with the BAAS, but when they organized the American Association for the Advancement of Science a different pattern emerged. The AAAS provided an institutional umbrella for individuals and was organized internally by developing disciplines.[24]

As it turned out, neither city nor metropolis shaped intellectual life. The collapse of intellectual vitality in American towns and cities coupled, perhaps, with an anti-urban resentment of the metropolis, opened

THE CULTURES OF INTELLECTUAL LIFE

the way for the rise of a multicentered and nonlocal system of professionalism stressing individual membership and the fragmentation of elites. That an urban-based metropolitanism failed to develop cannot, however, be blamed entirely upon provincial antipathy to the metropolis. Urban culture itself was in crisis. America's largest cities were no longer able to organize a vital, rigorous, and coherent intellectual life.

The culture of professionalism arose as an alternative to the disorganized urban culture characteristic of the third quarter of the nineteenth century, and it pointed in new directions. If urban culture had been centripetal, encouraging the convergence of specialisms, this new professionalism was centrifugal. Charles W. Eliot, whose reforms at Harvard helped to advance the new professionalism, was one of the earliest to notice this phenomenon. Writing in 1854, when he was twenty and apprehensive about his future, he observed: "What a tremendous question it is—what shall I be? . . . When a man answers that question he not only determines his sphere of usefulness in the world, he also decides in what *direction* his own mind shall be developed. The different professions are not different roads converging on the same end; they are different roads, which starting from the same vantage point *diverge* forever, for all we know."[25]

Intellectual specialization took on a new character in the process of becoming a system of disciplines. No longer an emphasis within a shared public culture, each new disciplinary profession developed its own conceptual basis. Each became a distinct "epistemic community."[26] Disciplinary peers, not a diverse urban public, became the only legitimate evaluators of intellectual work. If the civic institution pattern of intellectual life had woven together the various threads of intellectual life, the fabric of urban public culture was riven by the end of the nineteenth century. Knowledge and competence increasingly developed out of the internal dynamics of esoteric disciplines rather than within the context of shared perceptions of public needs. This is not to say that professionalized disciplines or the modern service professions that imitated them became socially irresponsible. But their contributions to society began to flow from their own self-definitions rather than from a reciprocal engagement with general public discourse.

The process of transition from urban-based to disciplinary intellectual life was complex, and its history reveals fleeting glimpses of what seem to have been alternatives. The American Social Science Association, for example, might be interpreted as a national version of civic professionalism. Its leaders represented traditional professions, and the organization's constitution expressed a hope of bringing together men and women at "both the local and national" level to address broad social

THOMAS BENDER

questions. Internal differentiation was based upon the definition of four areas of public concern rather than on disciplines or subdisciplines. By the end of the century, however, it was clear that the future for the social sciences belonged to professionalized disciplines associated with university departments.[27]

The community of scientists and intellectuals in Washington during the Gilded Age apparently had yet another model in mind. They tried to advance a disciplinary professionalism that was national in scope within the context of a shared urban culture by federating the disciplines in a local organization that offered public lectures. But the lectures and discussions associated with the urban culture component of this organizational strategy rather quickly lost significance.[28] Professional discourse was treated as a serious activity, while the manifestations of traditional urban culture were relegated to the status of mere entertainment.

The beginning of this schism can be seen as early as 1839, when Horace Mann praised the Lyceum and the public lectures typical of urban culture as "interesting and useful" while at the same time complaining that they tended toward "superficiality." He allowed that the "dim and floating notions" they offered might be acceptable for general topics, but he insisted that in areas that pertain to one's "immediate employment or profession" such knowledge would be "not simply useless, but ruinous."[29] Without precisely following Mann's analysis, a number of historians have also detected serious weaknesses in mid-century urban culture.[30] Such words as *flatness, superficiality, sentimentalism, ineffectual, confused, lax,* and *simplification* recur in historical writing about the period's thought. How can we explain the emergence of these intellectual problems? My argument is that a large part of the explanation can be attributed to changes in the city as a context for intellectual work. It no longer provided an effective audience.

Earlier, in the mid-eighteenth century, intellectual community had been available in American villages, towns, and cities. While a real distinction must be made between learned and popular traditions, the two could be bridged. Elite culture depended upon and extended popular culture. It was possible for intellectuals to speak to the pace of local thought and still address serious issues in a learned tradition that was at least dimly familiar to their local community of auditors or readers.[31] Yet this intellectual community was fragile. It was vulnerable to the changes in scale, the calculation and ambition, and the cultural diversity that emerged over the course of the nineteenth century. Although a variety of formal institutions maintained this intellectual community into the nineteenth century, it began to unravel after the 1830s, particularly

THE CULTURES OF INTELLECTUAL LIFE

in the larger cities that might have assumed the role of metropolis for the United States.

Intellect's clear association with general urban elites had achieved for it a certain legitimacy and hegemony within society in the eighteenth and early nineteenth centuries. The social fragmentation, isolation, and anonymity that characterized the chaotic mid–nineteenth-century city eroded these customary sources of intellectual authority. Neither personal knowledge nor clear social categories were available to organize and discipline intellectual life. Intellectual distinctions were blurred, and the identity of audiences became rather diffuse.

Urban intellectuals in the mid-nineteenth century confronted the difficult task of winning acceptance of their special competence in a milieu of strangers. With traditional rituals of accreditation abandoned, producers and consumers of intellectual work found it increasingly difficult to fix on the cues that made coherent intellectual discourse possible. Lacking a solid impersonal basis for establishing a relationship with their audience, urban intellectuals relied on their personalities and the appearance of intimate disclosure to establish the trust and authority essential for intellectual community.[32] But personality was a poor substitute for the shared intellectual framework and clear social categories that had earlier given shape to local intellectual life. In such a situation, the eighteenth-century penchant for argument gave way to the quest for "influence."[33]

Henry Ward Beecher exemplified this pattern of intellectual life and revealed its weakness. The structure of discourse within which he operated as one of New York City's most notable intellectuals did not demand—or allow—hard thinking and vigorous argument. Self-display, sentimentalism, posture, gesture, and preoccupation with external appearance characterized his thought and preaching style. In an important sense he was for theology what Barnum was for art and natural science.[34] And the new professionalism—whether manifested in academic theology or in the Metropolitan Museum of Art—represented an attempt to reform this disorderly pattern of intellectual life.

Those who sought a more penetrating and rigorous intellectual life rejected and withdrew from the general culture of the city in order to embrace a new model of professionalism. Intellectual purposes were thus clarified and made less complicated. Edwards A. Park, in a lecture in Boston to the Massachusetts Congregational Clergy, urged his colleagues to "conduct our scholastic disputes in a scholastic way" for "we do wrong to our own minds when we carry our scientific difficulties down to the arena of popular dissension." Rather conventional formulas were sufficient to fulfill their pastoral duties. Park proposed, in effect, to

THOMAS BENDER

separate the serious technical role of professionals from their responsibility of supplying usable philosophies for the general public. In time, as Bruce Kuklick has demonstrated in the case of Harvard philosophy, even this compromise was eroded by the complete triumph of the technical over the public role of philosophy.[35]

Intellectual life was tightened as people of ideas were inducted, increasingly through the emerging university system, into the restricted worlds of specialized discourse. The quest of professionals for the authority to define valid knowledge within disciplines is often interpreted as an expression of class interest, and to a degree it was.[36] But the new professionals were seeking intellectual security as much as social privilege and power. The new disciplines offered relatively precise subject matter and procedures at a time when both were greatly confused. The new professionalism also promised social guarantees of competence—certification—in an era when criteria of intellectual authority was vague and professional performance unreliable.[37]

Urban and professional cultures were also connected with alternative ways of defining and attempting to solve problems. The authority of disciplinary professionalism was linked to new perceptions of the nature of "reality." Representatives of urban culture—from Daniel Drake to P. T. Barnum—had assumed that reality was generally accessible to common observation.[38] However democratic, this naive empiricism was gradually rejected as inadequate. The new professions were associated with a growing sense that understanding must penetrate internal qualities, processes, and structures. Serious intellectual problems and procedures were largely reformulated, most notably in respect to scientific work and in the analysis of society (social science).[39] Valid knowledge, formerly concretized in individual relationships to nature and society, now seemed to be defined in forms and processes one step removed from direct human experience.

Certainly we must welcome the new power and rigor that the disciplinary professions brought to a disorganized nineteenth-century intellectual life. Yet the twentieth-century hegemony of the new professionalism remains problematical. As Edmund Wilson pointed out in *The Wound and the Bow*, powerful new weapons are often inseparable from serious disability. Rigor and intellectual security were gained at the cost of making the parts of American intellectual life more powerful than the whole. Was an intellectual community that comprehended the whole of life compatible with the new professions? When the character of modern professionalism's relation to the social whole was becoming apparent, Alfred North Whitehead pointedly observed: "Each profession makes progress, but it is progress in its own groove. But there is no groove . . . adequate for the comprehension of human life. . . . Of course, no one is

THE CULTURES OF INTELLECTUAL LIFE

merely a mathematician, or merely a lawyer. People have lives outside of their profession or their business. But the point is the restraint of serious thought within a groove. The remainder of life is treated superficially, with the imperfect categories of thought derived from one profession."[40]

The various patterns of intellectual community that have constituted effective audiences for American intellectuals deserve finer analysis than can be offered here. But even this necessarily schematic analysis of the city and the professions as alternative communities of discourse expands our understanding of the historical configurations of American intellectual life. And it suggests a fruitful approach for a history of the life of the mind in America.

When Merle Curti first presented his "social history of American thought" to the profession in 1943, his goal of linking social and intellectual history was not assumed to be at all problematical.[41] In recent years, however, social and intellectual history have been increasingly uncomfortable in each other's company. In looking for terms of rapprochement with social history, intellectual historians have been unduly attentive to the quantitative emphasis of much American and French social history.[42] A more fruitful approach to a social history of ideas is to focus on the way in which the social organization of knowledge affects the style, content, and social significance of intellectual activity.

By directing our attention to the social framework of intellectual life, the activity of the mind can be firmly located in time and place.[43] Writing intellectual history from a local standpoint becomes an exciting possibility. Here the full institutional matrix of intellectual life can be studied in sufficient detail to grasp the way in which specific ideas or ways of thinking develop, gain hegemony or lose significance, and are used in particular settings. We would learn much from studies of the changing social framework of knowledge in a particular locality over two or three centuries. How do various structures of discourse succeed each other over time and interact with each other? How are these changes related to the larger systems of ideas, social structures, and economies that find concrete articulation in a given locality?

These questions point toward a social history of ideas that can analyze the structures within which ideas are formulated, appropriated for use, and achieve hegemony in a given society. These issues are central to understanding the life of the mind because it is within these structures that reality is defined, and changes in the perception of reality are associated with changes in these structures over time. My emphasis here on the social foundations of intellectual life is not intended to deny that

THOMAS BENDER

the life of the mind is enmeshed in a world of ideas. The structure of ideas must be studied closely by historians, but this work must be matched by study of the structures within which ideas are developed, modified, and transmitted. Such a study will advance our understanding of how the various structures of discourse available to Americans for organizing intellectual life have enhanced (or hampered) their ability to penetrate "the nature of things."[44]

Notes

1. Thomas Kuhn's discussion of the paradigm in *The Structure of Scientific Revolutions*, rev. ed. (1962; Chicago: University of Chicago Press, 1970) suggests but does not quite say that a paradigm's significance flows from its institutionalization. See also Stephen E. Toulmin, *Human Understanding*, vol. I (Princeton, N.J.: Princeton University Press, 1972). For an example, see Frank Manuel's discussion of Newtonian science in his *Portrait of Isaac Newton* (Cambridge: Harvard University Press, 1968).

2. Daniel Bell writes: "Reality is a confirmation by 'significant others.'" (*The Cultural Contradictions of Capitalism* [New York: Basic Books, 1976], p. 90). More generally, see Bukart Holzner, *Reality Construction in Society* (Cambridge, Mass.: Schenkman, 1968); and Peter L. Berger and Thomas Luckmann, *The Social Construction of Reality: A Treatise in the Sociology of Knowledge* (Garden City, N.Y.: Doubleday, 1966).

3. Robert K. Merton, *Social Theory and Social Structure*, rev. ed. (New York: Free Press, 1957), pp. 482–83.

4. Quoted phrase from Georges Gurvitch, *The Social Frameworks of Knowledge*, trans. M. Thompson and K. Thompson (Oxford, England: Blackwell, 1971).

5. Thomas L. Haskell, *The Emergence of Professional Social Science: The American Social Science Association and the Nineteenth-Century Crisis of Authority* (Urbana: University of Illinois Press, 1977); Bruce Kuklick, *The Rise of American Philosophy: Cambridge, Massachusetts, 1860–1930* (New Haven, Conn.: Yale University Press, 1977); Burton J. Bledstein, *The Culture of Professionalism* (New York: W. W. Norton, 1976); Mary O. Furner, *Advocacy and Objectivity: A Crisis in the Professionalization of American Social Science, 1865–1905* (Lexington: University Press of Kentucky, 1975); Sally G. Kohlstedt, *The Formation of the American Scientific Community: The American Association for the Advancement of Science, 1848–1860* (Urbana: University of Illinois Press, 1976); Daniel H. Calhoun, *Professional Lives in America: Structure and Aspiration, 1750–1850* (Cambridge: Harvard University Press, 1965). See also two excellent review essays of some of this recent literature: Bari Watkins in *History and Theory* 15 (1976): 57–66; and Henrika Kuklick in *American Quarterly* 28 (1976): 124–41. Twenty-five years ago Donald Fleming wrote a brief (and not entirely successful) study that he presented as a model for further studies of the relationship of science and local communities, but the study seems to have been forgotten rather than built upon. See Donald Fleming, *Science and Technology in Providence, 1760–1914: An Essay in the History of Brown University in the Metropolitan Community* (Providence, R.I.: Brown University Press, 1952). Some provocative questions concerning the American city as a context for intellectual life are posed in Perry Miller, *The Raven and the Whale* (New York: Harcourt, Brace and World, 1956); and Martin Green, *The Problem of Boston* (New York: W. W. Norton, 1966). Although his focus is not quite on intellectual life, many stimulating perceptions on the changing character of urban culture can be

THE CULTURES OF INTELLECTUAL LIFE

gleaned from Neil Harris, "Four Stages of Cultural Growth: The American City," in *The History and Role of the City in American Life*, ed. Arthur Mann, et al. (Indianapolis: Indiana Historical Society, 1972), pp. 24–49. Manchester, England, is the subject of two interesting recent attempts to study intellectual history from an urban perspective, while Vienna is the subject of another. See Arnold Thackray, "Natural Knowledge in a Cultural Context: The Manchester Model," *American Historical Review* 79 (1974): 672–709; Robert H. Kargon, *Science in Victorian Manchester* (Baltimore, Md.: The Johns Hopkins University Press, 1977); and Allan Janik and Stephen Toulmin, *Wittgenstein's Vienna* (New York: Simon & Schuster, 1973).

6. On this process, see Thomas Bender, "Science and the Culture of American Communities: The Nineteenth Century," *History of Education Quarterly* 16 (1976): 63–77.

7. These issues are raised, in far broader contexts, in Gurvitch, *Social Frameworks of Knowledge*, and in Jürgen Habermas, *Knowledge and Human Interests* (Boston: Beacon Press, 1971).

8. Felix Gilbert, "Intellectual History: Its Aims and Methods," *Daedalus* 100 (Winter 1971): 80–97. Other conventional examples might be noted, including London coffee houses, Paris salons, or, later, cafés. See Lewis Coser, *Men of Ideas* (New York: Free Press, 1965).

9. Walter J. Ong is suggestive here. See his "Agonistic Structures in Academia: Past to Present," *Daedalus* 103 (Fall 1974): 229–38.

10. Nathan Reingold, "Definitions and Speculations: The Professionalization of Science in America in the Nineteenth Century," in *The Pursuit of Knowledge in the Early Republic*, ed. Alexandra Oleson and Sanborn C. Brown (Baltimore, Md.: The Johns Hopkins University Press, 1976), p. 48. Compare the assumption of continuity in Samuel Haber, "The Professions and Higher Education in America: A Historical View," in *Higher Education and the Labor Market*, ed. Margaret Gordon (New York: McGraw-Hill, 1974), pp. 237–80, with the argument of a distinctive form of professionalism in the era of industrial and corporate capitalism in Magali Sarfatti Larson, *The Rise of Professionalism: A Sociological Analysis* (Berkeley: University of California Press, 1977).

11. Florence provides the baseline for assessing civic culture; hence my notion of "civic professionalism" is intentionally reminiscent of the "civic humanism" so prominent in Florentine historiography. See especially Lauro Martines, *The Social World of the Florentine Humanists, 1390–1460* (Princeton, N.J.: Princeton University Press, 1963); Eugenio Garin, *Italian Humanism*, trans. Peter Munz (Oxford, England: Blackwell, 1965); and Gene Brucker, *Renaissance Florence* (New York: John Wiley, 1969), esp. chs. 3, 6. J. G. A. Pocock's recent book demonstrating the persistence of certain Florentine categories in early American republican thought suggests an interesting possibility for urban history; perhaps Florence also provided the central example for the basic social organization of intellectual life in a republic. See *The Machiavellian Moment: Florentine Political Thought and the Atlantic Republican Tradition* (Princeton, N.J.: Princeton University Press, 1975).

12. What follows is based is based upon my unpublished essay, "New York Hospital and the Culture of Cities." The most important secondary references are Calhoun, *Professional Lives*, ch. 2; and Donald H. Fleming, *William H. Welch and the Rise of Modern Medicine* (Boston: Little, Brown, 1954).

13. Eric Larrabee, *The Benevolent and Necessary Institution: The New York Hospital, 1771–1971* (Garden City, N.Y.: Doubleday, 1971), p. 2.

14. To some extent this movement reflects a quest for identity by a provincial elite. An essay that makes this point about Edinburgh, a city whose civic culture had deeply impressed Bard, is N. T. Phillipson's "Culture and Society in the 18th Century Province: The Case of Edinburgh and the Scottish Enlightenment," in *The University in Society*, ed. Lawrence Stone, 2 vols. (Princeton, N.J.: Princeton University Press, 1974), 2: 407–48.

THOMAS BENDER

15. David B. Tyack, *George Ticknor and the Boston Brahmins* (Cambridge: Harvard University Press, 1967), p. 27 and *passim*; Green, *Problem of Boston*, ch. 4. For Harvard as a local institution, see Ronald Story, "Harvard and the Boston Brahmins: A Study in Institutional and Class Development, 1800–1865," *Journal of Social History* 8 (1975): 94–121. Much the same can be said in the case of Boston for James Russell Lowell's slightly later generation. See Edward Everett Hale, *James Russell Lowell and His Friends* (Boston: Houghton, Mifflin, 1899), ch. 5.

16. Even in French intellectual history, where a concentration on Paris seems more justifiable, the data available on provincial intellectual life is beginning to force broader conceptions of French intellectual history. See Theodore Zeldin, *France, 1848–1945*, 2 vols. (Oxford, England: At the Clarendon Press, 1973–77), 2: 29–43.

17. Daniel Boorstin, *The Americans: The National Experience* (New York: Random House, 1965), pp. 113–68; Richard Wade, *The Urban Frontier* (Chicago: University of Chicago Press, 1964); Robert Wiebe, *The Segmented Society* (New York: Oxford University Press, 1975), p. 37.

18. Charles P. Cist, *Cincinnati in 1841* (Cincinnati: printed and published for the author, 1841), p. 129.

19. William Dean Howells, *Years of My Youth* [1916] (Bloomington: Indiana University Press, 1975), pp. 77, 92.

20. Charles Lyell, *Travels in North America*, 2 vols. (London: J. Murray, 1855), 1: 106–9. See also Alexis de Tocqueville, *Democracy in America*, 2 vols. (New York: Vintage, 1945), 2:47; Harriet Martineau, *Retrospect of Western Travel*, 2 vols. (London: Saunders & Otley, 1838), 2:91.

21. Henry D. Shapiro and Zane L. Miller, eds., *Physician to the West: Selected Writings of Daniel Drake on Science & Society* (Lexington: University Press of Kentucky, 1970), p. 59.

22. On the tariff function of poor transportation, see Julius Rubin, "Urban Growth and Regional Development," in *The Growth of Seaport Cities, 1790–1825*, ed. David Gilchrist (Charlottesville: University of Virginia Press, 1967), pp. 3–21. Antebellum communication patterns are discussed in relation to urban development in Allen R. Pred, *Urban Growth and the Circulation of Information, 1790–1840* (Cambridge: Harvard University Press, 1973).

23. Henry W. Bellows, "The Townward Tendency," *The City*, 1872, p. 38. For some general observations on the changing significance of locality in American culture, see Thomas Bender, *Community and Social Change in America* (New Brunswick, N.J.: Rutgers University Press, 1978), ch. 3.

24. Kohlstedt, *Formation of the American Scientific Community*, pp. 83–84. See also Henry D. Shapiro, "The Western Academy of Natural Sciences of Cincinnati and the Structure of Science in the Ohio Valley, 1810–1850," in *The Pursuit of Knowledge*, ed. Oleson and Sanborn, pp. 237–42; and Hamilton Cravens, "American Science Comes of Age: An Institutional Perspective, 1850–1930," *American Studies* 17 (1976): 49–70.

25. Quoted in Bledstein, *Culture of Professionalism*, p. 159.

26. Holzner, *Reality Construction in Society*, pp. 68–69.

27. See Haskell, *Emergence of Professional Social Science*, and Furner, *Advocacy and Objectivity*, ch. 1.

28. See J. Kirkpatrick Flack, *Desideratum in Washington: The Intellectual Community in the Capital City, 1870–1900* (Cambridge, Mass.: Schenkman, 1975).

29. Massachusetts Board of Education, *Third Annual Report* (Boston, 1839), pp. 78–79.

30. See, for example, Miller, *Raven and the Whale*; Daniel Calhoun, *Professional Lives*; idem, *The Intelligence of a People* (Princeton, N.J.: Princeton University Press, 1973); Neil Harris, *Humbug: The Art of P. T. Barnum* (Boston: Little, Brown, 1973); Green, *Problem of Boston*; Ann Douglas, *The Feminization of American Culture* (New York: Alfred A. Knopf, 1977).

THE CULTURES OF INTELLECTUAL LIFE

31. Calhoun, *Intelligence of a People*, pp. 229–30 and *passim*. See also David Hall, "The World of Print and Collective Mentality in Seventeenth-Century New England," chapter 10 of this volume.
32. Douglas, *Feminization of American Culture*, p. 142. More generally, see Richard Sennett, *The Fall of Public Man* (New York: Alfred A. Knopf, 1977). On the problem writers had in defining their audience, see William Charvat, *Literary Publishing in the United States, 1790–1850* (Philadelphia: University of Pennsylvania Press, 1959).
33. Douglas, *Feminization of American Culture*, pt. 1.
34. On Beecher's intellectual style, see the comments in Douglas, *Feminization of American Culture*, pp. 81–84, 132–41, 153–61; and Calhoun, *Intelligence of a People*, pp. 256–91. On Barnum, see Harris, *Humbug*.
35. Edwards A. Park, *Discourse Delivered in Boston. . . .* (Andover: Allen, Morrill, Wordwell, 1844), pp. 5–7; Kuklick, *Rise of American Philosophy*, see esp. pp. 560–72.
36. See, for example, Larson, *Rise of Professionalism*.
37. Surely after the Tilton affair, the moral and intellectual authority symbolized by Beecher's style was suspect. E. L. Godkin points this out in "Chromo-civilization," *The Nation* 19 (1874): 201–2. The embarassingly frequent collapses of built structures—from factories to bridges—called other types of competence into question.
38. See Bender, "Science and the Culture of American Communities," pp. 70–71.
39. See Calhoun, *Intelligence of a People*. pp. 319–22; and Haskell, *Emergence of Professional Social Science*.
40. Alfred North Whitehead, *Science and the Modern World* (1925; reprint ed., New York: Mentor Books, 1948), pp. 196–97.
41. Merle Curti, *The Growth of American Thought*, 2d ed. rev. (1943; New York: Harper, 1951), p. vi.
42. See Robert Darnton, "In Search of the Enlightenment: Recent Attempts to Create a Social History of Ideas," *Journal of Modern History* 43 (1971): 113–32. A dominant response of intellectual historians to social history is reflected in the concern for quantitative data on social structures and book distribution in Henry F. May, *The Enlightenment in America* (New York: Oxford University Press, 1976). The desire for rapprochement is clear in May's comment in p. 364n. The current concern for grounding ideas in the work of quantitative social history does not, however, produce a clear sense of the structure of discourse.
43. While the customary practice of studying ideas in a national context is difficult to defend, a study of intellectual life as a cultural activity within a given society is easily justified.
44. The phrase is originally from Paul Goodman; I have taken it from Thomas L. Haskell, "Power to the Experts," *New York Review of Books* 24 (13 October 1977): 28–33.

ICONOGRAPHY AND INTELLECTUAL HISTORY: THE HALF-TONE EFFECT

NEIL HARRIS

The relationship between iconography and American intellectual history has been cold and distant. Intellectual historians have used words rather than images to define their subjects and provide their evidence. This has by no means confined the discipline to the history of ideas as a disengaged subject; institutionalists, psychohistorians, and social historians have examined the history of consciousness and provided other historians with models, issues, and arguments. But the energy concentrated upon written texts as points of departure has accompanied an indifference toward those shifts of style and form that belong to physical objects. The history of stylistic change has been left in the care of art historians.

As the study of pictorial description, iconography has involved, for the most part, the examination of stylistic transformations. Its students, evaluating changing inclusions and exclusions, placements, techniques, and visual formulations, have therefore treated iconographic identity as a stylistic problem. The ability to detect changes in the manipulation of images quite obviously rests on familiarity with established conventions. The requisite discriminations belong to those who are habituated to the analysis of pictures and objects. The training of intellectual historians makes them unlikely candidates for substantial contributions, if iconography retains its current definition.

It would be possible, if time consuming, to explore the historiography systematically, and demonstrate how isolated the history of American art, architecture, and artifacts has been from the history of American thought. One could turn to classic texts and argue from omission, or supply samplings from major journals and discuss trends. The *Journal of the History of Ideas*, for example, reveals fewer than a dozen articles in more than twenty years that confront changes in physical style, and these are almost entirely concerned with non-American subjects. The end results of such a survey would be to point with alarm and make promises for the future. But the reasons for failure are, as I suggest, obvious, and not easily surmounted.

Although traditional iconographic analysis rests upon a level of

ICONOGRAPHY AND INTELLECTUAL HISTORY

training achievable only by substantial reorganization of our various disciplines, there still remain unexploited possibilities, changes in image-making so gross and dramatic that they do not require the peculiar competence of art historians for study. They can and should be confronted by historians of mind and consciousness. For American historians, who operate within a more compressed time frame than most colleagues, this means, practically, considering changes in image-making produced by technological innovation or adaption. This task is not necessarily easier than the analysis of more traditional objects or works of art. In some cases it is far more complex. It requires sensitivities that span several areas of interest, and a good deal of aggressive juxtaposition. But the integrative commitments of many intellectual historians, their concern for contextualizing, and their experience in establishing correspondences between mental processes and the possibilities or restrictions of social settings suggest their suitability for the task.

To indicate one such possibility I should like to examine an accomplishment that possesses great significance to the student of American thought and behavior during the late nineteenth and early twentieth centuries. So far as I know it has received little attention from anyone but historians of printing and photography. It is the coming of the half-tone engraving process to American magazines, books, and newspapers. First appearing in the 1880s and early nineties, by 1900 it was firmly established as a major reproductive method for publishers of mass illustrated materials.

The half-tone was developed to solve a problem that had bedeviled printers for a long time: securing a photomechanical method of reproducing images, and doing this by using a printing block that was applicable to the same paper that accepted type. Decades of experimentation preceded Stephen Horgan's production, in 1880, for the New York *Graphic*, of a half-tone reproduction of "A Scene in Shanty Town." In the newspaper's words, "There has been no redrawing of the picture. The transfer print has been obtained direct from the original negative." Horgan, according to Robert Taft, interposed "a screen of fine parallel rulings between the negative . . . made in the camera and the sensitive surface of bichromated gelatin. . . . The screen was made by photographing a mechanically ruled surface on the film of a wet collodion plate. . . . The film, after exposure and development, was stripped from the glass plate and became the half-tone screen."[1]

There were many improvements and refinements necessary before the invention could be put to daily use; Frederic Ives and Louis and Max Levy were among the Americans who helped perfect the screen. There were also many other experiments in photomechanical reproductions, in steady development since the middle of the nineteenth century. These

NEIL HARRIS

included the collotype, photogravure, the Woodburytype, process line
engraving, to name some of the major examples. But by the 1890s the
power of the half-tone to reproduce illustrations with shadows and tones,
most of all its ability to reproduce photographs, was beginning to sweep
all before it.

Until then photographs had been difficult to reproduce effectively in
type-compatible printing. Some publishers, wishing to use photographs
in books, had to slip in positive prints along with the pages of type.
Newspapers and magazines employed engravers to reproduce photographs and paintings. There were, of course, many methods. Wood
engraving, stipple and line engraving from metal plates, chromolithogra-
phy, all obtained brilliant levels of technical excellence. And, for various
purposes, these methods have been used in books and periodicals right
through the present time.

But then came the screen half-tone. This process, as several printing
historians have pointed out, was more than simply a technological innovation; it was an iconographical revolution as well. Because what the
half-tone did was translate—or code—the original picture in a new way.
It not only increased, geometrically, the mass of pictorial matter presented to the public, it also changed the quality of its appearance. It required adjustments and new expectations about appropriateness. And it
stimulated extended commentary. According to one historian of the process, Estelle Jussim, the heart of the iconographical shift was the disappearance of the "sign function" of the reproduction; it became "an
optical illusion with surrogate power."[2] Previously, Jussim argues, readers encountering illustrations were made aware of the subjective, contrived character of the pictures; these were obviously the product of an
artist's mind and tools. And they still were, when the half-tone repro-
duced a painting or print. But with the half-tone photograph, a photomechanical reproduction of a photochemical image, the illusion of seeing
an actual scene, or receiving an objective record of such a scene, was
immeasurably enhanced.

To further develop her point, Jussim argues that in the 1880s, when
the screen half-tone first appeared, magazines and books existed in a
state of reproductive limbo, containing true multimedia experiences:
wood engravings, full-process half-tones, white-line tonal wood engravings, line engravings, and combinations of all these type-compatible pictures were, in fact, mingled together. But inexorably, the processed
half-tones, appealing to some deeper level of psychological satisfaction,
began to drive out the wood engravings and pen drawings; phototech-
nology defeated the artist-mediated form of reproduction. In a fascinating
chapter that focuses on the picture books of world's fairs, Jussim presents
the scope of this change in the literature concerning Chicago's Columbian

ICONOGRAPHY AND INTELLECTUAL HISTORY

Exposition of 1893. Only 25 percent of the books published about the Exposition, she points out, contained any process other than process half-tone and process line engraving.[3] The popularity of these books today owes a good deal to this fact; with them, and with the periodicals that employed their systems of reproduction to publicize the fairs, we have entered the modern world of visual reproduction. The contrast with the visual reproductions of just a decade before is startling. Except for the addition of color, which would be developed by improved processes in the twentieth century, the illustrations match for persuasive power and technical impressiveness many of the photographic illustrations that appear in contemporary publications.

The Jussim argument may be a bit exaggerated. It fails to acknowl-edge an extremely important aspect of visual reproduction: the perma-nent continuity of nonphotographic reproductions as appropriate and popular illustrative and informative devices, in newspapers and maga-zines particularly. One of the most interesting results of this revolution, in fact, is the creation of categories of appropriateness, in which certain kinds of visual reproduction—photographic, drawn, painted—seem more valid in certain situations than others. I will return to this later. But despite this caveat, what Jussim and other historians of printing repro-duction point out is indisputable: in a period of ten or fifteen years the whole system of packaging visual information was transformed, made more appealing and persuadable, and assumed a form and adopted conventions that have persisted right through the present.

This then, is an iconographical revolution of the first order, and should be treated with careful attention. The single generation of Americans living between 1885 and 1910 went through an experience of visual reorientation that had few earlier precedents, although it would be matched by some twentieth-century experiences. The one earlier parallel that seemed to possess even greater scope and capacity for influence took place almost four centuries before, with the introduction of printing as a new code for transmitting verbal information. The Gutenberg Revo-lution has been the focus of sustained, elaborate, and controversial commentary, involving scholars from various disciplines. Some of its effects have been trumpeted too loudly, and more careful differentia-tions, distinctions, and tests have been introduced in the last few years to refine and qualify the glamorous generalizations 'that some associate with the name of McLuhan. And intellectual historians have played a major role in assessing the character of the printing revolution.

But American intellectual historians have done little with the history of our visual processing, although its impact, purely as a stylistic matter, was obviously great. The reasons for this failure are several, and their listing suggests, I think, some of the problems of subject definition that

NEIL HARRIS

have restricted the appeal of intellectual history. First of all, the coming of pictures, either as replacements for written words or enticing and subversive supplements to them, has seemed to many thoughtful people of the late nineteenth century, and today, artistically and intellectually suspect. As students of the word, with a large investment in careful verbal analysis, intellectual historians, like colleagues in other fields, have tended to deprecate surrogates thrown up by the Industrial Revolution, surrogates that threatened the primacy of printed communication and menaced the very concept of authenticity itself. The mass of inexpensive, sometimes sensational illustrations that took up increasing space in periodicals represented degeneration. Once the phenomenon had been noted, and deplored, it seemed unworthy of serious study. Art historians, with no necessary bias against graphic communication, did not pay much attention to the half-tone revolution, for one reason, because newspaper and magazine illustration in the prephotographic era was a minor art in itself, and for another, because photography, for a long time, seemed a mechanical device that did not require aesthetic analysis. So attention was given to other matters.

Secondly, the new reproductive methods were tied closely to commercialization, through both the forums that included them and the products associated with the pictures. The taint of money-making and profitable exploitation attached itself to this iconographic revolution; in general intellectual historians have given little effort to studying the history of American business and commerce. One evidence of that is the small number of serious studies of American advertising. European historians have, it must be admitted, been more assiduous in examining popularization processes and marketing, partly because their literary links have been better established, and partly because the longer period of time that has separated the manufacture of evidence from its study has more easily legitimized the subject.

A third reason for the failure to take greater note of this change lies in the character of the innovations themselves. They were technologically complex, and confusing in detail.[4] Assessment of their significance requires some absorption, not in the grand tradition of scientific theorizing, which historians of science do so well, but in minor, mundane, mechanical tinkering, bitterly disputed and often not explained with any degree of thoroughness. Since the history of technology in general has not formed a part of the usual training of American intellectual historians, but has remained in limbo as a semi-independent field of specialization, the vocabulary and interests necessary to integrate this praxis with the history of thought are not widely available. Joining iconography and intellectual history, for recent American history, requires a sensitivity to changing modes of visual transmission. Not only type-compatible repro-

ICONOGRAPHY AND INTELLECTUAL HISTORY

duction, but color photography, motion pictures, and television demand some immersion in operational details.

Fourth and finally, this kind of subject matter, once ignored, becomes provincial; its relationship to established issues within the field of intellectual history seems tenuous. What use is the demonstration of changes in visual coding unless some larger implications can be developed? This is, at the same time, the most important reason for the failure to develop historiographical ventures into new areas, and the most difficult to correct. It cannot be solved until the historiography itself develops.

Artistically suspect, commercially tainted, technically cumbersome, and intellectually isolated, the development of modern visual reproduction methods has failed to engage general historical interest. And until these problems are met, I believe that iconographical analysis will continue to suffer the isolation described at the beginning of the paper. The problem remains, however, of assessing the significance of the half-tone process itself. And here one can turn to the considerable debate that took place, in the late nineteenth century, about changes in media form.

The literature of controversy is abundant, but its uses have been somewhat narrow. Because of present interests in the development of photography and its elevation to an important art form, claiming equal dignity (and prices) with painting, the late–nineteenth-century discussion has been analyzed as combat about the aesthetic status of photography. It is this, to be sure, but it is also a dialogue about the nature of communication, and more particularly an early set of responses to the thrust of what would later be termed mass culture.

Starting from the early experiments of Daguerre, of course, painters and illustrators were concerned about the threat to their livelihood that photographers presented, particularly the portraitists.[5] If the creation of a memory piece was the principal motive powering a portrait commission, nonmediated, or apparently nonmediated, images possessed an objectivity that seemed more satisfying to many customers. Landscapes could be and were idealized by the painter; so were history, allegory, and scripture, generally unavailable to the photographer in any case. But the human face and figure, off which so many artists lived, could be idealized only in a more limited way. It was a natural subject for literalism. The idealizing was generally done by friends and relatives, who would endow the physical lineaments of the subject with the memories and associations that belonged to it. Moreover, the subject of a commission demanded self-recognition, and could not be transformed into total sublimity without some questions being asked. The solution of painters, in some instances, had been to keep the essential features, warts and all, but select a setting and costume that dignified, beautified, or exalted the sitter, or in the case of some of our early–nineteenth-century artists, proudly proclaimed doughty republican virtues and the advantages of a self-made background. Details of occupation and background added to conviction.

Daguerreotypists and photographic portraitists, however, could make the best of both worlds. While claiming objectivity for their cameras, they could establish studios that offered flattering trappings—exotic backdrops, lush foliage, interesting costumes and accessories. They did not have to abandon entirely those conventions of portraiture which added allurement, and yet they could protect themselves from the customer's angry protests about what had been done to his face.

Impressed by the threat, painters, illustrators, and critics joined a vigorous and often angry discussion about the capacity and status of the camera and its products, and this was extended, of course, to include photographic illustrations. Few defended the values of literalism and objectivity as such, save for "subordinate" uses such as scientific research, documentation, or medical diagnosis. Since art as a category enjoyed such high repute in Victorian America, it was crucial to determine whether or not the photograph could compete with the painting or drawing as an object. So defenders of photography insisted that the photographer, like the artist, had available a wide range of choices. The selection of lenses, apertures, lighting, distance, made personal decision-making and judgment as vital to his work as it was for the painter. This was the position of Charles H. Caffin, an art critic with broad tolerances who published *Photography as a Fine Art* at the turn of the century.[6]

But culturally conservative journals, like the *Nation*, disagreed. The photographer's landscapes, "however modified in effect, must be always topographical, his figures must be strictly naturalistic in form." Photography "is not a fine art because it can invent nothing. It can give us a true record or a muddled and falsified one," and that was the only choice available.[7] What worried many critics of photography was a loss of mastery over events and occasions, a diminution of the artist's ability to create a comprehensive and self-sufficient achievement. The photographer, in their eyes, seemed too passive, a responder rather than a shaper, accurate or inaccurate, but never inspired or original. The coming dominance of photography, like that of so many other areas of modern life, seemed to spell a shrinkage of human effectiveness, even while it opened up vast new areas for amusement and recreation.

The nature of this bias was revealed in a semihumorous comment made by the same journal, the *Nation*, entitled "The Perils of Photography."[8] Here it acknowledged the manly, even heroic status of news photographers, who courted danger to record war, violence, and disaster. If the photograph was passive, the photographers surely were not. Nonetheless, events perversely refused to "adopt themselves to the

ICONOGRAPHY AND INTELLECTUAL HISTORY

photographer's eye." The moment when he chose to make the picture might not be the optimal moment to record the event; and sudden accidents could destroy the value of the image. More traditional artists, however, faced no such problems. The history painter was more in command. "His barons never get in the way of a clear view of King John at Runnymede; nor has he to erase any of the Roman populace with gray pigment," to reveal what "Mark Antony is offering to Caesar."[9] What had been gained in personal status by the photographic journalists was lost by the contingent character of their craft. Will Irwin's piece, "The Swashbucklers of the Camera," for *Collier's*, made a similar kind of point, at least by implication. The news photographer had to be patient, thick skinned, indifferent to danger, and "retain enough self-poise after long runs, frantic climbing of fences, struggles with policemen, persuasion of reluctant victims." But he needed these heroic virtues "to ply with certainty one of the most delicate and complicated trades known to modern life."[10] He bore, in short, the same relationship to art that the journalist bore to literature, and, to conservatives at least, symbolized the way in which events were controlling man. All of this activity existed simply to record what was happening, simultaneously, to someone else.

The debate about loss of control, touched off by the reproductive improvements, was only one aspect of the cultural modernization that threatened to overwhelm older values. Distortion was another. The ease of reproducing images, drawn images as well as photographic images, excited attacks from those who felt that literary standards were being relaxed, perhaps fatally, by journals that would never have permitted these weaknesses to appear in their fiction or documentary reporting. Images were not only failing, in many instances, to complement the text, they were actually contradicting it. Tudor Jenks argued in the *Independent* that illustrators of fiction were exaggerating the purely pictorial aspects of stories and failing to supplement the plots. Modern illustrators, he insisted, were able to produce academically correct drawings, but they were a far cry from the greatness of John Leech, Felix Darley, and Doré; their work often bore little reference to the texts.[11] The *Atlantic Monthly* also argued that illustrators distorted fiction by raising passing details to unjustified importance and selecting the commonplace, instead of the unusual, as subject matter.[12] And one letter writer to the *Dial* protested against the deceptive and misleading illustrations to nonfiction. "Has not the time come," asked C. F. Tucker Brooke, "to demand that the pictures introduced into works on social and cultural conditions be subjected to the same investigation which is given to other testimony?" While Sidney Lanier was describing Tudor innyards, his illustrators presented eighteenth-century coaching inns; at other times hypothetical illustrations were passed off as an actual record. As "the

NEIL HARRIS

rage for illustration" had now passed from magazines to serious textbooks, Brooke continued, it must be realized that "pictures irresponsibly
selected, and inserted without adequate investigation, can easily lead to
more serious misapprehension than would result from glaring error in
the letter-press."[13] The picture's greater persuasive power made mistakes
more dangerous.

Vulgarization and error, loss of control, these were complemented by
another feature of mass culture: standardization. The increased number
of images being produced by illustrators was an apparent response to
categorical imperatives rather than to the needs of individual articles
and pieces. Some conservative critics saw the origins of this in the sensational political cartoons, which, in the hands of men like Nast, Opper,
Wales, and others, represented a pernicious influence. After words had
lost their significance, the Nation argued, "pictures had to come sooner
or later. The childish view of the world is, so to speak, 'on top.' " Soon
the illustrated cuts, in their turn, would pall "and have to be supple-
mented by something more infantile still. The reader will demand and
have to get a rattle, or a colored India-rubber balloon, or a bright ball of
worsted, or a jack-in-the-box, with each year's subscription."[14] The Atlantic proclaiming its horror of "the discolored supplement," and cartoons that defied "every maxim of morals and aesthetics," felt that the
"tendency to mere symbolism" in newspaper pictures had become characteristic and deadly. "Buster Brown's costume is as fixed as the green
tunic of St. Peter . . . Father Knickerbocker in buckled shoes, stockings,
breeches, long waistcoat, flaring frock . . . Pitt in something like court
costume; the late William Penn looking like an eighteenth-century publi-
can . . . these are examples of symbolic figures which are probably
destined to rival Uncle Sam and John Bull in permanence." Other cities
besides Philadelphia, New York, and Pittsburgh would soon be developing their own emblems. This tendency to fixed symbolic forms was
apparently a feature of "the decaying periods of all artistic nations," and
resulted from the recurrent discovery "that imitation and fixed formulas
were easier and more remunerative" than originality and initiative. Art,
in short, had become a consumer product, reduced to immediate titilla-
tion by reliance upon formulas. "Emblematism" was a trifling artistic
motive, raised to sudden importance by the mass audience.[15] The Bookman, surveying a recent rash of illustrations for romantic fiction, hinted
darkly at a "Heroine Trust," grafting its uniform versions of feminine
beauty on a range of unsuspecting readers.[16]

The case against the new iconography was summed up in a 1911
editorial in Harper's Weekly, entitled, significantly, "Over-Illustration."
"We can scarce get the sense of what we read for the pictures," complained Harper's. "We can't see the ideas for the illustrations. Our world

ICONOGRAPHY AND INTELLECTUAL HISTORY

is simply flooded with them. They lurk in almost every form of printed matter." There were ancient origins, of course. "The knight of old, the castle, city, province," each had its own pictorial device, but these were minor forerunners to what had become literally an avalanche. Subordinated, illustrations aided thought, but improperly used, they became "a mental drug." "And it would be safe to say that a young mind, overfed pictorially, will scarcely be likely to do any original thinking." Because so many illustrations failed to illuminate their subjects, they precluded thought and actually prevented visualization. Thinking was a living process, "the athletics of the mind," and standardized images were crutches that discouraged active exercise.[17]

Had there been a pronounced decline in the quality of American illustration in the previous years, Harper's position may have seemed more understandable. However, its assault shared another quality with some of the diatribes against mass culture that our own century has witnessed—misplacedness. For Harper's was reacting to an iconographical shift rather than to decay and degeneration. The previous twenty years or so are now seen as one of the great periods of American illustration. Among the artists working for periodicals like Collier's, Scribner's, Century, Judge, St. Nicholas, and for the publishing houses, were Blashfield, Bradley, Beard, Abbey, Christy, Frost, Castaigne, Davies, Fisher, Flagg, Parrish, Glackens, Luks, Sloan, Yohn, Denslow—some of the greatest names in the history of American graphic design.[18] Harper's itself had begun to use the half-tone for illustration by the late 1880s, and steady improvements meant the easier reproduction of oil paintings and wash drawings, to say nothing of the photographs. The new iconography, then, was capable of provoking outbursts on the general thrust of modernity and stimulating its discontents.

But the half-tone process did more than provoke comments on its belletristic aspects. It helped revolutionize the process of reporting news, and by the turn of the century the star photographer assumed a stance beside the crack journalist in purveying novelty to the mass audience. Now the unwanted snapshot took its place beside the aggressive interview as one of the hazards of American journalism. The connections between photography and illustration, on the one hand, and the new craze for publicity, on the other, were multiple and momentous.

One such relationship between the packaging of information and larger social values involved the growing debate over privacy. Several historians, Alan Westin and David Flaherty among them, have argued for the antiquity of the notion of privacy. Western civilization, writes Flaherty, "has . . . always incorporated personal privacy into its system of values. . . . Privacy can surely be identified in a general sense as one of the cultural goals of sixteenth- and seventeenth-century English society."

Colonial Americans carried on this older concern, and there was "no particular moment of decision in the country's history when the populace suddenly declared *de novo* that privacy was a good thing."[19]

Nonetheless, even if one allows this sometimes vulnerable argument validity, there was a moment when debates about personal privacy took on a special intensity. This moment began in the 1890s and continued through the period before World War I. The camera, and the ability to display and distribute accurate photographs, were vital elements in the new consciousness of the dangers—and benefits—of modern publicity.

The benefits had already been estimated by a number of social reformers. Jacob Riis, heavily involved in journalistic exposés, came in contact with flash photography in 1887. In the first published account describing the new technique, an article in the *New York Sun* of 12 February 1888, Riis explained that his object was to collect "a series of views for magic lantern slides, showing, as no mere description could, the misery and vice that he [Riis] had noticed in his ten years of experience." Aside from its strong human interest, he thought that this treatment of the topic would call attention to the needs of the situation, and suggest the direction in which much good might be done.[20] The *Sun* was still unable to reproduce the photographs by the half-tone process, and ran instead twelve line drawings that copied the photographs; *Scribner's* published "How the Other Half Lives" in December 1889, illustrating nineteen of Riis's photographs, again through line drawings rather than half-tones. His book, however, did not use only drawings; according to Alexander Alland it was the first American book to use a large number of half-tones, seventeen of them, in addition to eighteen line drawings.[21] This was in 1890, only a year or two after the first extensive use of the still expensive practice had developed in magazines. Starting in the 1890s more books were published with half-tones, and Robert Taft has chosen 1897 as "the advent of half-tone illustration as a regular feature of American newspaper journalism," with the *New York Tribune* and *Chicago Tribune* pioneering in their use.[22] Once Riis had set the pattern, others followed, especially Lewis D. Hine, whose photographs were published in the *Charities and Commons* and *Boyhood and Lawlessness*. Hine's work was soon being commissioned by *Everybody's*, *McClure's*, and the *Outlook*, and helped contribute to the general progressive sense that dramatic publicity was the way to ensure public action and solve problems like child labor, slum housing, and industrial safety. The spirit of liberal reform was exemplified by muckraking efforts to make public the private business practices of American bankers and manufacturers, to force them to reveal the nature of interlocking and conflicting interests. It was difficult to argue with the dramatic results achieved by publication of revelations, accompanied,

ICONOGRAPHY AND INTELLECTUAL HISTORY

where possible, as in the *Pittsburgh Survey*, with photographs. Public astonishment fed upon this nurture, and along with it demands for legal and social changes grew.

But the same spokesmen for the public's right to greater knowledge were often anxious about how far the limits of this interest extended. The irony of Louis Brandeis's authorship of the first major discussion of the legal right to privacy just a few years before his published revelations of American finance released a firestorm of controversy was only the most theatrical of these paradoxes. The line had become blurred, warned the *Century* in 1913, between "the publicity which is for the good of the people, for the terror of offenders, and the publicity which is only gossip and scandal printed for no other purpose than to sell the papers and make money." Without proposing any remedy, the *Century* went on to argue that honest rights to privacy had been imperiled. "If Lady Godiva were to ride through the streets of Coventry to-day, there would be Peeping Toms in groups at every window with cameras and machines for making motion pictures."[23] The growth of gossip columns, and the assault on the private lives of businessmen, socialites, athletes, actors, and actresses accompanied the camera's march and that of the illustrated supplement. John Gilmor Speed angrily protested these tendencies in an 1896 article for the *North American Review*. Disagreeing with court decisions that removed the right of privacy from public figures, he insisted that "the habit indulged in by so many actors of thrusting their portraits before the public, and filling the columns of daily newspapers with the most intimate as well as most trivial of their private affairs, does not take away from any member of the profession the right to be let alone." What drew his ire most severely was the new illustrated journalism, built upon surreptitiously taken photographs. "Indeed, it is a well-known fact that at least one of the newspapers of New York keeps a photographer busy in the streets of the metropolis taking 'snap shots' at every person who appears to be of consequence. These are used at once, or filed away."[24] The snapshot was still being taken "at" rather than "of" a subject.

But protests about intrusion came from both the innocent and the guilty. A developing press agentry and advertising managers sensed the rewards planted news and rehearsed photographs could bring. And they worked for politicians on the highest level. Both Theodore Roosevelt and Woodrow Wilson proved skillful at meeting the challenges of the new mass journalism and turning the public attention brought by photography to their own account. This meant inviting cameras in to record normal days at the White House and details of family living. As early as 1903 the *Century* noted the new willingness of government, at home and abroad, to encourage the publication of intimate glimpses of official life.

NEIL HARRIS

Even the Pope had permitted a photographer to enter his private chambers for a magazine article, and had subsequently allowed cinematographers and gramophone records to create publicity. The *Century* foresaw only good effects from this kind of self-advertisement, for mystery and dread were bound to recede under the new enlightenment. "When the mind is no longer awed and clouded by the dim and the unknown the appeal to reason must be reinforced. So far as publicity has to do with authority, secular or sacred, we believe the change effected is very great and likely to increase; and we believe that this change is, on the whole, better for humanity."[25]

Once again, it was easy to mistake the direction of change. Executive authority was not necessarily diluted by greater publicity; the cultivation of a more personalized relationship with the mass public was capable, if anything, of augmenting authoritarian power. But the expectation that a technological innovation would enhance the power of democratic, rational thought reappeared in commentaries on later inventions. Radio, for example, seemed to hold out the same promise. Isolated listeners, protected from the excesses of crowd psychology that were inevitably induced by mass meetings and political rallies, would listen dispassionately to the statements of elected leaders and candidates for office. No longer permitted the rhetorical bombast and exaggeration that the crowd loved, politicians would be forced to eschew demagoguery and offer clear-headed and restrained statements to their listening audiences.[26] By the mid-1930s this fallacy had been completely exploded by political demagogues who found they could exploit the radio waves as easily as predecessors had manipulated the laws of collective imitation. The passion for deliverance by machine dies hard.

Thus the debate about mass culture and a series of strategies toward it were furthered by the half-tone revolution and the spread of pictorial journalism. The private lives of the great filled the new Sunday supplements and popular monthlies, orchestrated by their public relations experts and press managers. But issues of social reform, personal privacy, and political authority do not exhaust the effect of the outburst of pictorialism. Commodity advertising, school textbooks, pornography, and architectural and interior design were also affected. Not always evenly, of course. But few studies have attempted to chart the differing rates by which fields of thought and action were penetrated by the new coding system and the changing pace of specialized communication.

Some experiments were not successful. The illustrated novel, for example, a major source of illustrated commission during the nineteenth century, attempted to adjust by substituting photographs, often of staged versions; but this ploy was doomed by the effective competition of the photoplay. Photographed fiction could not match the silver screen,

ICONOGRAPHY AND INTELLECTUAL HISTORY

although in Europe the photographed serial seemed to do much better. And in magazines and newspapers, the photograph did not carry all before it; half-tone reproduction of artist drawings continued to be popular, as the twentieth-century success of illustrators like Leyendecker, Parrish, Rockwell, Flagg, Pitz, Artzybasheff, and the work commissioned by *Fortune*, the *New Yorker*, *Collier's*, and the *Saturday Evening Post* demonstrate.[27] But half-tone photography was necessary accompaniment to certain kinds of stories—news, documentary, and travel, in particular.

All this, of course, requires much more research if the arguments are to be given appropriate conviction and precision. The question, I suppose, is who shall carry on the research, and how it shall be organized. Until now, historians of journalism and of art, along with the social scientist analysts of mass and popular culture, have not shown great interest in the history of nonmediated reproductive techniques and their intellectual and social impact. The literature of commentary upon the threats and promises of mass culture is now extensive and well established, its roots and conventions going back one hundred years or more. This in itself seems to me an important problem for intellectual historians to consider, but when it is combined with the specific stylistic changes in illustrated communication developed by technical innovators, it offers an opportunity to integrate aspects of commercial, industrial, technological, and administrative history with the history of taste, opinion, and artistic style. The study of these changes, treated narrowly, can result in a new antiquarianism, as recondite and self-limiting as the most abstruse problems of medieval, Byzantine, or Hellenistic reconstructions. Some recent work in the study of popular culture suggests this possibility. But viewed analytically by intellectual historians who are committed to explaining not only the origins of stylistic transformation but also their relationship to contemporary thought and opinion, they offer a way of incorporating iconography with classic subjects within the discipline. Models of analysis exist in dizzying number, provided, in general, by the anthropological and literary wings of the semiological schools. A great deal of highly personalized or overdetermined commentary has already appeared. Much of it needs correction and specification, in the same way that the McLuhanesque interpretation of the Gutenberg Revolution required evaluation and restriction. All this would, I fear, require another paper. It seems best, then, to stop with the proposal now. Arguments from abundance have a way of becoming their own worst enemies.

NEIL HARRIS

Notes

1. Robert Taft, *Photography and the American Scene: A Social History, 1839–1889*, reprint ed. (1938; New York: Dover, 1964), pp. 437–38.
2. Estelle Jussim, *Visual Communication and the Graphic Arts: Photographic Technologies in the Nineteenth Century* (New York: Bowker, 1974), p. 288. This is the most complete modern analysis of the problem.
3. Ibid., ch. 9.
4. The varieties of photomechanical and other reproductive processes developed in the late nineteenth century are too complex to be adequately summarized in a few paragraphs. Dozens of newly patented methods appeared within a short time, promoted energetically by groups of supporters. Some of these varieties are detailed in the many periodicals and annuals devoted to printing and reproductive methods that appear about this time, among them the *Inland Printer*, which started publication in Chicago in 1883; *Printing Art*, published in Cambridge, Massachusetts, from 1903; and *The Graphic Arts and Crafts Year Book*, printed in Hamilton, Ohio, from 1907. Other serials of importance appeared in Britain and on the Continent. Extensive commentaries and bibliographies can be found in Harold Curwen (revised by Charles Mayo), *Processes of Graphic Reproduction in Printing* (London: Faber, 1967); Helmut and Alison Gernsheim, *The History of Photography, from the Earliest Use of the Camera Obscura in the Eleventh Century Up to 1914* (London: Oxford University Press, 1955); Jussim, *Visual Communication and the Graphic Arts*, particularly pp. 45–76; and Geoffrey Wakeman, *Victorian Book Illustration: The Technical Revolution* (Newton Abbot: David and Charles, 1973).
5. Further discussion of this issue can be found in Gernsheim and Gernsheim, *The History of Photography*; E. H. Gombrich, *Art and Illusion: A Study of the Psychology of Pictorial Representation* (New York: Pantheon, 1960); Richard Rudisill, *Mirror Image: The Influence of the Daguerreotype on American Society* (Albuquerque: University of New Mexico Press, 1971); and Robert Taft, *Photography and the American Scene*.
6. Charles H. Caffin, *Photography as a Fine Art: The Achievements and Possibilities of Photographic Art in America* (New York: Doubleday, Page, 1901).
7. *Nation* 73 (19 December 1901): 475–76.
8. "The Perils of Photography," *Nation* 85 (11 July 1907): 28–29.
9. Ibid., p. 29.
10. Will Irwin, "The Swashbucklers of the Camera," *Collier's* 48 (3 February 1912): 11.
11. Tudor Jenks, "The Decadence of Illustration," *Independent* 51 (28 December 1899): 3487–89. For a more sympathetic view in the same journal, see Ella R. Boult, "The Illustration of Books by Artistic Photography," *Independent* 61 (13 December 1906): 1414–20.
12. "Handsomely Illustrated," *Atlantic Monthly* 93 (January 1904): 136–37.
13. *Dial* 51 (1 October 1911): 245–46. See also "The Illustrations That Do Not Illustrate," *Critic* 48 (June 1906): 498–99.
14. "Newspaper Pictures," *Nation* 56 (27 April 1893): 307.
15. "A Growl for the Unpicturesque," *Atlantic Monthly* 98 (July 1906): 141–42.
16. Laurence Burnham, "The Modern Heroine in Illustration," *Bookman* 25 (April 1907): 199.
17. "Over-Illustration," *Harper's Weekly* 55 (29 July 1911): 6. Articles about "over-illustration" had been appearing since the 1880s.
18. Many of these illustrators are represented in the Delaware Art Museum catalogue, *The Golden Age of American Illustration, 1880–1914* (Wilmington: Wilmington Society of the Fine Arts, 1972). For more on American illustration see

ICONOGRAPHY AND INTELLECTUAL HISTORY

Walt Reed, ed., *The Illustrator in America, 1900–1960's* (New York: Reinhold, 1966); and *A Century of American Illustration*, a catalogue of an exhibition at the Brooklyn Museum in 1972.
19. David H. Flaherty, *Privacy in Colonial New England* (Charlottesville: University of Virginia Press, 1972), pp. 6–7. See also Alan F. Westin, *Privacy and Freedom* (New York: Atheneum, 1967), ch. 2.
20. Alexander Alland, Sr., *Jacob A. Riis: Photographer & Citizen* (New York: Aperture, 1974), pp. 26–27.
21. Ibid., p. 29. For a listing of books illustrated with photographs in the second half of the nineteenth century see Julia Van Haaften, " 'Original Sun Pictures': A Check List of the New York Public Library's Holdings of Early Works Illustrated with Photographs, 1844–1900," *Bulletin of the New York Public Library* 80 (Spring 1977): 355–415. Before the late 1880s these books have mounted plates bound into them, and tend to be in limited and expensive editions.
22. Robert Taft, *Photography and the American Scene*, p. 446.
23. "Newspaper Invasion of Privacy," *Century* 86 (June 1913): 310–11.
24. John Gilmor Speed, "The Right of Privacy," *North American Review* 163 (July 1896): 64–74. See also George D. Richards, "Pictorial Journalism," *The World To-Day* 9 (August 1905): 845–52.
25. "Some Effects of Modern Publicity," *Century* 67 (November 1903): 156.
26. See, for example, E. F. Barnard, "Radio Politics," *New Republic* 38 (19 March 1924): 91–93.
27. For a survey of later illustrators and their autobiographical experiences, see Ernest W. Watson, *Forty Illustrators and How They Work* (New York: Watson-Guptill, 1946). See also Susan E. Meyer, *America's Great Illustrators* (New York: Abrams, 1978).

"PERSONALITY" AND THE MAKING OF TWENTIETH-CENTURY CULTURE

WARREN I. SUSMAN

> Perhaps the greatest problem which any historian has to tackle is neither the cataclysm of revolution nor the decay of empire but the process by which ideas become social attitudes.
>
> —*J. H. Plumb*

> I have always observed a singular accord between supercelestial ideas and subterranean behavior.
>
> —*Montaigne*

> The whole history of ideas should be reviewed in the light of the power of social structures to generate symbols of their own.
>
> —*Mary Douglas*

> No ideas but in things.
>
> —*William Carlos Williams*

One of the things that makes the modern world "modern" is the development of consciousness of self. The European world that produced the Reformation, the new capitalist order, and the growing system of nation-states also gave us a new vocabulary that revealed a new vision of the self. *Consciousness* itself became a key word in the seventeenth century; the new language of self announced what Owen Barfield has called "the shifting of the centre of gravity of consciousness from the cosmos around him into the personal human being himself."[1] The results of a such a shift were significant. Impulses that control human behavior and destiny were felt to arise more and more *within* the individual at the very time that the laws governing the world were seen as more and more impersonal. Not only was it more difficult to feel spiritual life and activity immanent in the world outside the self; as the rituals of the external church grew feebler, the needs of inner self grew stronger.

This story is familiar to the historian of modern thought. He has charted the way of this newly developed self in a stormy and changing world from its beginnings in Luther and Calvin, Descartes and Locke. To insist that the history of thought in the modern era is the history of thinking about that self may be an exaggeration. But the consequences of this vision of a self set apart have surely been felt in every field of

212

"PERSONALITY" AND TWENTIETH-CENTURY CULTURE

inquiry, whether it be psychology or political theory, epistemology or economics. Freud, in one of his rare moments of historical analysis, pointed in 1917 to a series of blows that had been administered by modern science to the fragile self. In the sixteenth century Copernicus gave it a cosmological buffeting by removing man from the center of the universe and insisting that he dwells on a small fragment of matter, only one of a countless number of them. In the nineteenth century Darwin made a biological assault on the self when he argued man's essential affinity to all animals and brought into doubt the special role of reason and civilization. The final blow, Freud thought, was that delivered on our own century, the psychological blow. This vision (his own) denied that the center of personality was the ego or the soul, and it further suggested, from its new view of the unconscious, that man in the traditional sense did not have full control over himself.[2] In Freud's special vision the history of science is especially important because of its effect on man's view of himself.

All of this has been the stuff of the intellectual historian. He has studied each "crisis"—as he calls it—in thought brought about by a newer vision of new knowledge. He has attempted to assess the "influence" of major and even minor "thinkers" and has examined new "patterns" of thought emerging from the reconsideration of old problems in new contexts or from new problems arising in changed circumstances. On occasion he has made an effort to relate "ideas" to the particular social structure in which they appear to have been generated. We have "seen" ideas become social attitudes. We have been made aware of the "impact" of Locke, Darwin, and Freud. Seldom do we even ask the question whether social attitudes do indeed become "ideas." When the historian talks of "popular" ideas he rarely sees them as part of the world in which "ideas" (real ideas?) are born.

Yet that world—that combination of new social, economic, political, and religious structures—in which the new idea of self-consciousness developed belonged to others than just Hobbes and Locke—and I do not mean Descartes and Pascal! The same problems of self so important in the systematic thinking of the modern era were already widely felt. The changes in language and usage, the new words and word forms we find in the seventeenth and eighteenth centuries, are at least suggestive. It is striking, for example, to see the interest as early as the seventeenth century in what was called "character" and how significant a cultural form character study became. Surely by the nineteenth century *character* was a key word in the vocabulary of Englishmen and Americans.

Philip Rieff has pointed out that as cultures change so do the modal types of persons who are their bearers.[3] By 1800 the concept of character had come to define that particular modal type felt to be essential for

WARREN I. SUSMAN

the maintenance of the social order. The term itself came to mean a group of traits believed to have social significance and moral quality, "the *sine qua non* of all collective adjustment and social intercourse."[4] In the age of self-consciousness a popular vision of the self defined by the word *character* became fundamental in sustaining and even in shaping the significant forms of the culture. Such a concept filled two important functions. It proposed a method for both mastery and development of the self. In fact, it argued that its kind of self-control was the way to fullest development of the moral significance of self. But it also provided a method of presenting the self to society, offering a standard of conduct that assured interrelationship between the "social" and the "moral." The importance of character can be most easily established by examination of the hundreds of books, pamphlets, and articles produced during the century, the character studies providing examples for emulation, and the manuals promising a way to character development and worldly success. These were clearly a popular and important cultural form, but further examination of other aspects of the culture—literature, the arts, popular music, and the like—helps reinforce the importance of the concept of character to the culture of the nineteenth century. It was a culture of character.

It is significant in this context to call attention to the other key words most often associated with the concept of character. A review of over two hundred such items reveals the words most frequently related to the notion of character: *citizenship, duty, democracy, work, building, golden deeds, outdoor life, conquest, honor, reputation, morals, manners, integrity,* and above all, *manhood.* The stress was clearly moral and the interest was almost always in some sort of higher moral law. The most popular quotation—it appeared in dozens of works—was Emerson's definition of character: "Moral order through the medium of individual nature."

The problem of self, even as vaguely defined as it is in this paper, thus becomes a fundamental one for almost all modern cultural development. The effort to achieve both a moral and a social order and a freely developing self shapes the cultural products of the times—high, middle, low, culture. The very existence of manuals (obviously necessary among the middle class in terms of their numbers and sales) indicates the reality of the problem. Further investigation would establish, I think, that the patterns of behavior, the institutions developed, the persistence in nineteenth-century America of a predominantly Arminian vision, the insistence on the so-called Protestant Ethic with emphasis on work as essential in a society that was constantly stressing producer values—all these are part of what I have suggested is a culture of character.

These are assertions, not proofs; these are not established propositions.

"PERSONALITY" AND TWENTIETH-CENTURY CULTURE

Yet they illustrate my conviction that we can best understand modern cultural developments in all forms if we see and define the particular vision of the self basic to each cultural order. But my fundamental interest in the culture of character lies in the signs of its disappearance and the resulting call for a new modal type best suited to carry out the mission of a newer cultural order. It was not that the culture of character died suddenly or that books and manuals stressing the "character" vision of the self disappeared. In fact they are still being published. But, starting somewhere in the middle of the first decade of the twentieth century, there rapidly developed another vision of self, another vision of self-development and mastery, another method of the presentation of self in society. First, there is clear and growing evidence of an awareness of significant change in the social order, especially after 1880. Symptoms are easily suggested: what was called "American nervousness" and the various efforts at its diagnosis; the rash of utopian writings; the development of systematic sociological and economic analysis in the academic world; the development in government and public journals of a view of the need for "objective" and "scientific" gathering of data and treatment of social ills; and even more important, the development of psychological and psychiatric studies. This awareness of change also suggested the need for a new kind of man, a new modal type to meet the new conditions. Perhaps few were as specific as Simon Patten and his *The New Basis of Civilization* (1909), in which he argued that a society moving from scarcity to abundance required a new self. But it is hard to read the social theorists of the period—Sumner, Ward, Veblen—without some sense of their keen interest in the relation between social orders and psychological types, the sense that people in the change of the social order almost demanded a change in the people in it.

Writing in the middle of the century about the Renaissance in Italy, Jacob Burckhardt, the greatest of cultural historians, suggested:

In the Middle Ages both sides of human consciousness—that which was turned within as well as that which was turned without—lay dreaming or half awake beneath a common veil. The veil was woven of faith, illusion, and childish prepossession. . . . Man was conscious of himself only as a member of a race, people, party, family, or corporation—only through some general category. In Italy this veil was first melted into air; an *objective* treatment and consideration of the State and all of the things of this world became possible. The *subjective* side at the same time asserted itself with corresponding emphasis. Man became a spiritual *individual* and recognized himself as such. . . . It will not be difficult to show that this result was due above all to the political circumstances of Italy.[5]

This analysis is valuable to us as a model. There is general agreement among historians that some significant material change occurred in the

WARREN I. SUSMAN

period we are considering. Whether it is a change from a producer to a consumer society, an order of economic accumulation to one of dis-accumulation, industrial capitalism to finance capitalism, scarcity to abundance, disorganization to high organization—however that change is defined, it is clear that a new social order was emerging. But even more important than this was the growing awareness on the part of those living through the change that it was in fact occurring and that it was fundamental. The ability to treat this change with increasing "objectivity" made it possible to face the subjective or psychological changes that seemed to be mandated.

All of this is preface to the discovery of the beginnings of a radical shift in the kind of advice manuals that appeared after the turn of the century, and to new preoccupations, which strike at the heart of the basis of the culture of character. In an important sense, however, the transition began in the very bosom of the old culture. For it was what might be called the other side of Emerson—his vision of a transcendent self—that formed the heart of that New Thought or Mind Cure movement so important in the process from a culture of character to a culture of personality. The key figures—Ralph Waldo Trine, Ella Wheeler Wilcox, Annie Payson Call, Horatio Dresser, ʼOrison Swett Marden—attempted to combine the qualities of the works on character with a religious and even mystical stress on a spiritual vision of the self; they insisted not only on a higher moral order but also on the fulfillment of self by a striving to become one with a higher self. As New Thought work proceeded it was possible to note an increasing interest in self-development along these lines, with a somewhat less interest in moral imperatives.

Meanwhile, in the American heartland, a careful reader of Ralph Waldo Trine was developing a method of production along with a new philosophy of industry. The results in all areas were revolutionary. When he made his famous 1907 announcement promising a motor car for the great multitude, he was favoring production, mass consumption, mass society. But he also stressed both the family (it would be a family car) and the individual (the owner could run and care for it). Everyone could have one. It would be made of the best materials by the best men. It would be simple in design. And what was its purpose? To "enjoy . . . the blessings of hours of pleasure in God's open spaces." A machine for pleasure. How much Ford's world sounds like that of Simon Patten. No more austerity and sacrifice but rather leisure and rational enjoyment for all.[6] The world of the man of Dearborn—with its new ideas of production, consumption, and use—is not part of the culture of character.

It is further a striking part of that turn-of-the-century decade that interest grew in personality, individual idiosyncrasies, personal needs and interests. The vision of self-sacrifice began to yield to that of self-realization. There was fascination with the very peculiarities of the self, especially the sick self. Miss Beauchamp, in Dr. Morton Prince's 1905 study *The Dissociation of Personality*, became a figure of popular discussion. At least five major studies of Jesus appeared in the same decade. But in these works the Nazarene is not the healer, the social problem-solver, the achieving man of character and moral exemplar. Rather he is a sick personality, a miserably maladjusted fanatic. So serious was the debate on this analysis that Albert Schweitzer felt called upon to reply to these studies in 1913 with his *The Psychiatric Study of Jesus*. And our literature produced the strange heroine of William Vaughan Moody's *The Great Divide* (1909), with her peculiar problems of personality (in its way a precursor of the drama of Eugene O'Neill), and Gertrude Stein's remarkable portrait of *Three Lives* (1906), perhaps in its way a model for Sherwood Anderson's *Winesburg, Ohio* (1919). Literature was interested increasingly in probing personality .and less in studying moral or social achievement in the more traditional way of a culture of character.

But even without these hints the evidence is readily available in hundreds of manuals and guides for self-improvement published between 1900 and 1920. One of Raymond Williams's "keywords," *personality*, is a modern term.[7] It appears in the late eighteenth century, and there is some evidence of its modern usage in the nineteenth century. While there are examples of its use by Emerson and Henry Adams, Walt Whitman alone, to my knowledge, made frequent and consistent use of the word in its current sense in the last century. By the first decade of this century it was an important part of the American vocabulary. It is in that decade as well that a series of volumes and articles began to appear addressed to the problem of helping people develop their personalities. From the start *personality* was distinguished from *character*. In 1915 Funk and Wagnalls published a series of self-help books, their *Mental Efficiency Series*. (*Efficiency* and *energy* are also important words with significant increased usage in the new culture of personality.) The series contains volumes on both character ("How to Strengthen It") and personality ("How to Build It"). From the beginning the adjectives most frequently associated with personality suggest a very different concept from that of character: *fascinating, stunning, attractive, magnetic, glowing, masterful, creative, dominant, forceful*. These words would seldom if ever be used to modify the word *character*. One writer himself makes the point: character, he insists, is either good or bad; personality, famous or infamous.[8]

WARREN I. SUSMAN

"Personality is the quality of being Somebody."[9] This definition—repeated in various ways in almost all of the manuals I have analyzed—is also a major theme of this literature. The problem is clear. We live now constantly in a crowd; how can we distinguish ourselves from others in that crowd? While the term is never used, the question is clearly one of life in a mass society ("crowd" is the most commonly used word). Since we live in such a world it is important to develop one's self—that is, those traits, "moral, intellectual, physical, and practical," that will enable us to think of ourselves and have others think of us as "somebodies." "To create a personality is power," one manual writer insists.[10] One does this by being "conscious of yourself and of others," by being discerning and sincere, by showing energy, by paying attention to others so that they will pay attention to you.

To be somebody one must be oneself (whatever that means). It is an almost too perfect irony that most of the works published and sold in large numbers as self-help in developing an effective personality insist that individuals should be "themselves" and *not* follow the advice or direction of others. The importance of being different, special, unusual, of standing out in a crowd—all of this is emphasized at the same time that specific directions are provided for achieving just those ends. In virtually the same breath the reader is also urged repeatedly to "express your individuality" and to "eliminate the little personal whims, habit, traits that make people dislike you. Try in every way to have a ready command of the niceties, the manners, the ways of speech, etc. which make people think 'he's a mighty likable fellow.' That is the beginning of a reputation for personality."[11] Thus "personality," like "character" is an effort to solve the problem of self in a changed social structure that imposes its own special demands on the self. Once again, such a popular view of self proposes a method of both self-mastery and self-development as well as a method of the presentation of that self in society. Both methods differed from those proposed in the culture of character and they underpin the development of a new culture, the culture of personality.

This was also, of course, the age of Freud and psychoanalysis. Philip Rieff has argued that "psychoanalysis defends the private man against the demands of both culture and instinct." He asserts that this era was one dominated by a new character type, "psychological man."

> We will recognize in the case history of psychological man the nervous habits of his father, economic man, he is anti-heroic, shrewd, carefully counting his satisfactions and dissatisfactions, studying unprofitable commitments as the sins most to be avoided. From this immediate ancestor, psychological man has constructed his own careful economy of the inner life ... and lives by the mastery of his own personality.[12]

"PERSONALITY" AND TWENTIETH-CENTURY CULTURE

In a general sense the popular personality manuals I have investigated establish essentially the same new character type Rieff sees as the consequence of Freud's influence. I do not mean to suggest that Freudian theory is implicit in these works (although in the 1920s Freud was often explicitly cited on occasion to support the general position advanced). I mean rather that a vision of the self and its problems generated in large part by an awareness of a significant change in the social structure contains certain basic attitudes comparable to those of Rieff's "psychological man." Freud, an intellectual genius without doubt, lived after all in the social world. What I am suggesting is that general social attitudes exist in popular thought before formal "ideas" expressing them rise to the level of general understanding. This is perhaps why so many ideas of major thinkers do finally win popular acceptance.

In the particular case under study there is a striking example. Even in the early personality manuals in the first decade of the century there is singular emphasis not only on the need for self-confidence but also on the importance of not feeling "inferior." Not only are there constant warnings against the dangers of feeling inferior (if one harbors such feelings, one can never impress others and will always exhibit, as a result, a weak personality), but there is a positive injunction to appear superior (but not overly or aggressively so). This attitude was important long before Alfred Adler explained to the world the significance of the "inferiority complex" late in the 1920s.

A brief examination of two works by one of the most popular writers of the period will serve to press home the importance of the change in emphasis from character to personality. In 1899 Orison Swett Marden published *Character, The Greatest Thing in the World*. Crowded with character studies of special historical heroes as exemplars, this book dwells most particularly on the "mental and moral traits," the "high ideals," the "balance" that makes character and therefore brings success in the world. Being a true Christian gentleman, pure, upright, intelligent, strong, and brave, possessing a sense of duty, having benevolence, moral courage, personal integrity, and the "highest kinship of soul," devoting service to mankind, being attentive to the "highest and most harmonious development of one's powers" to achieve "a complete and consistent whole"—these are the key words and phrases used in support of the argument. In the course of the volume Marden stresses the basic values necessary in a producer-oriented society, including hard work (the "sacredness of one's work") and thrift. He ends the book with a powerful appeal. Quoting President Garfield ("I must succeed in making myself a man"), Marden insists that character above all means, for those interested in developing it, "Let him first be a Man."

In 1921 Marden published *Masterful Personality*. It suggests a re-

WARREN I. SUSMAN

markably different set of interests. In this book Marden addresses himself to "man's mysterious atmosphere," the aura and power of personality that can "sway great masses." Against the profound dangers of feeling inferior, he proposes a search for supremacy. Much attention is focused on "personal charm." He urges women not only to rely on physical beauty but also to develop "fascination." The ability to attract and hold friends is important. "You can," Marden insists, "compel people to like you." "So much of our success in life depends upon what others think of us." Manners, proper clothes, good conversation ("to know *what* to say and *how* to say it"), energy, "life efficiency," poise—these are the concerns of this volume. In the course of twenty years Marden had come to see the need for a different character type.[13]

The older vision of self expressed in the concept of character was founded in an inner contradiction. That vision argued that the highest development of self ended in a version of self-control or self-mastery, which often meant fulfillment through sacrifice in the name of a higher law, ideals of duty, honor, integrity. One came to selfhood through obedience to law and ideals. Brilliantly sustaining the human needs of a producer-oriented society, it urged in effect a sublimation of self-needs or their redefinition in Arminian terms. But the newer vision of personality also had its paradox. It stressed self-fulfillment, self-expression, self-gratification so persistently that almost all writers as an afterthought gave a warning against intolerable selfishness, extreme self-confidence, excessive assertions of personal superiority. But the essentially antinomian quality vision of this, with its view not of a higher law but of a higher self, was tempered by the suggestion that the self ought to be presented to society in such a way as to make oneself "well liked." There is an obvious difficulty here. One is to be unique, distinctive, follow one's own feelings, make oneself stand out from the crowd, and at the same time appeal—by fascination, magnetism, attractiveness—to it.

Both visions of self—visions I argue shaped the very nature of the culture—are assumed from the start not to be natural but to be things that can be learned and practiced, through exercise and by study of guidebooks, to success. Both visions relate to the needs of a particular social structure and do not develop in an atmosphere of pure philosophical speculation. The older vision no longer suited personal or social needs; the newer vision seemed particularly suited for the problems of the self in a changed social order, the developing consumer mass society.

The new personality literature stressed items that could be best developed in leisure time and that represented in themselves an emphasis on consumption. The social role demanded of all in the new culture of personality was that of a performer. Every American was to become a performing self. Every work studied stressed the importance of the

"PERSONALITY" AND TWENTIETH-CENTURY CULTURE

human voice in describing methods of voice control and proper methods of conversation or public speaking. Everyone was expected to impress and influence with trained and effective speech. Special books and courses were developed to meet demands in this area alone. In these books and articles exercise, proper breathing, sound eating habits, a good complexion, and grooming and beauty aids were all stressed. At the same time, clothing, personal appearance, and "good manners" were important, but there was little interest in morals. Poise and charm top the list of necessary traits, and there was insistence that they could be learned and developed through careful practice. The new stress on the enjoyment of life implied that true pleasure could be attained by making oneself pleasing to others.

Often the books stressed the role of personality in business success. *Personality in Business*, a series of fifty articles on every aspect of business activity by some of the most distinguished businessmen and publicists of the period, was first issued in 1906 and then reprinted in 1910 and 1916. The new stress on personality in business, in fact, led to a reaction by some of the older character-based authors. George Horace Lorimer, in his 1902 best seller, *Letters from a Self-Made Merchant to His Son*, specifically warned against the attempt to be popular, suggesting that the effort took too much time and was not always successful in a business way. But in general the personality manuals move away from an interest in business or even financial success and provide a newer definition of what constitutes genuine success in life.[14]

The new interest in personality—both the unique qualities of an individual and the performing self that attracts others—was not limited to self-help authors in this period. It extended to participants in the high culture as well. In 1917 Ezra Pound pleaded for the struggle that would assure what he called "the rights of personality," and even earlier he had insisted to a friend that mass society created a world in which man was continually being used by others. For him, *the* issue of the modern world was "the survival of personality." Earlier, Herbert Croly explained in *The Promise of American Life* (1909) that "success in any . . . pursuit demands that an individual make some sort of personal impression." Painters, architects, politicians, all depend "upon a numerous and faithful body of admirers." Emancipation, self-expression, excellent work, are all meaningless unless such gifted individuals have the support of a following. This is only one of many works in the period that stresses the role of personal magnetism in leadership. And in 1913 Randolph Bourne pleaded with young radicals to understand the new order of things, which included the importance of personality, sincerity, and the like, and which is interpreted in terms of these attainments. In stressing the importance of influence Bourne proposed that nothing was so important

WARREN I. SUSMAN

as a "most glowing personality." Self-cultivation, he maintained, "becomes almost a duty, if one wants to be effective towards the great end (the regeneration of the social order). And not only personality, but prestige."[15]

At the outset of the century, Nathaniel Southgate Shaler wrote in his *The Individual* (1900), which he insisted was a purely scientific analysis, a central chapter on "Expression of the Individuality." Here he demonstrated the importance of what he called "modes of externalization," the ways people gain the attention of others. He believed these things are done, not simply for gain or esteem but because there is an instinctive need "to externalize the self." He saw this in dress and fashion, in song and speech, in the richness of language. Each culture, he suggested, has different "motives of self-presentation." The key to all expression of self, however, is the face. We are, in Shaler's view, all actors, and the face has the power of an instrument able to express intellect as well as emotion.

The test of the general approach proposed in this paper would be a more specific analysis of the cultural forms of our century to see whether they in fact share the characteristics of a culture of personality, whether they can be examined as manifestations of the working out of the basic ideas central to this vision of self. Investigations have convinced me that most cultural forms studied to date reveal a kinship in the culture of personality. Comic strips, radio programs, even beauty pageants have yielded evidence of significant dependence on these ideas. For purposes of this paper, however, I want to offer only one example. I am convinced that the nature and form of the modern motion picture as it developed as a middle-class popular art between 1910 and 1915 clearly shows its participation in the culture of personality. Technically the film, most especially in the hands of its major developer as a middle-class art, D. W. Griffith, and those who followed him, depended on two major modes and used them dramatically in startling juxtaposition. The first was the handling of vast groups of people. Vachel Linsday in his brilliant 1915 book on film speaks of the role of what he calls "crowd splendor" in motion pictures.[16] Films are not only a mass medium, they also represent one of the major ways in which a mass society can examine itself as mass. There was from the start of serious motion pictures an intimate relationship between it and the portraying of the role of crowds. To the depiction of the crowd, and often in striking contrast to it, Griffith added the extraordinary form of the "close-up." Almost as if following the teachings of Shaler, the face, bigger than life and abstracted from it, provides a brilliant expression of self, of an individual. The importance of this contrast—the mass and the isolated individual apart from that mass—to the development of film, and thus of film's role in the culture of personality, cannot be exaggerated.

"PERSONALITY" AND TWENTIETH-CENTURY CULTURE

Up to 1910 motion picture studios generally concealed the identity of most screen players. In 1910, however, the idea of the movie star was born. The creation of the star changed the nature of the role of motion pictures in our society. It brought into even more prominent use the press agent and modern advertising. "Henceforth, a screen player was to be marketed for her admirers as a personality, an image and, to an increasingly sinister extent, an object," the historian of the star system suggests.[17] This immediately leads to fan magazines and to a new consciousness of the importance of personality. It leads, in fact, to a new profession—that of being a movie star or a celebrity. In the culture of character the public had insisted on some obvious correlation between achievement and fame. Now that insistence is gone. The very definition of reality was altered, as Richard Schickel explains in his suggestive study of Douglas Fairbanks, Sr. "Indeed, it is now essential that the politician, the man of ideas, and the non-performing artist become performers so that they may become celebrities so that in turn they may exert genuine influence on the general public."[18] Fairbanks himself was dedicated not to his art but to himself. As early as 1907 a famous actress said of him that he would be famous in films. "He's not good looking. But he has worlds of personality."

Fairbanks is important to us in this analysis. He becomes one of those symbols social structures generate—and in this case an active agent as well. Not only was he a star and a topnotch public relations man, but he also wrote his own kind of self-help books (*Make Life Worth-While, Laugh and Live*) and a column in one of the leading movie magazines. He provided a link between the pioneers of the new self-help literature and the new social world that Henry Ford was building. In 1928 Ralph Waldo Trine published *The Power That Wins*, the report of an intimate talk on life with Henry Ford. Trine begins his conversation with Ford by recalling a trip to Hollywood and a visit to Douglas Fairbanks. He assumes, of course, that Fairbanks doesn't know who he is.

> "Don't I?" he replied. "Just wait until I show you a specially inscribed copy of *In Tune with the Infinite* that Henry Ford sent me."
> Mr. Ford. Yes, I remember sending that book to Mr. Fairbanks. Back in 1914, when my associates and I were working out some very difficult problems here, some of your books were of great help to me. I used to keep a stock of your books in my office, to give to friends or associates who, I thought would be benefited by them the same as I.[19]

Trine, Ford, Fairbanks, three major figures in the transition from a culture of character to a culture of personality, are here neatly linked together.

If Fairbanks was at the beginning of this world of stars and press

WARREN I. SUSMAN

agents, we know that it was only the beginning. There *are* ideas in things (maybe *only* in things, as William Carlos Williams insists), but we are only beginning to understand our cultural developments in terms of the system of ideas on which they are in fact based, the system of ideas inherent in the very cultural forms we study. Movies suggest many explorations not yet undertaken. For films have been an agency fundamental for the generation of the key symbols of our social structure. Complete with stars and even gods and goddesses, housed in places that (even down to the massive organ) resemble huge cathedrals, motion pictures became for thousands a new religion (perhaps a special religion for the antinomians of the twentieth century). No wonder some more fundamentalist Protestant religionists forbid movie-going to their congregants. They know a surrogate or competing religious order when they see one.

A Concluding, Most Unscientific, Postscript

Some unproven assertions about the emergence of a culture of personality in twentieth-century America lead me to attempt to confirm these speculations. Convinced that the nature of cultural development specifically depends for its forms on the existing vision of self—in terms of its definition of its problem in development and presentation in society—I am also anxious to press the analysis further and account for the significant changes clearly visible in our cultural history during the century. Thus within the culture of personality there are divisions based on special readings of the problem of personality at different times within the whole range and in response to shifts in social structure. In the period from 1910 through the late 1920s the problem was most often defined in terms of guilt and the need to eliminate guilt. One might think of this period, at least metaphorically, as an Age of Freud—not so much in terms of direct influence but rather in terms of the point of view from which the culture viewed its problem of self. I have already argued elsewhere that the period from 1929 to 1938 might be seen as one dominated by the problem of shame, and I have, again metaphorically, called this the Age of Alfred Adler. From 1939 through the late 1940s we do not need to invent a name. The period self-consciously thought of itself as The Age of Anxiety. The major concern for moral, national identity and character led increasingly to an interest in myth, to a search for some collective unconscious brought to awareness. Let me call this the Age of Jung. From the end of the 1940s to almost the end of the 1950s the problem was fundamentally redefined as that of personal identity. Who could object to seeing this as the Age of Erik Erikson? The 1960s

"PERSONALITY" AND TWENTIETH-CENTURY CULTURE

and the profound interest in liberation, especially sexual liberation, provided still another modification in the culture of personality. Perhaps this will be known as the Age of Wilhelm Reich. I refuse to speculate on the immediate present for fear I will be regarded as irresponsible. Yet, wild as these speculations may seem, I remain convinced that the changes in culture do mean changes in modal types of character and that social structures do generate their own symbols. Intellectual historians would do well to begin to see ideas in things and to see that there is in fact some connection between the most ethereal of ideas and common, and even basic, human behavior.

Notes

1. Owen Barfield, *History in English Words*, new ed. (London: Methuen, 1954), p. 166.
2. The essay "A Difficulty in the Path of Psycho-Analysis" is reprinted in *Standard Edition of the Collected Psychological Works of Sigmund Freud*, 23 vols. (London: Hogarth Press, 1955), 17: 135–44.
3. Philip Rieff, *The Triumph of the Therapeutic Uses of Faith after Freud* (New York: Harper & Row, 1966), p. 2.
4. A. A. Roback in the article "Character" in the *Encyclopaedia of the Social Sciences*, 14 vols. (New York: 1930), 3:335.
5. Jacob Burckhardt, *The Civilization of the Renaissance in Italy*, reprint ed. (1860; New York: Modern Library, 1954), pp. 100–101.
6. I have developed this analysis at greater length in a piece on Henry Ford, in "Piety, Profits, and Play: the 1920s," in *Men, Women, and Issues in American History*, ed. A. Quint and M. Cantor, 2 vols. (Homewood, Ill.: Dorsey Press, 1975), vol. 2, ch. 10.
7. Raymond Williams, *Keywords: A Vocabulary of Culture and Society* (New York: Oxford University Press, 1976), pp. 194–97. The word *character* does not appear in Mr. Williams's study.
8. Henri Laurent, *Personality: How to Build It* (New York: Funk and Wagnalls, 1915), p. iv. This volume was translated from the French by Richard Duff.
9. Ibid., p. 25.
10. Ibid., pp. iv, 29. I have used this manual as typical. Part 1 deals with the "building" of personality, and part 2 with "how to impress." It stresses self-control as a way to control others. I find all of the themes of other manuals studied stated here more boldly and precisely.
11. B. C. Bean, "Power of Personality" (Meridan, Conn.: Pelton Publishing, 1920), p. 3. This is one of a series of pamphlets called *The Science of Organizing Personal Powers for Success*.
12. Philip Rieff, *Freud: The Mind of a Moralist* (New York: Viking Press, 1961), pp. 391–92. The whole of chapter 10, "The Emergence of Psychological Man," makes an important statement.
13. Orison Swett Marden, *Character, The Greatest Thing in the World* (New York: T. Y. Crowell, 1899), pp. 7, 11, 16, 21, 25, 30, 37, 50; idem, *Masterful Personality* (New York: T. Y. Crowell, 1921), pp. 1, 3, 17, 23, 33, 68, 291.
14. George Horace Lorimer, *Letters from a Self-Made Merchant to His Son* (New York: Small, Maynard, 1902). See especially pp. 40, 88–89. This is striking in almost all the self-help manuals studied. There is clearly a relationship between

WARREN I. SUSMAN

thin new definition of success and the contemporary religious interest in personality. I address this issue in another paper, "The Religion of Personality and Personality as a Religion." This issue is of considerable importance to the theme I am attempting to develop. In this context let me cite only one of many theologians and philosophers on the importance of personality, J. Herman Randall, in his *The Culture of Personality* (New York: ?1912), p. xiii: "[Personality] is by far the greatest work in the history of the human mind. [It is the key] that unlocks the deeper mysteries of Science and Philosophy, of History and Literature, of Art and Religion, of all of man's ethical and social relationships."

15. Ezra Pound, "Provincialism the Enemy" *The New Age* 21 (19 July 1917): 268–69. See also letter to Margaret Anderson, reprinted in her *My Thirty Years War* (New York: Alfred A. Knopf, 1930), p. 171. Herbert Croly, *The Promise of American Life* (New York: Macmillan, 1909), p. 432. His whole analysis of individualism and leadership can be best understood in terms of the premises of this paper. In another paper, "Leadership and Public Opinion in a Culture of Personality," I deal with the implications in political theory and especially in political rhetoric in the period from 1890 to 1920. Randolph Bourne, *Youth and Life* (New York: Houghton, Mifflin, 1913), p. 294.

16. Nathaniel Southgate Shaler, *The Individual: A Study of Life and Death* (New York: D. Appleton, 1900), ch. 7. Vachel Lindsay, *The Art of the Moving Picture* (New York: Macmillan, 1915). There was a revised edition in 1922. It remains a classic work for all cultural historians.

17. Alexander Walker, *Stardom, The Hollywood Phenomenon* (New York: Stein and Day, 1970), p. 36.

18. Richard Schickel, *His Picture in the Papers: A Speculation on Celebrity in America Based on the Life of Douglas Fairbanks, Sr.* (New York: Charterhouse, 1974), p. 9.

19. Ralph Waldo Trine, *The Power That Wins* (Indianapolis, Ind.: Bobbs-Merrill, 1928), pp. 2–3.

AFTERWORD

PAUL K. CONKIN

These essays document the maturity but certainly not the senility of American intellectual history. Gone are some of the vigor and enthusiasm of youth, but gone also are the illusioned hopes of the 1950s. If these contributors are at all representative, intellectual historians are now aware, possibly all too aware, of the limitations of their tools and of all the hazards that lie in wait for those who would try to understand broadly shared beliefs in the American past. As participants in an established subdiscipline, they are increasingly self-conscious about their methods. They are thus more cautious, more careful, and at times more defensive than their predecessors. This often means a more narrowed focus but improved quality. They attend more carefully than their progenitors to clarity in concepts, good logic in inferences, and confirming evidence in their descriptions and explanations.

Definitional problems remain. Several contributors wrestle with definitions of intellectual history, particularly Veysey, Hollinger, Welter, and Wood. Others clearly assume specific definitions. Yet, these essays document the lack of a common defining language. Are intellectual historians concerned with ideas, concepts, percepts, beliefs, attitudes, assumptions, or presuppositions, or with the form or configuration or style of a thinking process? The definitional difficulty, at least in part, reflects the intellectual historian's lack of an exclusive subject. Historians in all areas have to attend to the content of language, to symbolic meanings, for these condition almost all human behavior. Intellectual historians are thus distinct, not by their subject, but only by their more concentrated focus upon meanings and thus upon culture, or by their willingness to work with highly specialized or technical systems of belief that are beyond the competence of other historians. They cultivate an unusual receptiveness to subtlety and nuance in meaning, or develop special competence in such areas as philosophy, theology, political and economic theory, literary criticism, art, or one or more of the physical or social sciences.

Continuities with the past are as striking as the new directions explored in these essays. Perhaps more than they realize, the contributors remain in the tradition of Merle Curti. With one exception (Bercovitch),

227

they represent history departments. Most have research interests or teaching responsibilities outside intellectual history, even as their training encompassed other historical fields. They share many of the concerns of historians in general, including a cautious fascination with new research tools or with fashionable theories in the social sciences. Most revealing of all, they still share the absorbing interest in social context and the concern for the practical role of even rigorous and systematic thought that so distinguished Curti's *Growth of American Thought*.

The concerns of these essays stand out when contrasted with the types of intellectual history absent or underrepresented. At one extreme is the more sweeping efforts at cultural synthesis by the myth and image school, or at political synthesis by Richard Hofstadter and others who seek to integrate intellectual themes with more traditional political, diplomatic, or economic subjects. Bercovitch, from his disciplinary home in literature, and Susman, with his interpretive verve, are closest to those traditions, while Welter defends broad and ambitious subjects for intellectual historians. But most contributors stress the difficulty of verifying sweeping characterizations of a national mind or character, and show skepticism about general assertions based on limited literary evidence. Revealingly, the most precautionary warnings come from Murphey, the participant closest to the other excluded extreme—those who work with narrowly specialized and technically demanding beliefs, and who often find their academic home outside history departments. His work in the history of philosophy only points up the absence of any specialized historian of science, theology, art, or political and economic theory. As a whole, the contributors are not hostile to a specialized history of ideas, to efforts to explain complex beliefs by purely ideational preconditions in isolation from a broader biographical or social context. But neither do they applaud such efforts or show much concern with the problems of such specialized inquiry. In summary, these contributors cluster around scholarly commitments halfway between the more soaring interpretations of Perry Miller and the often tedious analytical excursions of Arthur O. Lovejoy.

The middle way has its risks. Intimidated by all the dangers of broad subjects, historians may back away from any effort at synthesis, leaving this to the inadequate caricatures of textbooks. At least Welter and May are aware of these dangers. On the other side, highly specialized work in the history of ideas requires the highest level of semantic precision and logical rigor. These contributors have advanced far in this direction if judged by the standards of even a decade ago. Loose labels, such as "democracy" or "liberalism," no longer stand at the center of their debates. But ambiguities of language still haunt even these essays, as attested by the varied meanings that confusingly mingle behind words such as *determinism*.

In the perspective of even the recent past, what is most conspicuously missing in these essays is any general preoccupation with either the role of something called ideas or the larger purposes of intellectual history. The role of ideas is central only in the essay by Gordon Wood. Surprisingly, none of the Wingspread Conference discussions focused upon the complex range of issues suggested by this old issue. In one sense this surely documents a new level of sophistication, an appreciation of the antiquated and simplistic mind-body dualities that formerly haunted any consideration of the status or role of ideas. Perhaps it also reflects a working consensus on these issues among this center group of American intellectual historians.

The "role of ideas" has always served as an elliptical way of referring to a whole series of issues. Even the word *idea* is, in its use by historians, all but hopelessly ambiguous. If one means by *idea* a specific image or concept tied to some conventional symbol, and thus a part of a language, then Wood's essay exemplifies the most influential American response to the general or encompassing problem of role—that of John Dewey. Dewey viewed the use of a symbolic language (talking or thinking) as a form of adaptive, socially acquired behavior distinctive to man, which was always fully interactive with other, nonlinguistic forms of behavior. Moreover, language use depends upon a developed body of transmitted and conventional meanings, or an all but objective mind or culture. This largely shapes the content of any individual thought. Yet, meaning systems do change, and always of necessity through the creative innovations of individuals. The world of meaning is, to this extent, open, for in the stress and strain of life individuals slowly change the meanings of words and even change the words and syntax of a language. Such a functional perspective on language and meaning dissolves all older dualisms, and makes any challenge to the efficacious role of such meanings seem hopelessly naive. Who would deny the adaptive superiority of language-using animals over nonlinguistic animals?

Surely the old puzzles are not so easily unraveled. They are not because the problem of role always encompassed other issues than the ultimate role of language. For example, how often, or to what extent, are the most crucial and determinant meanings at a level of conscious awareness? How often are they residual in habit? Most "social forces," to fall back on that lame and elusive analogue from physics so long appealed to by historians, are the direct constraints of neither physical environment nor genetic endowments, but are reasonably stable and learned habits broadly exemplified by people in society. These habits,

AFTERWORD

however far back their development, still reflect the past role of symbolized meanings. To the extent that conditioning meanings are residual,
no longer conscious, and thus hidden in the unknown past, they are not
in any immediate sense a component of one's conscious assessment of a
situation or one's conscious selection of one goal over another. Such
meanings are beyond any present control, but surely not beyond recovery. This clarifies a key task for an intellectual historian—to seek out
residual purposes, to recover for a contemporary audience the cultural
content of their most conventional and habitual behavior. In this way
historians contribute to self-awareness, help transform hidden purposes
into conscious ones and thus open them to critical appraisal and bring
them into the arena of moral responsibility.

A rather inadequately formulated issue haunts most discussions of the
role of ideas. It even muddied up a bit of the dialogue at the conference.
To what extent do people behave "rationally"? Obviously, this begs some
precise criteria of rationality. Historians use the word *rational* in at least
three ways. In its most behavioral sense, rational behavior entails successful behavior, that which most efficiently leads an animal to the satisfaction of a need or want. In this sense, either instinctual or conditioned
behavior might be completely rational, while that based on conscious
choice, even when informed by much reflection, might end in frustra-
tion, particularly when a person has to adapt himself to completely new
circumstances.

Secondly, *rational* may refer to the appropriateness of intentional
and thoughtful behavior. In this case, it also entails an efficient and
effective response to circumstances, but one in line with orienting goals
or purposes. Without knowing those, we cannot judge the rationality of
an action. In this instrumental sense, to be rational requires a grasp of
relevant knowledge and an ability to draw logical inferences, or what
most people mean by *intelligence*. To distinguish this type of rational
behavior—that which is carefully and successfully related to conscious
purposes—is not to argue that it is easy for historians to infer these
purposes from surviving artifacts. But unless they can infer them, they
cannot understand purposeful behavior at all.

Finally, the word *rational* may qualify ends, not means. In this normative sense, irrational behavior is not inefficient, but abnormal or immoral, such as suicidal or destructive acts. The tastes or moral
preferences of an observer necessarily enter into such judgments about
the goals of other people. In this sense of misdirection, people may be
irrational even when they are fully informed and impeccably logical.

None of these three uses of *rational* and *irrational*—behavioral, instrumental, or normative—suggests any profound implications about the
role of ideas. Purely behavioral judgments skirt the possible role of lan-

AFTERWORD

guage and meaning. They do not preclude such a role, although one who is always content to stop with such an external analysis of human behavior, one who refuses in any context to accept the burden of the intellectual historian to search out embodied meanings, has probably already embraced a metaphysical position that denies any role for thought. Clearly, both the instrumental and the normative uses of *rational* entail the efficacy of thought. Ill-informed choices and illogical judgments exemplify the role of meanings as much as do rational decisions, unwise goals as much as wise ones. In fact, perverse behavior usually reflects the role of long and agonizing thought, however such thinking interacts with physiological or environmental determinants. It makes no sense to talk of an instinctual or even a habitual suicide. Such irrational choices pose a difficult challenge to intellectual historians—how to unearth the strange beliefs that conditioned them.

Claims about the role of ideas in a society often identify a much narrower problem—the role of people called intellectuals or the role of formal and systematic bodies of thought, such as the theoretical content of a physical science. These issues haunt at least half of the questions addressed in these essays- -the status of intellectuals in America, the role of professions, the particular environment or context of specialized intellectual activity, the diversity of beliefs in America, the interaction or overlap of belief between an intellectual elite and ordinary folk, the sense in which we can speak of a collective mentality, and the value of nonverbal sources for identifying such mentalities. If these essays are indicative, here are the role problems that presently challenge American intellectual historians. Much more than the overarching problem of the role of language and thought, or the varied issues posed by "rationality," these questions beg contextual rather than general answers. One has to look, not at man in general, but at particular groups of people in particular societies. These questions parallel the empirical and national focus of these essays. Even in their borrowings from the social sciences, these authors characteristically turn to restrained, empirical, and historically oriented anthropological theories, and not to more general and determinant theories, such as structuralism in anthropology and forms of behaviorism in psychology.

The "role of" anything suggests causality. If meanings do condition behavior, then in some sense of that loaded word they are "causes." But if thinking is a quite natural but context-limited mode of behaving that is always related to nonlinguistic behavior, then by definition a particular belief about matters either of fact or of desire can never be a sufficient condition for any human action. A belief in itself never assures that an act will take place. Many other factors have to cooperate. Yet, without a belief, entertained consciously or entombed in learned habits, the act could not have occurred. In this sense of cause as necessary precondition, or the most common use of causal language by historians, ideas do have a causal role. Why back away from that fact? If they did not have this role, then language and meaning would be epiphenomena, adequate only for recording what happens to or through man. To deny this type of causality for ideas is, therefore, to deny any significant subject matter for intellectual historians. More important, any significant, socially justified role for intellectual historians directly depends upon such an efficacy in ideas.

This suggests a second issue largely ignored in these essays. What is the role, not of ideas, but of intellectual history? What audience does it inform? Of what use is it to anyone? This is an oblique way of asking what criteria historians use to select and justify their topics. In a direct way, historians rarely address these thorny questions. Yet, even in these essays, judgments about topical significance abound. For example, we need to know more about the beliefs of common folk. One can only ask, why? Or, we will explore more significant issues if we look at the discourse of intellectuals, at the important questions they mutually confront, and not just at abstracted beliefs. But significant for whom, and in relation to what purposes? Clearly, such questions ask for normative or evaluative answers, not cognitive ones. It is hard to think of any logical or methodological justification for selection of one topic over another, so long as each topic yields itself to historical inquiry. Conversely, no conceivable personal or moral reason for selecting a topic need threaten the integrity of an inquiry. In fact, one might expect deep moral concern to so increase the stakes involved in historical inquiry as to deepen a commitment to honesty and integrity.

Selective judgment would be of minimal interest if historians expected an early understanding of all dimensions of the American past. Of course they will never have the time to explore more than a small percentage of that past now open to historical understanding. Perhaps fortunately, at any one time most of the past does not seem worth exploring. No one is interested. But shifting problems and concerns in the larger society continuously reorient interest in the past, and insure the ascendence of subjects long deemed insignificant. What presently exists in American intellectual history, as in other historical fields, is a jumbled mosaic. Historians have clustered their efforts, as in the case of Puritan studies. This documents how often the interests of scholars relate to a professional community. Each new question about the Puritans has been father to ten new ones, and each new refinement of method has opened up new subtleties of understanding. The game has no end. For such a community of scholars, the stimulating issues, and thus the criteria of historical significance, are often communal, parochial, and internal. Often the only audience for such inquiry is other historians. Such historians value and reward either novelty or new rigor. Every historian wants to fill in missing gaps or revise and refine the received understanding. In such well-cultivated and fruitful fields as Puritan thought, historians do come close to the goal of completion. They really do aspire to the whole story, and gladly applaud even the most narrow topics if they contribute to that whole.

Professionalism can isolate scholars even as it supports the highest standards of truthfulness. In well-explored areas, and by the very fact of a mature historiography, the valuative issues external to the community of scholars tend to drop out of sight and out of mind. The same is true in exceedingly fashionable new areas of scholarship, even when these originate in the concerns of the larger community. Soon fashions help delimit the range of applauded topics to those that insure status within the profession. How many authors of dissertations in intellectual history can vindicate their topic by criteria external to purely practical imperatives or to those set by the profession? How many chose and developed a topic in order to help students gain a new level of self-awareness or in order to add perspective and depth to debates about public policy, to cite only two traditional moral justifications for historical understanding?

I do not mean to damn such internal criteria of significance. I am too much a part of a scholarly community for that. I enjoy our games. More important, the larger concerns of the community play a major role in establishing historical fashions. Look at how both black and women's history have flowered in the past two decades. Thus, even dissertation candidates, often to their own pleasant surprise, retrospectively find plenty of justifying uses for their labor. Even when not calculated for such ends, our inquiry often informs textbooks, reaches a wider audience, and surely helps fulfill some of the social benefits of historical understanding. But the sway of internal, professionally oriented criteria do not dignify our topical selection, for then other people choose for us. Often, our scholarly predecessors chose, because they first launched the enduringly fascinating lines of inquiry. And it is notable that the pioneers of American intellectual history often had overt, compelling moral purposes in mind, as illustrated by the political goals of a Parrington or the insecurities about self and national identity that inspired the work of Perry Miller. The other obvious drawback of ascendent scholar fashion is that it directs our attention away from subjects that may be of great importance to a student or lay audience.

I believe intellectual historians should become more self-conscious about criteria of topical significance. They might profitably share some of those with their audience. Such self-consciousness might either decrease, or make more explicit the grounds of, deprecating judgments about the significance of other historians' work. It is surely difficult to judge the appropriateness of a topic until one understands the goals of a historian. If one wants to encourage intellectual rigor in students, or develop their commitment to a chosen discipline, then the history of a few technical philosophic doctrines, or a detailed exploration of the intellectual biography of an outstanding philosopher, may be the perfect vehicle. Who would say these are mean or insignificant goals? In such a context, either understanding broader or more popular beliefs, or even grasping the social context of such elite beliefs, might be completely irrelevant. By the same teleological standards, and they are the only standards that should determine choice, a bold and risky effort to unearth fundamental, shared, but largely unconscious beliefs for a whole nation or even a whole civilization may alone enable readers to confront their most basic presuppositions and to come to a clear sense of their broadest communal identity. And who would deprecate such a purpose in writing history?

As a whole, the preceding essays reveal the ascendent concerns of intellectual historians. The authors explore with great subtlety the relationship of their work to that of historians in other fields and to that of social scientists, suggest challenging new ways of using sources, and in illustrative essays bring refreshing new insights to older problems. But to the extent that they have ignored the broader use or role of intellectual history, they have offered few clues as to how historians should allocate their ever scarce supply of time and talent. Perhaps these problems of significance and topic selection, since they have an inescapably moral dimension, should best be confronted by individual historians.

THE CONTRIBUTORS

THOMAS BENDER (Ph.D., University of California, Davis, 1971) is Samuel Rudin Professor of the Humanities at New York University and codirector of the New York Institute for the Humanities. His first book, *Toward an Urban Vision: Ideas and Institutions in Nineteenth-Century America* (1975), received the Frederick Jackson Turner Award of the Organization of American Historians.

SACVAN BERCOVITCH (Ph.D., Claremont Graduate School, 1965) is professor of English and American Literature at Columbia University. The essay in this volume is an outgrowth of his earlier studies, *The Puritan Origins of the American Self* (1975) and *The American Jeremiad* (1978).

PAUL K. CONKIN (Ph.D., Vanderbilt University, 1957) is Merle Curti Professor of History at the University of Wisconsin. Now working entirely in intellectual history, he has also written on recent American history and the philosophy of history. His best-known book is *Puritans and Pragmatists: Eight Eminent American Thinkers* (1968).

DAVID D. HALL (Ph.D., Yale University, 1964) is professor of History at Boston University. His principal work is *The Faithful Shepherd: A History of the New England Ministry in the Seventeenth Century* (1972).

NEIL HARRIS (Ph.D., Harvard University, 1965) is professor of History at the University of Chicago and a member of the Board of Directors of the American Council of Learned Societies. His varied writings on American cultural history include *The Artist in American Society* (1966).

THOMAS L. HASKELL (Ph.D., Stanford University, 1973) is associate professor of History at Rice University and author of *The Emergence of Professional Social Science: The American Social Science Association and the Nineteenth-Century Crisis of Authority* (1977).

235

THE CONTRIBUTORS

JOHN HIGHAM (Ph.D., University of Wisconsin, 1949) is John Martin Vincent Professor of History at The Johns Hopkins University. His major interests have been in historiography and American ethnic history. Most recently he published *Send These to Me: Jews and Other Immigrants in Urban America* (1975).

DAVID A. HOLLINGER (Ph.D., University of California, Berkeley, 1970) is professor of History at the University of Michigan and author of *Morris R. Cohen and the Scientific Ideal* (1975). The essay in this volume was written at the Institute for Advanced Study, Princeton, New Jersey.

HENRY F. MAY (Ph.D., Harvard University, 1947) is Margaret Byrne Professor of History at the University of California, Berkeley. His major works are *The End of American Innocence: A Study of The First Years of Our Own Time, 1912–1917* (1959) and *The Enlightenment in America* (1976).

MURRAY G. MURPHEY (Ph.D., Yale University, 1954) is chairman of the American Civilization Department at the University of Pennsylvania. His writings deal with the history of philosophy, the history of society, and historical methodology. Most recently he coauthored (with Elizabeth Flower) *A History of Philosophy in America* (1973).

DOROTHY ROSS (Ph.D., Columbia University, 1965) is currently associate professor of History at the University of Virginia in Charlottesville. She has published *G. Stanley Hall: The Psychologist as Prophet* (1972) and other studies of social scientists in the Progressive era.

WARREN I. SUSMAN (Ph.D., University of Wisconsin, 1958) is professor of History at Rutgers University. His influential essays have dealt chiefly with the period between the two world wars.

LAURENCE VEYSEY (Ph.D., University of California, Berkeley, 1961) is professor of History at the University of California, Santa Cruz. His book, *The Emergence of the American University* (1965), is the standard authority on the subject.

RUSH WELTER (Ph.D., Harvard University, 1951) is professor of History at Bennington College. He has written *Popular Education and Democratic Thought in America* (1962) and *The Mind of America, 1820–1860* (1975).

GORDON S. WOOD (Ph.D., Harvard University, 1964) is professor of History at Brown University. His book, *The Creation of the American Republic, 1776–1787* (1969) won the Bancroft Prize for history.

INDEX

INDEX

INDEX

INDEX

INDEX

INDEX

INDEX

INDEX

Library of Congress Cataloging in Publication Data

Wingspread Conference on New Directions in
   American Intellectual History, Racine, Wis.,
   1977.
   New directions in American intellectual history.

   Papers presented at the Wingspread Conference
on New Directions in American Intellectual History
held in 1977 at Racine, Wis.
   Includes bibliographical references and index.
   1.   United States—Intellectual life—Congresses.
I.   Higham, John.   II.   Conkin, Paul Keith.
III.   Title.
E169.1.W558   1977   973.9   78–21563
ISBN 0–8018–2183–5 (hardcover)
ISBN 0–8018–2460–5 (paperback)